The Law of Tax-Exempt Organizations

Ninth Edition
2010 Cumulative Supplement

Update Service

BECOME A SUBSCRIBER!
Did you purchase this product from a bookstore?

If you did, it's important for you to become a subscriber. John Wiley & Sons, Inc. may publish, on a periodic basis, supplements and new editions to reflect the latest changes in the subject matter that you need to know in order to stay competitive in this ever-changing industry. By contacting the Wiley office nearest you, you'll receive any current update at no additional charge. In addition, you'll receive future updates and revised or related volumes on a 30-day examination review.

If you purchased this product directly from John Wiley & Sons, Inc., we have already recorded your subscription for this update service.

To become a subscriber, please call **1-877-762-2974** or send your name, company name (if applicable), address, and the title of the product to:

mailing address: **Supplement Department**
John Wiley & Sons, Inc.
One Wiley Drive
Somerset, NJ 08875

e-mail: **subscriber@wiley.com**
fax: **1-732-302-2300**

For customers outside the United States, please contact the Wiley office nearest you:

Professional & Reference Division
John Wiley & Sons Canada, Ltd.
22 Worcester Road
Etobicoke, Ontario M9W 1L1
CANADA
Phone: 416-236-4433
Phone: 1-800-567-4797
Fax: 416-236-4447
Email: canada@wiley.com

John Wiley & Sons, Ltd.
The Atrium
Southern Gate, Chichester
West Sussex PO 19 8SQ
ENGLAND
Phone: 44-1243-779777
Fax: 44-1243-775878
Email: customer@wiley.co.uk

John Wiley & Sons Australia, Ltd.
33 Park Road
P.O. Box 1226
Milton, Queensland 4064
AUSTRALIA
Phone: 61-7-3859-9755
Fax: 61-7-3859-9715
Email: brisbane@johnwiley.com.au

John Wiley & Sons (Asia) Pte., Ltd.
2 Clementi Loop #02-01
SINGAPORE 129809
Phone: 65-64632400
Fax: 65-64634604/5/6
Customer Service: 65-64604280
Email: enquiry@wiley.com.sg

The Law of Tax-Exempt Organizations

Ninth Edition
2010 Cumulative Supplement

Bruce R. Hopkins

WILEY

John Wiley & Sons, Inc.

Library of Congress Cataloging-in-Publication Data:

ISBN: 978-0-470-03760-7; ISBN: 978-0-470-45704-7 (supplement)

Printed in the United States of America

10 9 8 7 6 5 4 3 2 1

About the Author

BRUCE R. HOPKINS is a senior partner in the law firm of Polsinelli Shughart PC, practicing in the firm's Kansas City, Missouri, and Washington, D.C., offices. He specializes in the representation of tax-exempt organizations. His practice ranges over the entirety of law matters involving exempt organizations, with emphasis on the formation of nonprofit organizations, acquisition of recognition of tax-exempt status for them, governance and the law, the private inurement and private benefit doctrines, the intermediate sanctions rules, legislative and political campaign activities issues, public charity and private foundation rules, unrelated business planning, use of exempt and for-profit subsidiaries, joint venture planning, tax shelter involvement, review of annual information returns, Internet communications developments, the law of charitable giving (including planned giving), and fundraising law issues.

Mr. Hopkins served as Chair of the Committee on Exempt Organizations, Tax Section, American Bar Association; Chair, Section of Taxation, National Association of College and University Attorneys; and President, Planned Giving Study Group of Greater Washington, D.C.

Mr. Hopkins is the series editor of Wiley's Nonprofit Law, Finance, and Management Series. In addition to *The Law of Tax-Exempt Organizations, Ninth Edition*, he is the author of the *Planning Guide for the Law of Tax-Exempt Organizations: Strategies and Commentaries; IRS Audits of Tax-Exempt Organizations: Policies, Practices, and Procedures; The Tax Law of Charitable Giving, Fourth Edition; The Law of Fundraising, Fourth Edition; The Tax Law of Associations; The Tax Law of Unrelated Business for Nonprofit Organizations; The Nonprofits' Guide to Internet Communications Law; The Law of Intermediate Sanctions: A Guide for Nonprofits; Starting and Managing a Nonprofit Organization: A Legal Guide, Fifth Edition; Nonprofit Law Made Easy; Charitable Giving Law Made Easy; Private Foundation Law Made Easy; Fundraising Law Made Easy; 650 Essential Nonprofit Law Questions Answered; The First Legal Answer Book for Fund-Raisers; The Second Legal Answer Book for Fund-Raisers; The Legal Answer Book for Nonprofit Organizations; The Second Legal Answer Book for Nonprofit Organizations*; and *The Nonprofit Law Dictionary*; and is the co-author, with Jody Blazek, of *Private Foundations: Tax Law and Compliance, Third Edition*; also with Ms. Blazek, of *The Legal Answer Book for Private Foundations*; with David O. Middlebrook, of *Nonprofit Law for Religious Organizations: Essential Questions and Answers*; with Thomas K. Hyatt, of *The Law of Tax-Exempt Healthcare Organizations, Third Edition*; with Douglas K. Anning, Virginia C. Gross, and Thomas J. Schenkelberg, of *The New Form 990: Law, Policy, and Preparation*; and with Ms. Gross, of *Nonprofit Governance:*

Law, Practices & Trends. He also writes *Bruce R. Hopkins' Nonprofit Counsel,* a monthly newsletter, published by John Wiley & Sons.

Mr. Hopkins maintains a Web site providing information about the law of tax-exempt organizations, at www.nonprofitlawcenter.com. Material posted on this site includes current developments, outlines concerning this aspect of the law, summaries of court opinions, discussions of his book, various indexes for his newsletter, and a "What's New" listing of recent developments in exempt organizations law.

Mr. Hopkins received the 2007 Outstanding Nonprofit Lawyer Award (Vanguard Lifetime Achievement Award) from the American Bar Association, Section of Business Law, Committee on Nonprofit Corporations. He is listed in *The Best Lawyers in America,* Nonprofit Organizations/Charities Law, 2007–2010.

Mr. Hopkins earned his J.D. and L.L.M. degrees at the George Washington University National Law Center and his B.A. at the University of Michigan. He is a member of the bars of the District of Columbia and the state of Missouri.

Contents

Note to the Reader: Sections not in the main bound volume, *The Law of Tax-Exempt Organizations, Ninth Edition* (978-0-470-03760-7), are indicated by "(New)" after the title. Material from the main bound volume that has been updated for this supplement is indicated by "(Revised)" after the title. Material new to or modified in *this* supplement is indicated by an asterisk (*) in the left margin in the Contents and throughout the supplement.

CONTENTS

Part Four   Other Tax-Exempt Organizations 91

CONTENTS

CONTENTS

PART SEVEN   INTERORGANIZATIONAL STRUCTURES AND OPERATIONAL FORMS   187

*Chapter Twenty-Eight: Tax-Exempt Organizations and Exempt Subsidiaries   189

Chapter Twenty-Nine: Tax-Exempt Organizations and For-Profit Subsidiaries   190

CONTENTS

Preface

This is the third cumulative supplement to accompany this ninth edition of *The Law of Tax-Exempt Organizations*, which, I freely admit, got somewhat out of control (the book, not the cumulative supplement (although a case can be made for both)). At 1,259 pages, the book weighs in as the largest of the nine editions. (Somehow, the tenth edition will be thinner.) Excessive writing is not the principal reason for this capacious volume. The bulk of the blame for the book's size is attributable to the many recent developments that have substantially augmented the law of tax-exempt organizations. It really is a lawyer's dream to try to keep up with and chronicle all of these contemporary accretions to this fascinating body of law. This supplement generally covers developments since the book was published, which basically means developments from 2007 through 2009.

The paramount reason underlying all of this law expansion lies with the IRS. Not that Congress has not done its part; it has, of course, most obviously with enactment of the Pension Protection Act of 2006 (PPA), plus some interesting tidbits in the Tax Technical Corrections Act of 2007, the American Recovery and Investment Act of 2009, and the unfolding Tax Extenders Act of 2009. But the PPA is bones; the IRS (and the Treasury Department) has, in the last handful of months, added much flesh: regulations (mostly proposed and temporary), announcements, notices, and press releases. In addition, the agency has produced a goodly amount of revenue rulings, revenue procedures, and private letter rulings.

This assessment of what sounds like blame is merely an objective observation; it is not criticism of the IRS—a government agency has gotta do what it has gotta do. There is no question but that the PPA heaped much work on the IRS; the agency has responded in that regard admirably (and more guidance is on its way). (We remain troubled, however, by the IRS giving supporting organizations safe passage to another category of public charity status to sidestep the PPA rules.) An enormous amount of assistance and direction from the IRS has been produced since publication of the ninth edition, and these efforts have considerably fueled the number of pages of this supplement.

The most recent star of this show, of course, is the new Form 990 (see §§ 5.6(l) and 27.2A of this cumulative supplement). Despite its size, complexity, and overreaching, this thing is a work of art. For large organizations, proper preparation of this return is a mighty feat. But that is not the stuff of law development, although it will entail considerable lawyering.

There should be no mistake—the revamped Form 990 is no mere government form. The issuance of the redesigned Form 990 is akin to publication of a mammoth set of regulations. Much new "law" is embedded in this return. In the context of nonprofit law, there has never been anything like this new Form 990. Touted by its handlers as a means for acquiring information and promoting transparency, the real story is the enormous impact this return is having in modifying the behavior of the leaders, managers, and representatives of tax-exempt organizations, particularly in terms of development of policies and procedures and other forms of alterations in governance. (Much more information about the revamped annual information return is available in *The New Form 990: Law, Policy, and Preparation*, by yours truly, Doug Anning, Virginia Gross, and Tom Schenkelberg.)

Speaking of governance, this subject has emerged as one of the top law issues in today's law of tax-exempt organizations. The new Form 990 has much to do with this, but there is more. (The biggest misstep by the IRS came in 2007 when the draft of the agency's good governance principles emerged (see § 5.6(i) of this cumulative supplement)—an unhelpful, poorly written document that should never have been issued (the principles, not the supplement), if only because the Exempt Organizations Division has more important things to do. Mercifully, this enumeration of principles was allowed a quiet demise.) In the absence of law mandating various policies, independent boards, and the like, the IRS is applying the private benefit doctrine in its efforts to impose governance requirements (see § 5.6(o) of this cumulative supplement), issuing a raft of private letter rulings that are simply flatly erroneous. (Much more on governance principles and the faint law underpinnings for them is explored in *Nonprofit Governance: Law, Practice, and Trends*, by yours truly and Virginia Gross.)

As impressive as all this PPA guidance and revamped Form 990 is, there is much more to the workings of today's IRS TE/GE Division. Other sets of rules are flowing, such as those pertaining to tax-exempt organizations and prohibited tax shelter transactions. Private letter rulings, some of them quite interesting, continue to tumble out of the agency. The IRS has made considerable progress in reducing its inventory of pending applications for recognition of exemption. IRS audits of exempt organizations, along with a host of compliance check projects, are on the rise.

And speaking of compliance checks, the recently launched compliance initiative involving tax-exempt colleges and universities will have an enormous impact on the sector. This compliance check questionnaire, elevated to the level of an IRS form (number 14018), while no Form 990, is still an impressive document. It, too, contains much in the way of "law," pertaining to executive compensation, endowment fund operations, and the unrelated business rules. (We thought about a book on this form but decided to pass.)

One of the most significant and well-prepared products from the IRS in the exempt organizations context in recent months is the Exempt Organization's annual report, which includes the agency's EO work plan for fiscal year

2009. Elements of the work plan include a charitable spending initiative (read: application of the commensurate test), continued work in the governance area (including a long-overdue program of educating agents about this area of the law), inquiries into valuation issues concerning noncash gifts, a look at student loan organizations, and a summary of the compliance programs.

As far as can be determined, all of this law development will continue merrily on in 2010. The courts will add their measure of opinions. The wild card is Congress (the 111th (2009–2010)); no one yet knows what will happen on the legislative front, concerning nonprofit law, in the coming months. (One distinct possibility: legislation to establish charity care and community benefit standards for exempt hospitals.) Back to the IRS, there is another momentous development in the making. It is the IRS's growing reliance on technology in the exempt organizations area, such as development of an electronic determinations case processing and tracking system (the TE/GE Determination System (TEDS)), the emerging Cyber Assistant to guide preparers of applications for recognition of exemption, and Internet-based workshops and educational material.

On January 21, 2010 (and after the pages of Appendix H were completed), the U.S. Supreme Court issued its opinion in Citizens United v. Federal Election Comm'n (No. 08-205). In this case, the Court held that corporations, including nonprofit corporations, may make expenditures from their general treasuries in support of or in opposition to political candidates in furtherance of their free speech rights. To arrive at this decision, the Court overruled Austin v. Michigan Chamber of Commerce (see App. H, n. 50) and the portion of McConnell v. Federal Election Comm'n (*id.*) that facially upheld limits on electioneering communications.

These developments and many more that are certain to come will continue to enhance and enervate the law of tax-exempt organizations. All bodes well in this regard for nonprofit lawyers (and for the tenth edition). Shrinkage of this book and its supplements gets consistently tougher.

My thanks are extended to Susan McDermott, senior editor, and Laura A. Cherkas, production editor, for their valuable assistance in producing this 2010 cumulative supplement.

Bruce R. Hopkins
January 2010

Book Citations

p. xxxv. Replace "Book Citations" page with the following:

Throughout this book, 11 books by the author (in some instances as co-author), all published by John Wiley & Sons, are referenced as follows:

1. *IRS Audits of Tax-Exempt Organizations: Policies, Practices, and Procedures* (2008): cited as *IRS Audits*.

2. *The Law of Fundraising, Fourth Edition* (2009): *Fundraising*.

3. *The Law of Intermediate Sanctions: A Guide for Nonprofits* (2003): *Intermediate Sanctions*.

4. *The Law of Tax-Exempt Healthcare Organizations, Third Edition* (2008): *Healthcare Organizations*.

5. *The Nonprofits' Guide to Internet Communications Law* (2003): *Internet Communications*.

6. *Planning Guide for The Law of Tax-Exempt Organizations: Strategies and Commentaries* (2004): *Planning Guide*.

7. *Private Foundations: Tax Law and Compliance, Third Edition* (2008): *Private Foundations*.

8. *Starting and Managing a Nonprofit Organization: A Legal Guide, Fifth Edition* (2009): *Starting and Managing*.

9. *The Tax Law of Associations* (2006): *Associations*.

10. *The Tax Law of Charitable Giving, Third Edition* (2005): *Charitable Giving*.

11. *The Tax Law of Unrelated Business for Nonprofit Organizations* (2005): *Unrelated Business*.

The second, fourth, seventh, and tenth of these books are annually supplemented. Also, updates on all of the foregoing subjects (plus *The Law of Tax-Exempt Organizations*) are available in *Bruce R. Hopkins' Nonprofit Counsel*, the author's monthly newsletter, also published by Wiley.

PART ONE

Introduction to the Law of Tax-Exempt Organizations

CHAPTER ONE

Definition of and Rationales for Tax-Exempt Organizations

§ 1.1 DEFINITION OF *NONPROFIT* ORGANIZATION

p. 4, *second complete paragraph.* Delete last sentence.

p. 4, *third complete paragraph.* Move n. 3 to end of last sentence of paragraph; renumber as n. 4.

p. 4, *third complete paragraph.* Renumber n. 4 to n. 3.

p. 4, *second complete paragraph.* Insert n. 2 in place of former n. 3.

p. 5, *second complete paragraph.* Delete last sentence.

p. 5. Insert as third complete paragraph:

In addition to the prohibition on private inurement, several state nonprofit corporation acts require the nonprofit entity to devote its profits to ends that are beneficial to society or the public, such as purposes that are arts promotion, agricultural, athletic, beneficial, benevolent, cemetery, charitable, civic, cultural, debt management, educational, eleemosynary, fire control, fraternal, health promotion, horticultural, literary, musical, mutual improvement, natural resources protection, patriotic, political, professional, religious, research, scientific, and/or social.

§ 1.2 DEFINITION OF *TAX-EXEMPT* ORGANIZATION

p. 8, *first complete paragraph.* Insert as third sentence:

Thus, in a private letter ruling, the IRS wrote that "[e]xemption from federal income taxation is not a right, it is a matter of legislative grace that is strictly construed."[24.1]

*p. 9, n. 38, *first paragraph, last sentence.* **Delete and substitute:**

The staff of the Joint Committee on Taxation estimated that, for the federal government's fiscal years 2009–2013, the tax expenditure for the income tax charitable contribution deduction will be $237.6 billion, of which $32.4 billion is in connection with the deduction for gifts to educational institutions and $21.1 billion is for gifts to health care organizations (Estimates of Federal Tax Expenditures for Fiscal Years 2009–2013 (JCS-1-10)).

*p. 9, n. 38. Insert as second paragraph:

The Joint Committee on Taxation has changed its approach for the identification and classification of tax law provisions as tax expenditures, with goals of improving the utility of tax expenditure analysis and reemphasizing its neutrality. The committee issued an extensive report, on May 12, 2008, that stated that tax expenditure analysis "can and should serve as an effective and neutral analytic tool for policymakers in their consideration of individual tax proposals or larger tax reforms" (A Reconsideration of Tax Expenditure Analysis (JCX-37-08)). This report formally presented the committee's "new paradigm" for tax expenditures classification (as does the report referenced in the preceding paragraph, dated January 13, 2010), by which these expenditures are now divided into *tax subsidies* and *tax-induced structural distortions*; tax subsidies are divided into three subcategories, one being *social spending*. The charitable contribution deduction is a social spending tax subsidy.

p. 9, n. 38, *last paragraph.* **Insert as last sentences:**

Under the new Joint Committee staff approach, however, tax exemption for credit unions (see § 19.7) is treated as a tax subsidy, in the subcategory of *business synthetic spending* (this tax expenditure currently is $7.9 billion). Also, exceptions to the rules for the taxation of unrelated business income (see §§ 24.6, 24.7) are now business synthetic spending tax subsidies.

§ 1.3 TAX-EXEMPT ORGANIZATIONS LAW PHILOSOPHY

p. 10, *first complete paragraph, third line.* **Delete** *has very* **and insert** *however, has.*

§ 1.4 POLITICAL PHILOSOPHY RATIONALE

p. 19, *last line.* **Insert note following** *subsidy:*

[101.1]Cf. *supra* note 38, second paragraph.

p. 21, *second line.* **Insert** *and those who fund it* **following** *sector.*

24.1. Priv. Ltr. Rul. 200830028, citing New Dynamics Found. v. United States, 2006-1 U.S.T.C. ¶ 50,286 (Ct. Fed. Cl. 2006).

CHAPTER TWO

Overview of Nonprofit Sector and Tax-Exempt Organizations

*p. 29, *second paragraph, eighth line.* **Insert following existing text:**

U.S. in the

*p. 29, *second paragraph, last line.* **Delete text before period and substitute:**

for 2008, the amount of charitable giving was an estimated $307.65 billion.

*p. 29, *third paragraph, third line.* **Delete text after** *almanac* **and substitute:**

published by

*p. 30, *first line.* **Delete** *Sector and.*

*p. 30, *first complete paragraph, fifth line.* **Delete** *defines* **and insert** *defined.*

*p. 30, *second complete paragraph, first line.* **Delete** *defines* **and insert** *defined.*

*p. 30, n. 4. **Delete text and substitute:**

The most recent version of this almanac is Wing, Pollak, & Blackwood, *The Nonprofit Almanac 2008* (Wash., D.C.: The Urban Institute Press) (*Nonprofit Almanac*).

*p. 30, n. 8, *last line.* **Delete and substitute:**

other analyses of this nature

*p. 30, n. 11, *second line.* **Insert following** *in*:

the 2002 edition of the

∗p. 30, n. 11. Insert following existing material:

Today, the *Nonprofit Almanac* does not attempt a definition of the sector but instead surveys the "nonprofit landscape" (*Nonprofit Almanac* at 3-5).

∗p. 30, n. 12. Insert *(2002)* before *at*.

§ 2.1 PROFILE OF NONPROFIT SECTOR

∗p. 31, *first complete paragraph, fifth line*. Delete *354,000* and insert *350,000*.

∗p. 31, *first complete paragraph, last line*. End sentence following *IRS*, preserve note 19, and delete remainder of line.

∗p. 31, *first complete paragraph*. Insert as last sentence:

Small organizations are not required to file annual information returns with the IRS but are required to electronically submit a short notice as to their existence.[20]

∗p. 31, n. 16. Delete *5* and insert *139*.

∗p. 31, n. 16. Insert following existing material:

See § 10.3(a).

∗p. 31, n. 18. Delete *25.5* and insert *25.6*.

∗p. 31, *second complete paragraph, last sentence*. Delete and substitute:

The most recent analysis posited the number of exempt organizations registered with the IRS (based on 2005 data) at about 1.4 million.[23] This analysis also stated that 528,024 exempt organizations report to the IRS.[23.1]

∗p. 31. Insert as third and fourth complete paragraphs:

Because a "price cannot be placed on the output of most nonprofit organizations," their percent of the gross domestic product is difficult to assess; the best estimate is that it is about 5 percent.[23.2] When the measure is in terms of wages and salaries paid, the percentage arises to approximately 8 percent.[23.3] Other ways to measure the size of the sector are its revenue (about $1,006.7 billion in 2006),[23.4] its outlays (about $915.2 billion (2005)),[23.5] and its paid employment

---

∗   20. See § 27.3. The IRS has not, as of the close of 2009, published any data resulting from this notification requirement.

∗   23. *Nonprofit Almanac* at 3, 140.

∗   23.1. *Id*. at 3.

∗   23.2. *Id*. at 9.

∗   23.3. *Id*. at 10.

∗   23.4. *Id*. at 115.

∗   23.5. *Id*.

(12.9 million (2005)).[23.6] Most of the sector's revenue is in the form of fees for services provided, followed by contributions and grants.[23.7] As to outlays (2006 data), the funds are expended by the organizations (88.7 percent), granted (8), or invested or used as a buffer for cash flow (3.3 percent).[23.8]

The number of public charities (in 2005) is said to be 876,164; the number of public charities that reported to the IRS was set at 310,683.[23.9] Public charities had (in 2005) $1.1 trillion in expenses and $2 trillion in total assets.[23.10] The number of public charities increased by 66.1 percent during the period 1995–2005.[23.11] During that period, the revenue of public charities increased by 99.5 percent.[23.12] Financial support for public charities swelled from $107 billion in 1995 to $244 billion in 2005—an increase of 128.3 percent.[23.13] During this period, the total assets of public charities grew from $843 billion to nearly $2 trillion, an increase of 134.3 percent.[23.14]

*p. 31, *third complete paragraph, first line.* **Delete** *Approximately* **and substitute:**

The breakdown as to these tax-exempt organizations[23.15] shows that approximately

*p. 31, *third complete paragraph, first line.* **Insert** *(984,386)* **before** *are.*

*p. 31, *third complete paragraph, second line.* **Delete** *20* **and insert** *100.*

*p. 31, *third complete paragraph, third line.* **Delete** *7,000* **and insert** *5,850.*

*p. 31, *third complete paragraph, fourth line.* **Delete** *1,200* **and insert** *1,133.*

*p. 31, *third complete paragraph, fourth line.* **Delete** *140,000* **and insert** *116,890.*

*p. 31, *third complete paragraph, fifth line.* **Delete** *65,000* **and insert** *56,819.*

*p. 31, *third complete paragraph, fifth line.* **Delete** *90,000* **and insert** *71,878.*

*p. 31, *third complete paragraph, sixth line.* **Delete** *68,000* **and insert** *56,369.*

*p. 31, *third complete paragraph, sixth line.* **Delete** *82,000* **and insert** *63,318.*

*p. 32, *carryover paragraph, first line.* **Delete** *24,000* **and insert** *20,944.*

---

* 23.6. *Id.* at 18, 27.
* 23.7. *Id.* at 115. Fees for services and goods were estimated to be 70.3 percent of the total; contributions and non-government grants were said to be 12.3 percent of the total (*id.* at 143–144).
* 23.8. *Id.* at 121.
* 23.9. *Id.* at 140.
* 23.10. *Id.* at 141.
* 23.11. *Id.* at 148.
* 23.12. *Id.* at 152.
* 23.13. *Id.*
* 23.14. *Id.* at 158.
* 23.15. *Nonprofit Almanac* at 2-3.

*p. 32, *carryover paragraph, first line.* Delete *14,000* and insert *10,088.*

*p. 32, *carryover paragraph, second line.* Delete *15* and insert *14.*

*p. 32, *carryover paragraph, second line.* Delete *6,500* and insert *5,901.*

*p. 32, *carryover paragraph, third line.* Delete *10,000* and insert *9,808.*

*p. 32, *carryover paragraph, third line.* Delete *4,500* and insert *3,565.*

*p. 32, *carryover paragraph, fourth line.* Delete *1,400* and insert *1,646.*

*p. 32, *carryover paragraph, fourth line.* Delete *25* and insert *16.*

*p. 32, *carryover paragraph, fifth line.* Delete *500* and insert *300.*

*p. 32, *carryover paragraph, fifth line.* Delete *35,000* and insert *35,113.*

*p. 32, *carryover paragraph, sixth line.* Delete *30* and insert *28.*

*p. 32, *carryover paragraph, seventh line.* Delete *9* and insert *12.*

*p. 32, *carryover paragraph, eighth line.* Delete *130* and insert *160.*

*p. 32, *carryover paragraph, eighth line.* Delete *40* and insert *18.*

*pp. 32–33. **Delete first complete paragraph on p. 32 (including footnote) and subsequent paragraph that carries over to p. 33, and substitute:**

Charitable giving in the United States in 2008 is estimated to be $307.65 billion, a decrease of 2 percent (–5.7 percent when adjusted for inflation) compared to the revised estimate of $314.07 billion for 2007.[52] Giving by living individuals in 2008 totaled an estimated $229.28 billion; this level of giving constituted an estimated 75 percent of all charitable giving for the year. Gifts in the form of charitable bequests in 2008 are estimated to be $22.66 billion (7 percent of total giving). Grantmaking by private foundations was an estimated $41.21 billion in 2008 (13 percent of the total). Gifts from corporations in 2008 totaled an estimated $14.5 billion (5 percent of total giving for that year).

Giving to religious organizations amounted to an estimated $106.89 billion in 2008, accounting for about 35 percent of total giving during that year. In the realm of education, giving totaled an estimated $40.94 billion for 2008 (13 percent of the total). Giving to human services organizations was an estimated amount of $25.88 billion in 2008 (9 percent of the total). Giving to health-care entities in 2008 totaled an estimated $21.64 billion (7 percent of the total). Public-society benefit organizations received an estimated $23.88 billion in 2008 (8 percent of the total). Giving to organizations in the arts, culture, and

---

* 52. These data are from *Giving USA 2009*, published by the Giving USA Foundation, researched and written by the Center on Philanthropy at Indiana University.

humanitarian fields was about $12.79 billion in 2008 (4 percent of the total). Giving to international affairs organizations was about $13.3 billion in 2008 (4 percent of the total). Giving in 2008 to environment/animal organizations was an estimated $6.58 billion (2 percent of the total).

§ 2.2 ORGANIZATION OF IRS

(a) IRS in General

*p. 35, *fourth paragraph.* **Insert as last sentence:**

These divisions are the Large and Mid-Size Business, the Small Business/ Self-Employed, the Tax Exempt/Government Entities, and the Wage and Investment Divisions.

*p. 35. **Insert as last paragraph:**

This reorganization of the IRS, in the form of a four-division structure, resulted in delegation to each division the responsibility for developing procedures and establishing priorities for servicing its customers. In the words of a Treasury Inspector General for Tax Administration report, this organizational methodology "enabled each division to establish end-to-end accountability for its respective customer base."[70.1] This report, however, also stated that this "fragmented approach" to IRS operations is a "weakness" that frustrates the accomplishments intended by the creation of "IRS-wide" programs, one of which is the National Fraud Program.[70.2]

(b) Tax Exempt and Government Entities Division

*p. 36, *second paragraph, last line.* **Insert footnote at end of line:**

[71.1] This office has initiated an academic program for the purpose of collaborating with academic institutions that offer degrees related to the nonprofit sector, to promote education as to the law of tax-exempt organizations. Ann. 2009-26, 2009-14 I.R.B. 755.

p. 36, n. 72. Insert before existing material:

More technically, the term *Exempt Organizations* (EO) *Determinations* refers to the office of the IRS that is primarily responsible for processing initial applications for recognition of tax-exempt status; it includes the main EO Determinations office in Cincinnati, Ohio, and other field offices that are under the direction and control of the Manager, EO Determinations (Rev. Proc. 2009-9, 2009-2 I.R.B. 256 § 1.01(3)).

---

* 70.1. TIGTA, "A Corporate Approach Is Needed to Provide for a More Effective Tax-Exempt Fraud Program," at 2 (no. 2009-10-096, July 6, 2009).
* 70.2. *Id.* See text accompanied by *infra* note 76.1.

∗p. 36, *third paragraph, line 10.* **Insert footnote following period:**

^{72.1}More technically, the term *EO Technical* refers to the office of the IRS, in Washington, D.C., that is primarily responsible for issuing letter rulings to taxpayers on exempt organizations matters, and for providing technical advice or technical assistance to other offices of the IRS on exempt organizations matters (Rev. Proc. 2009-9, 2009-1 C.B. 256 § 1.01(4)).

p. 36, *last paragraph, second line.* **Delete** *review projects* **and insert** *compliance checks.*

p. 36, last paragraph, fifth line. Delete *noncompliance* **and insert** *compliance.*

p. 36, last paragraph, fifth and sixth lines. Delete *using correspondence and telephone contacts* **and accompanying footnote, and insert** *by conducting compliance checks.*

p. 37, *carryover paragraph.* **Insert as last two sentences:**

A Review of Operations unit engages in follow-up reviews of tax-exempt organizations. The Compliance Strategies Critical Initiative coordinates the Division's strategic planning, monitors progress of critical initiatives, and analyses the results of these projects.

∗p. 37. Insert as second and third complete paragraphs:

As of the close of the government's fiscal year 2008, the Exempt Organization's Division had a staff of 838 employees. The Customer Education and Outreach core staff consisted of 10 fulltime employees, the Rulings and Agreements office had 355 employees, and the Examinations office had 461 employees. Twelve employees are in the Exempt Organizations Division's Director's office.

Also within the TE/GE Division are the Employee Plans and Government Entities functions. Within the latter are the Federal, State, and Local Governments; Indian Tribal Governments; and Tax Exempt Bonds offices.

p. 37, *second complete paragraph, sixth line.* **Delete** *issues* **and insert** *issued.*

∗p. 37, *second complete paragraph.* **Insert as last sentence:**

Beginning with fiscal year 2009, however, the implementing guidelines were replaced with an Exempt Organizations Annual Report, which includes a work plan for the forthcoming fiscal year.

∗p. 37. Insert as last complete paragraph before heading:

The IRS has a National Fraud Program, which entails the coordination of the establishment of IRS-wide fraud strategies, policies, and procedures to enhance enforcement of the federal tax law.^{76.1} This program, which is within

---

∗ 76.1. This program is the subject of the TIGTA report referenced in *supra* note 70.1.

the Small Business/Self-Employed Division, facilitates coordination for all IRS divisions to identify and develop fraud cases. The Treasury Inspector General for Tax Administration criticized the TE/GE Division for ineffectiveness in implementing its share of the fraud program and caused the Division to implement a more centralized approach to fraud cases across the five offices in the Division.[76.2]

p. 38, *last paragraph.* Insert as last sentence:

This program has disappeared from the IRS's list of projects, although the market segment concept lives on in the agency's compliance check programs.[97.1]

p. 39, n. 105. Delete *F* and insert *G*.

§ 2.3   CHARITABLE CONTRIBUTION DEDUCTION RULES

p. 41, *third complete paragraph, last line.* Insert footnote at end of line:

[139.1] In general, see *Charitable Giving*; Hopkins, *Charitable Giving Law Made Easy* (Hoboken, NJ: John Wiley & Sons 2007).

---

* 76.2. *Id.*
  97.1. See § 26.6(a)(ii), text accompanied by notes 308.1–308.6.

PART TWO

Fundamentals of the Law
of Tax-Exempt Organizations

CHAPTER THREE

Source, Advantages, and Disadvantages of Tax Exemption

§ 3.2 *RECOGNITION* OF TAX EXEMPTION

*p. 52, *first complete paragraph, seventh line.* **Insert footnote following period:**

> [25.1] The IRS procedures state that an organization seeking recognition of tax-exempt status must file the appropriate application (Rev. Proc. 2009-9, 2009-1 C.B. 256 § 3.01) but are silent on the fact that recognition is not always required.

p. 52, *first complete paragraph.* Delete fourth sentence (including footnote) and substitute:

That is, in order for an organization to be exempt as a charitable entity (with exceptions), such as a credit counseling organization that desires exemption as a social welfare entity, or as an employee benefit entity, it must file an application for recognition with the IRS and receive a favorable determination.[26]

p. 52, n. 27. Delete 25.7 and insert 25.8.

§ 3.3 ADVANTAGES OF TAX-EXEMPT STATUS

(b) Deductibility of Contributions

p. 54, *fourth paragraph, second line.* Insert footnote following period:

> [43.1] See § 3.3(b).

*p. 58, n. 89, *third line.* **Delete *administration* and insert *administrative*.**

---

26. IRC §§ 508(a), 501(q)(3), 505(c), respectively. See §§ 25.2, 25.4, 25.5, respectively.

CHAPTER FOUR

Organizational, Operational, and Related Tests and Doctrines

§ 4.1 FORMS OF TAX-EXEMPT ORGANIZATIONS

(a) General Rules

*p. 66, n. 2. Insert following existing material:

In the context of religious organizations (see Chapter 10), state law may recognize the *corporation sole*, which is an entity "composed of a series of natural persons who, one after another, hold the office of the religious leader of the particular religious organization" (*In re Catholic Bishop of Spokane*, 329 B.R. 304 (U.S. Bankr. Ct. E.D. Wash. 2005), *rev'd, in part, on other grounds*, 364 B.R. 81 (E.D. Wash. 2006)). Also in this context, entities can be established in dubious forms, such as *ministerial trusts* (e.g., United States v. Hovind, 2009 WL 2369340 (N.D. Fl. July 29, 2009)), which can be or edge close to being fraudulent tax schemes (e.g., United States v. Stoll, 2005 WL 1763617 (W.D. Wash. June 27, 2005)) or *personal ministries* (see § 10.2(c)).

*p. 67, n. 24, *eighth line*. Insert following semicolon:

United States v. Hovind, 2009 WL 2369340 (N.D. Fl. July 29, 2009);

(b) Check-the-Box Regulations

(i) Basic Rules.

p. 68, n. 28, *fourth line*. Insert following first closing parenthesis:

, *aff'd*, 484 F.3d 372 (6th Cir. 2007).

§ 4.3 ORGANIZATIONAL TEST

(a) Statement of Purposes

p. 75, *second paragraph.* **Insert as fifth sentence:**

Likewise, the IRS will likely revoke a charitable organization's tax exemption for removal of a dissolution clause, with the revocation retroactive to the date the clause was deleted.[91.1]

§ 4.4 PRIMARY PURPOSE TEST

*p. 85, n. 163. **Insert following existing material:**

Similarly, an organization with the primary purpose of fostering networking between vendors and prospective clients within the legal profession was held to not qualify as an exempt social club (Priv. Ltr. Rul. 200906057).

*p. 85, *second paragraph.* **Insert as last sentence:**

In addition, the IRS ruled that (1) an organization, formed to promote soccer, was ineligible for exemption as a charitable or educational organization because its primary purpose was the promotion of recreational sports for adults;[167.1] (2) an organization, established to "spread the gospel of Jesus Christ through professionally run fishing tournaments," did not qualify as an exempt religious entity because its primary purpose was socializing;[167.2] (3) an organization could not be tax-exempt on the basis of operating a religious camp because its primary activities are fishing and socializing;[167.3] (4) an organization, formed as an "Italian culture club," did not constitute a charitable or educational entity, in that it was more akin to a fraternal organization;[167.4] (5) an organization, the primary purpose of which was enjoyment of the art of riding motorcycles with members, could not qualify as an exempt social welfare entity because social activities were its substantial function,[167.5] and (6) an organization that sought exempt status as a charitable and educational organization could not qualify for the exemption because its activities were conducted exclusively for recreational and/or social purposes.[167.6]

91.1. E.g., Priv. Ltr. Rul. 200842047.
* 167.1. Priv. Ltr. Rul. 200849018.
* 167.2. Priv. Ltr. Rul. 200851040.
* 167.3. Priv. Ltr. Rul. 200905028.
* 167.4. Priv. Ltr. Rul. 200905029.
* 167.5. Priv. Ltr. Rul. 200909072.
* 167.6. Priv. Ltr. Rul. 200930049.

§ 4.5 OPERATIONAL TEST

(a) Basic Rules

p. 90, *carryover paragraph.* **Insert as last sentence:**

On occasion, tax exemption will be revoked for inactivity (failure of an organization to operate at all).[200.1]

§ 4.7 COMMENSURATE TEST

*p. 96, *first complete paragraph.* **Insert as last sentence:**

Yet a public charity had its tax exemption revoked, by application of the commensurate test, because, in the two years under examination, although bingo gross income was 73 percent and 92 percent of total gross income, only a small of amount of this income was distributed for charitable purposes.[246.1]

*p. 96. **Insert as second complete paragraph, before heading:**

Thereafter, the IRS announced, as one of its new compliance initiatives for fiscal year 2009, a *charitable spending initiative,* which is a "long-range study to learn more about sources and uses of funds in the charitable sector and their impact on the accomplishment of charitable purposes."[246.2] The IRS said it will be looking at fundraising, contributions, grants, revenue from related and unrelated businesses, types and amounts of direct and indirect unrelated business expenses, and officer compensation, and the effect each of these elements has on funds available for charitable activities. The first stage of this initiative will focus on "organizations with unusual fundraising levels and organizations that report unrelated trade or business activity and relatively low levels of program service expenditures."[246.3]

§ 4.11 COMMERCIALITY DOCTRINE

(a) Origin of Doctrine

*p. 114, n. 377. **Delete 27.9 and insert 27.13.**

(b) Contemporary Application of Doctrine

p. 121, *last complete paragraph, line 12.* **Delete** *and to.*

200.1. E.g., Priv. Ltr. Rul. 200646020.
246.1. Priv. Ltr. Rul. 200825046.
246.2. IRS Exempt Organizations 2009 Annual Report, at 20.
246.3. *Id.*

p. 121, *last complete paragraph, penultimate line.* **Delete period and insert semicolon; following footnote number insert:**

and an organization that maintained a golf course open to the public on a fee-for-service basis.[443.1]

p. 121, n. 444. Insert following existing material:

In applying the commerciality doctrine, the IRS may compound its adverse (from the standpoint of the applicant or exempt organization) findings by borrowing a precept from the unrelated business rules (see § 24.4(b)) and hold that the commercial operation is being conducted on a scale larger than is reasonably necessary for the conduct of the activities as exempt functions (e.g., Priv. Ltr. Rul. 200815035).

(c)   Contemporary Perspective on Doctrine

∗p. 123. Insert as third paragraph:

The IRS provided a unique application of the commerciality doctrine, holding that a community foundation can, in furtherance of charitable purposes, sell grantmaking services to charitable organizations in its community, although the sale of administrative and clerical services was held to be a nonexempt function.[457.1] The IRS suggested that the purchasing charitable entities constituted a charitable class,[457.2] a fact that trumped the "commercial nature of the service." The IRS dismissed the matter of the charging of fees,[457.3] stating that the fees would be reasonable.

§ 4.12   SOCIAL ENTERPRISE MOVEMENT

p. 126, n. 477, *third line.* **Insert following third period:**

Also Wexler, "Social Enterprise: A Legal Context," 54 *Exempt Org. Tax Rev.* (No. 3) 233 (Dec. 2006).

443.1. Priv. Ltr. Rul. 200815035.
∗   457.1. Priv. Ltr. Rul. 200832027.
∗   457.2. See § 6.3(a).
∗   457.3. See §§ 6.3(h), 24.2(e).

CHAPTER FIVE

Boards of Directors and Governance Principles

§ 5.1   BOARDS OF DIRECTORS BASICS

(b)   Number

p. 129. Insert as last sentence of carryover paragraph:

In a nonsensical private letter ruling, the IRS asserted that unwarranted private benefit [7.1] was inherent in the fact of a board of directors, of an organization that unsuccessfully sought recognition of exemption as a charitable entity, consisting of two related individuals. [7.2]

§ 5.2   BOARD COMPOSITION AND TAX LAW

p. 132, *first paragraph, first line*. Insert *public revenue* before *rulings*.

p. 132, *first paragraph fourth line*. Delete *prominent*.

p. 132, *first paragraph, last line*. Insert footnote at end of line:

[24.1]The redesigned annual information return (Form 990) issued by the IRS (see § 27.2A) includes a question requiring the organization to report the number of its voting board members who are *independent* (Form 990, Part I, question 4), in the absence of any federal law requirement that there be any independent board members.

§ 5.3   DUTIES AND RESPONSIBILITIES

(a)   Principles of Fiduciary Responsibility

p. 134, *first complete paragraph, first line*. Delete *One* and insert *Two*.

p. 134, *penultimate line*. Delete second *and* and insert *the*.

(b)   Duties of Directors

(ii)   Duty of Loyalty.

p. 135, *fifth paragraph, last line*. Delete *information* and insert *organization*.

§ 5.5   SARBANES-OXLEY ACT

(b)   Principal Features of Act

(xiii)   Real-Time Disclosures.

p. 144, *eighth complete paragraph, first line*. Insert *law* following *securities*.

7.1. See § 20.11(a).

7.2. Priv. Ltr. Rul. 200736037. The redesigned annual information return (Form 990) issued by the IRS (see § 27.2A) includes a question requesting the number of voting members of the organization's governing body (Form 990, Part I, question 3).

§ 5.6   NONPROFIT GOVERNANCE PRINCIPLES

p. 152. Insert following existing text:

(i)   IRS Draft of Good Governance Principles (New)

The IRS, in 2007, unveiled a draft of the agency's "Good Governance Practices" for charitable organizations.[91] The agency is of the view that governing boards of charitable organizations should be composed of persons who are informed and active in overseeing the organizations' operations and finances. If a governing board tolerates a climate of secrecy or neglect, charitable assets are more likely to be used to advance an impermissible private interest. Successful governing boards include individuals who are not only knowledgeable and passionate about the organization's programs but also have expertise in critical areas involving accounting, finance, compensation, and ethics.

Organizations with very small or very large governing boards may be problematic: Small boards generally do not represent a public interest; large boards may be less attentive to oversight duties. If an organization's governing board is very large, it may want to establish an executive committee with delegated responsibilities or establish advisory committees.

The IRS suggests that charitable organizations review and consider the following to help ensure that directors understand their roles and responsibilities, and actively promote good governance practices. While adopting a particular practice is not a requirement for tax exemption, the agency believes that an organization that adopts some or all of these practices is more likely to be successful in pursuing its exempt purposes and earning public support.

The proposed principles, essentially reproduced verbatim, are as follows:

(i) Mission Statement.   A clearly articulated mission statement that is adopted by an organization's board of directors will explain and popularize the charity's purpose, and serve as a guide to the organization's work. A well-written mission statement shows why the charity exists, what it hopes to accomplish, and what activities it will undertake, where, and for whom.

(ii) Code of Ethics.   The public expects a charity to abide by ethical standards that promote the public good. The board of directors bears the ultimate responsibility for setting ethical standards and ensuring that they permeate the organization and inform its practices. To that end, the board should consider adopting and regularly evaluating a code of ethics that describes behavior it wants to encourage and discourage. The code of ethics should be a principal

---

91. The occasion was a presentation on February 2, 2007, by the Chief, EO Technical, IRS Office of Rulings and Agreements. See Bureau of Nat'l Affairs, *Daily Tax Report* (No. 33) TaxCore® (Feb. 2, 2007); 24 *Bruce R. Hopkins' Nonprofit Counsel* (no. 4) 1 (April 2007).

means of communicating to all personnel a strong culture of legal compliance and ethical integrity.

(iii) Whistleblower Policy.   The board of directors should adopt an effective policy for handling employee complaints and establish procedures for employees to report in confidence suspected financial impropriety or misuse of the charity's resources.

(iv) Due Diligence.   The directors of a charity must exercise due diligence consistent with a duty of care that requires a director to act in good faith, with the care an ordinarily prudent person in a like position would exercise under similar circumstances, and in a manner the director reasonably believes to be in the charity's best interests. Directors should see to it that policies and procedures are in place to help them meet their duty of care, such as by (1) being familiar with the charity's activities and knowing whether the activities promote the charity's mission and achieve its goals, (2) being fully informed about the charity's financial status, and (3) having full and accurate information to make informed decisions.

(v) Duty of Loyalty.   The directors of a charity owe it a duty of loyalty. This duty requires a director to act in the interest of the charity rather than in the personal interest of the director or some other person or organization. In particular, the duty of loyalty requires a director to avoid conflicts of interest that are detrimental to the charity. To that end, the board of directors should adopt and regularly evaluate an effective conflict-of-interest policy that (1) requires directors and staff to act solely in the interests of the charity without regard for personal interests; (2) includes written procedures for determining whether a relationship, financial interest, or business affiliation results in a conflict of interest; and (3) prescribes a certain course of action in the event a conflict of interest is identified. Directors and staff should be required to disclose annually in writing any known financial interest that the individual, or a member of the individual's family, has in any business entity that transacts business with the charity.

(vi) Transparency.   By making full and accurate information about its mission, activities, and finances publicly available, a charity demonstrates transparency. The board of directors should adopt and monitor procedures to ensure that the charity's Form 990, annual reports, and financial statements are complete and accurate, are posted on the organization's public Web site, and are made available to the public on request.

(vii) Fundraising Policy.   Charitable fundraising is an important source of financial support for many charities. Success at fundraising requires care and honesty. The board of directors should adopt and monitor policies to ensure that fundraising solicitations meet federal and state law requirements and solicitation materials are accurate, truthful, and candid. Charities should keep their fundraising costs reasonable. In selecting paid fundraisers, a charity should use those that are registered with the state and that can provide good references. Performance of professional fundraisers should be continuously monitored.

(viii) Financial Audits. Directors must be good stewards of a charity's financial resources. A charity should operate in accordance with an annual budget approved by the board of directors. The board should ensure that financial resources are used to further charitable purposes by regularly receiving and reading up-to-date financial statements, including Form 990, auditor's letters, and finance and audit committee reports. If the charity has substantial assets or annual revenue, the board of directors should ensure that an independent auditor conduct an annual audit. The board can establish an independent audit committee to select and oversee the independent auditor. The auditing firm should be changed periodically (e.g., every five years) to ensure a fresh look at the financial statements. For a charity with lesser assets or annual revenue, the board should ensure that an independent certified public accountant conduct an annual audit. Substitute practices for very small organizations would include volunteers who would review financial information and practices. Trading volunteers between similarly situated organizations who would perform these tasks would also help maintain financial integrity without being too costly.

(ix) Compensation Practices. A successful charity pays no more than reasonable compensation for services rendered. Charities should generally not compensate persons for service on the board of directors, except to reimburse direct expenses of such service. Director compensation should be allowed only when determined to be appropriate by a committee composed of persons who are not compensated by the charity and have no financial interest in the determination. Charities may pay reasonable compensation for services provided by officers and staff.

(x) Document Retention Policy. An effective charity will adopt a written policy establishing standards for document integrity, retention, and destruction. The document retention policy should include guidelines for handling electronic files. The policy should cover backup procedures, archiving of documents, and regular checkups of the reliability of the system.[92]

---

92. In general, Silk, "Good Goverance Practices for 501(c)(3) Organizations: Should the IRS Become Further Involved?," 57 *Exempt Org. Tax Rev.* (No. 2) 183 (Aug. 2007).

(j) American National Red Cross Governance Modernization Act (New)

The American National Red Cross Governance Modernization Act of 2007 was signed into law on May 11, 2007.[93] This legislation amended the congressional charter of the Red Cross to modernize its structure and otherwise strengthen its governance. Changes include a substantial reduction in the size of the organization's board, delegation to management of the day-to-day operations of the organization, elimination of distinctions as to how board members are elected, and transition of some board members into an advisory council.

The essence of the legislation is unique to the National Red Cross entity. Yet, there are elements of the act with larger significance. For example, the legislation refers to the governing board as a "governance and strategic oversight board."[94] It outlines the board's responsibilities (a checklist for boards in general):

- Review and approve the organization's mission statement
- Approve and oversee the organization's strategic plan and maintain strategic oversight of operational matters
- Select, evaluate, and determine the level of compensation of the organization's chief executive officer
- Evaluate the performance and establish the compensation of the senior leadership team and provide for management succession
- Oversee the financial reporting and audit process, internal controls, and legal compliance
- Ensure that the chapters of the organization are geographically and regionally diverse
- Hold management accountable for performance
- Provide oversight of the financial stability of the organization
- Ensure the inclusiveness and diversity of the organization
- Provide oversight of the protection of the brand of the organization [this is a responsibility rarely found in a list of this nature]
- Assist with fundraising on behalf of the organization[95]

This legislation contains the following "sense of Congress" that (1) "charitable organizations are an indispensable part of American society, but these organizations can only fulfill their important roles by maintaining the trust of the American public," (2) "trust is fostered by effective governance and transparency," and (3) "Federal and State action play an important role in

---

93. Pub. L. No. 110-26, 110th Cong., 1st Sess. (2007).
94. *Id.* § 2(a)(5).
95. *Id.*

ensuring effective governance and transparency by setting standards, rooting out violations, and informing the public."[96]

(k) Panel on Nonprofit Sector Good Governance Principles (New)

The Panel on the Nonprofit Sector, convened by Independent Sector, issued, on October 18, 2007, its principles for good governance for public and private charitable organizations.[97] The principles are predicated on the need for a "careful balance between the two essential forms of regulation—that is, between prudent legal mandates to ensure that organizations do not abuse the privilege of their exempt status, and, for all other aspects of sound operations, well-informed self-governance and mutual awareness among nonprofit organizations." These principles, organized under four categories, are as follows (slightly edited for brevity):

(i) Legal Compliance and Public Disclosure

- An organization must comply with applicable federal, state, and local laws. If the organization conducts programs outside the United States, it must abide by applicable international laws and conventions that are legally binding on the United States.

- An organization should have a formally adopted, written code of ethics with which all of its directors, staff, and volunteers are familiar and to which they adhere.

- An organization should implement policies and procedures to ensure that all conflicts of interest, or appearance of them, within the organization and its board are appropriately managed through disclosure, recusal, or other means.

- An organization should implement policies and procedures that enable individuals to come forward with information on illegal practices or violations of organizational policies. This whistleblower policy should specify that the organization will not retaliate against, and will protect the confidentiality of, individuals who make good-faith reports.

- An organization should implement policies and procedures to preserve the organization's important documents and business records.

- An organization's board should ensure that the organization has adequate plans to protect its assets—its property, financial and human resources, programmatic content and material, and its integrity and

---

96. *Id.* § 2(b). In general, Josephson, "American Red Cross Governance," 55 *Exempt Org. Tax Rev.* (No. 1) 71 (Jan. 2007).
97. Panel on the Nonprofit Sector, "Principles for Good Governance and Ethical Practice—A Guide for Charities and Foundations" (Independent Sector (Oct. 2007)).

reputation—against damage or loss. The board should regularly review the organization's need for general liability and directors' and officers' liability insurance, as well as take other actions to mitigate risk.

- An organization should make information about its operations, including its governance, finances, programs, and other activities, widely available to the public. Charitable organizations should also consider making information available on the methods they use to evaluate the outcomes of their work and sharing the results of the evaluations.

(ii) Effective Governance

- An organization must have a governing body that is responsible for approving the organization's mission and strategic direction; annual budget; and key financial transactions, compensation practices, and fiscal and governance policies.

- The board of an organization should meet regularly to conduct its business and fulfill its duties.

- The board of an organization should establish its size and structure, and periodically review these. The board should have enough members to allow for full deliberation and diversity of thinking on organizational matters. Except for very small organizations, this generally means there should be at least five members.

- The board of an organization should include members with the diverse background (including ethnic, racial, and gender perspectives), experience, and organizational and financial skills necessary to advance the organization's mission.

- A substantial majority of the board (usually at least two-thirds) of a public charity should be independent. Independent members should not be compensated by the organization, have their compensation determined by individuals who are compensated by the organization, receive material financial benefits from the organization except as a member of a charitable class served by the organization, or be related to or reside with any person described above.

- The board should hire, oversee, and annually evaluate the performance of the chief executive of the organization, and should conduct such an evaluation prior to any change in that individual's compensation, unless a multiyear contract is in force or the change consists solely of routine adjustments for inflation or cost of living.

- The board of an organization that has paid staff should ensure that separate individuals hold the positions of chief staff officer, board chair, and board treasurer. Organizations without paid staff should ensure that the position of board chair and treasurer are separately held.

- The board should establish an effective, systematic process for educating and communicating with board members to ensure that they are aware of their legal and ethical responsibilities, are knowledgeable about the programs and other activities of the organization, and can effectively carry out their oversight functions.

- Board members should evaluate their performance as a group and as individuals no less than every three years, and should have clear procedures for removing board members who are unable to fulfill their responsibilities.

- The board should establish clear policies and procedures, setting the length of terms and the number of consecutive terms a board member may serve.

- The board should review the organization's governing instruments at least every five years.

- The board should regularly review the organization's mission and goals, and evaluate at least every five years the organization's goals, programs, and other activities to be sure they advance its mission and make prudent use of its resources.

- Board members are generally expected to serve without compensation, other than reimbursement for expenses incurred to fulfill their board duties. An organization that provides compensation to its board members should use appropriate comparability data to determine the amount to be paid, document the decision, and provide full disclosure to anyone, on request, of the amount and rationale for the compensation.

(iii) Strong Financial Oversight

- An organization must keep complete, current, and accurate financial records. Its board should review timely reports of the organization's financial activities and have a qualified, independent financial expert audit or review these statements annually in a manner appropriate to the organization's size and scale of operations.

- The board of an organization must institute policies and procedures to ensure that the organization (and, if applicable, its subsidiaries) manages and invests its funds responsibly, in accordance with requirements of law. The full board should approve the organization's annual budget and monitor performance against the budget.

- An organization should not provide loans (or the equivalent, such as loan guarantees, purchasing or transferring ownership of a residence or office, or relieving a debt or lease obligations) to its directors or officers.

- An organization should spend a significant portion of its annual budget on programs that pursue its mission. The budget should provide sufficient resources for effective administration of the organization and, if it solicits contributions, for appropriate fundraising activities.

- An organization should establish clear, written policies for paying or reimbursing expenses incurred by anyone conducting business or traveling on behalf of the organization, including the types of expenses that can be paid or reimbursed and the documentation required. These policies should require that travel on behalf of the organization be undertaken in a cost-effective manner.

- An organization should neither pay for nor reimburse travel expenditures for spouses, dependents, or others who are accompanying someone conducting business for the organization unless they are also conducting the business.

(iv) Responsible Fundraising

- Solicitation materials and other communications addressed to prospective donors and the public must clearly identify the organization, and be accurate and truthful.

- Contributions must be used for purposes consistent with the donor's intent, whether as described in the solicitation materials or as directed by the donor.

- An organization must provide donors with acknowledgments of charitable contributions, in accordance with federal tax law requirements, including information to facilitate the donor's compliance with tax law requirements.

- An organization should adopt clear policies to determine whether acceptance of a gift would compromise its ethics, financial circumstances, program focus, or other interests.

- An organization should provide appropriate training and supervision of the people soliciting funds on its behalf to ensure that they understand their responsibilities and applicable law, and do not employ techniques that are coercive, intimidating, or intended to harass potential donors.

- An organization should not compensate internal or external fundraisers on the basis of a commission or percentage of the amount raised.

- An organization should respect the privacy of individual donors and, except where disclosure is required by law, should not sell or otherwise make available the names and contact information of its donors without providing them an opportunity to at least annually opt out of use of their names.

*(l)   Redesigned Form 990 (New)

The redesigned annual information return (Form 990) issued by the IRS in 2007[98] includes a series of questions that directly reflect the agency's views as to governance principles applicable to tax-exempt organizations. Indeed, this return, particularly in Part VI, is designed to influence and modify exempt organizations' behavior, by in essence forcing them to adopt certain policies and procedures so they can check "yes" rather than "no" boxes. Almost none of these policies and procedures is required by the federal tax law.

An organization filing this return is required to report the total number of voting members of its governing body and the number of these members who are *independent*.[99] The organization must indicate whether a trustee, director, officer, or key employee has a family relationship or a business relationship with any other trustee, director, officer, or key employee.[100] It must report whether it delegated control over management duties customarily performed by or under the direct supervision of trustees, directors, officers, or key employees to a management company or other person.[101] The organization must indicate whether a copy of the annual information return was provided to its governing body before it was filed.[102] The organization is required to indicate whether it contemporaneously documented the meetings held or written actions undertaken during the year by its governing body and/or each committee with authority to act on behalf of the governing body.[103] The organization must describe whether and, if so, how it makes its governing documents, conflict-of-interest policy, and financial statements available to the public.[104]

This annual information return references 12 types of written policies or procedures that tax-exempt organizations may be expected to adopt. The filing exempt organization is asked whether it has a conflict-of-interest

---

98. See § 27.2A.
99. Form 990, Part VI, Section A, questions 1a, 1b. It may be anticipated that the second of these questions will increase the likelihood that IRS agents, when reviewing applications for recognition of exemption and during examinations, will insist that at least a majority of the board of charitable (and perhaps other exempt) organizations consist of "independent" members, even though there is no basis for the requirement in the law.
100. Form 990, Part VI, Section A, question 2.
101. *Id.*, question 3.
102. *Id.*, question 10. An organization must describe, in Form 990, Schedule O, the process, if any, the organization uses to review the annual information return.
103. Form 990, Part VI, Section A, question 8.
104. Form 990, Part VI, Section C, question 19. This description is provided in Schedule O. There is no requirement in federal law that an exempt organization's conflict-of-interest policy or financial statements be made available to the public.

policy,[105] a whistleblower policy,[106] and a document retention and destruction policy.[107] If the organization reports that it has chapters, branches, or affiliates,[108] it must indicate whether it has policies and procedures governing the activities of these entities to ensure that their operations are consistent with those of the organization.[109] A filing organization is asked whether it invested in, contributed assets to, or participated in a joint venture or similar arrangement with a taxable entity during the year.[110] If the answer to this question is "yes," the organization must report whether it has adopted a written policy or procedure requiring it to evaluate its participation in joint venture arrangements under the federal tax law and has taken steps to safeguard its exempt status with respect to such arrangements.[111] The organization must state whether the process for determining compensation of its chief executive officer, executive director, top management official, and/or other officers or key employees included a review and approval by independent persons, comparability data, and contemporaneous substantiation of the deliberation and decision.[112] If an organization reports that it holds one or more conservation easements, it is required to indicate whether it has a policy regarding the periodic monitoring, inspection, and enforcement of the easement or easements.[113] If the organization makes grants to recipients outside the United States, it is required to describe its procedures for monitoring use of the grant funds.[114] If the organization is functioning as a hospital, it must report whether it has a charity care policy[115] and a debt collection policy.[116] An organization must indicate whether it is following a policy regarding payment or reimbursement of expenses incurred by trustees, directors, officers, and key employees regarding first-class or charter travel, travel for companions, tax indemnification and gross-up payments, a discretionary spending account, a housing allowance or residence for personal use, payments for business use of personal residence,

---

* 105. Form 990, Part III, question 3a. If the answer to this question is "yes," the organization will be required to report the number of transactions the organization reviewed under the policy and related procedures during the year (*id.*, question 3b).
* 106. Form 990, Part III, question 4.
  107. *Id.*, question 5.
  108. *Id.*, question 7a.
  109. *Id.*, question 7b.
  110. Form 990, Part VI, Section B, question 16a.
  111. *Id.*, question 16b.
  112. *Id.*, question 15. This process must be described in Schedule O.
  113. Form 990, Schedule D, Part II, question 5.
  114. Form 990, Schedule F, Part I, question 2. The description is provided in *id.*, Part IV.
  115. Form 990, Schedule H, Part I, question 1.
  116. *Id.*, Part III, question 9a. If the answer is "yes," the organization must report whether its collection policy contains provisions on the collection practices to be followed for patients who are known to qualify for charity care or financial assistance (*id.*, question 9b).

health or social club dues or initiation fees, and/or personal services (such as for a maid, chauffeur, or chef).[117]

(m) IRS Life Cycle Educational Tool (New)

The IRS abandoned its draft of good governance practices for charitable organizations,[118] stating that current IRS positions on nonprofit governance "are best reflected in the reporting required by the revised Form 990"[119] and the components in this document as part of the agency's Life Cycle educational tool. The IRS, on its website, proclaimed: "Good governance is important to increase the likelihood that organizations will comply with the tax law, protect their charitable assets and, thereby, best serve their charitable beneficiaries."

(i) Introduction. The IRS believes that a well-governed charity is more likely to obey the tax laws, safeguard charitable assets, and serve charitable interests than one with poor or lax governance. A charity that has clearly articulated purposes that describe its mission, a knowledgeable and committed governing body and management team, and sound management practices is more likely to operate effectively and consistent with tax law requirements. Although the tax law generally does not mandate particular management structures, operational policies, or administrative practices, it is important that each charity be thoughtful about the management practices that are most appropriate for that charity in assuring sound operations and compliance with the tax law.

(ii) Mission. The IRS encourages every charity to establish and regularly review its mission. A clearly articulated mission, adopted by the board of directors, serves to explain and popularize the charity's purpose and guide its work. It also addresses why the charity exists, what it hopes to accomplish, and what activities it will undertake, where, and for whom.

(iii) Organizational Documents. Regardless of whether a charity is a corporation, trust, unincorporated association, or other type of organization, it must have organizational documents that provide the framework for its governance and management. State law often prescribes the type of organizational document and its content. State law may require corporations to adopt bylaws. Organizational documents must be filed with applications for recognition of exemption.

---

117. Form 990, Schedule J, question 3. Relevant information concerning any of these 8 items, or an explanation as to why the organization did not follow such a policy, is provided in *id.*, Part III. In general, Nilles & Meier, "IRS Places New Emphasis on Nonprofit Corporate Governance Policies: Are You Ready for the New Form 990?," 57 *Exempt Org. Tax Rev.* (No. 3) 283 (Sep. 2007).
118. See § 5.6(i).
119. See § 5.6(l).

(iv) Governing Body.   The IRS encourages an active and engaged board, believing that it is important to the success of a charity and to its compliance with applicable tax law requirements. Governing boards should be composed of persons who are informed and active in overseeing a charity's operations and finances. The IRS is concerned that, if a governing board tolerates a climate of secrecy or neglect, charitable assets are more likely to be diverted to benefit the private interests of insiders at the expense of public and charitable interests. Successful governing boards include individuals who are not only knowledgeable and engaged but selected with the organization's needs in mind (e.g., accounting, finance, compensation, and ethics).

Attention should also be paid to the size of the board, ensuring that it is the appropriate size to effectively make sure that the organization obeys tax laws, safeguards its charitable assets, and furthers its charitable purposes. Small boards run the risk of not representing a sufficiently broad public interest, and of lacking the required skills and other resources required to effectively govern the organization. On the other hand, very large boards may have a more difficult time getting down to business and making decisions.

A governing board should include independent members and not be dominated by employees or others who are not independent individuals because of family or business relationships. The IRS reviews the board composition of charities to determine whether the board represents a broad public interest; to identify the potential for insider transactions that could result in misuse of charitable assets; to determine whether an organization has independent members, stockholders, or other persons with the authority to elect members of the board or approve or reject board decisions; and to ascertain whether the organization has delegated control or key management authority to a management company or other persons.

If an organization has local chapters, branches, or affiliates, the IRS encourages it to have procedures and policies in place to ensure that the activities and operations of these subordinates are consistent with those of the parent organization.

(v) Governance and Management Policies.   Although the federal tax law does not require charities to have governance and management policies, the IRS will nonetheless review an organization's application for recognition of exemption and annual information returns to determine whether it has implemented policies relating to executive compensation, conflicts of interest, investments, fundraising, documenting governance decisions, document retention and destruction, and whistleblower claims.

Persons who are knowledgeable in compensation matters and who have no financial interest in the determination should determine a charity's executive compensation. The federal tax law does not, however, require charities to follow a particular process in ascertaining the amount of this type of compensation. Organizations that file Form 990 will find that Part VI, Section B, line 15 asks whether the process used to determine the compensation of an organization's top management official and other officers and key employees included a review and approval by independent persons, comparability data, and contemporaneous substantiation of the deliberation and decision. In addition, the Form 990 solicits compensation information for certain trustees, directors, officers, key employees, and highest compensated employees.

The IRS encourages reliance on the *rebuttable presumption*, which is part of the intermediate sanctions rules.[120] Under this test, payments of compensation are presumed to be reasonable if the compensation arrangement is approved in advance by an authorized body composed entirely of individuals who do not have a conflict of interest with respect to the arrangement, the authorized body obtained and relied on appropriate data as to comparability prior to making its determination, and the authorized body adequately documented the basis for its determination concurrently with making the determination.

The duty of loyalty, which requires a director to act in the interest of the charity, requires a director to avoid conflicts of interest that are detrimental to the charity.[121] The IRS encourages a charity's board of directors to adopt and regularly evaluate a written conflict-of-interest policy that requires directors and staff to act solely in the interests of the charity without regard for personal interests; includes written procedures for determining whether a relationship, financial interest, or business affiliation results in a conflict of interest; and prescribes a course of action in the event a conflict of interest is identified.[122]

Increasingly, charities are investing in joint ventures, for-profit entities, and complicated and sophisticated financial products or investments that require financial and investment expertise and, in some instances, the advice of outside investment advisors. The IRS encourages charities that make these types of investments to adopt written policies and procedures requiring the charity to evaluate its participation in these investments, and to take steps to safeguard the organization's assets and tax-exempt status if they could be affected by the investment arrangement. The Form 990 inquires as to whether an organization has adopted this type of policy. Also, the form asks for detailed information about certain investments.

The IRS encourages charities to adopt and monitor policies to ensure that fundraising solicitations meet federal and state law requirements, and that solicitation materials are accurate, truthful, and candid. Charities are encouraged to keep their fundraising costs reasonable, and to provide information about fundraising costs and practices to donors and the public. The Form 990 solicits information about fundraising activities, revenues, and expenses.

---

120. See § 21.9.
121. See § 5.3.
122. See 5.6(f).

The IRS encourages the governing bodies and subcommittees to take steps to ensure that minutes of their meetings, and actions taken by written action or outside of meetings, are contemporaneously documented. The Form 990 asks whether an organization contemporaneously documents meetings or written actions undertaken during the year by its governing body and committees with authority to act on behalf of the governing body.

The IRS encourages charities to adopt a written policy establishing standards for document integrity, retention, and destruction. This type of policy should include guidelines for handling electronic files; it should also cover backup procedures, archiving of documents, and regular checkups of the reliability of the system. The Form 990 asks whether an organization has a written document retention and destruction policy.

The IRS also encourages a charity's board to consider adopting and regularly evaluating a code of ethics that describes behavior it wants to encourage and behavior it wants to discourage. A code of ethics will serve to communicate and further a strong culture of legal compliance and ethical integrity to all persons associated with the organization.

The IRS further encourages the board to adopt an effective *whistleblower policy* for handling employee complaints and to establish procedures for employees to report in confidence any suspected financial impropriety or misuse of the charity's resources. The Form 990 asks whether the organization became aware during the year of a material diversion of its assets and whether an organization has a written whistleblower policy.

(vi) Financial Statements and Form 990 Reporting. The IRS is of the view that a charity with substantial assets or revenue should consider obtaining an audit of its finances by an independent auditor. The board may establish an independent audit committee to select and oversee an auditor. The Form 990 asks whether the organization's financial statements were compiled or reviewed by an independent accountant, audited by an independent accountant, and subject to oversight by a committee within the organization. Also, the Form 990 asks whether, as the result of a federal award, the organization was required to undergo an audit.

Practices differ widely as to who sees the Form 990, when they see it (before or after its filing), and the extent of the reviewers' input, review, or approval. Some organizations provide copies of the return to the members of the board and other governance or management officials. The Form 990 asks whether the organization provides a copy of the return to its governing body and requires the organization to explain any process of review by its directors or management.

(vii) Transparency and Accountability. By making full and accurate information about its mission, activities, finances, and governance publicly available, a charity encourages transparency and accountability to its constituents.

The IRS encourages every charity to adopt and monitor procedures to ensure that its Form 1023, Form 990, Form 990-T, annual reports, and financial statements are complete and accurate, are posted on its public website, and are made available to the public on request.

*(n) IRS Official's Speeches (New)

The policy of the IRS concerning tax-exempt (particularly public) charities and matters of governance has evolved over recent months. Perhaps the best evidence of the contours of this evolution is the content of three speeches delivered by the TE/GE Commissioner during 2007–2008.

When the TE/GE Commissioner first began talking about the IRS's role in nonprofit governance, in an April 2007 speech, he conceded that for the IRS to propound and enforce good governance principles, the agency would have to go "beyond its traditional spheres of activity."[123] The Commissioner on that occasion revealed that he was pondering the question of "whether it would benefit the public and the tax-exempt sector to require [by the IRS] organizations to adopt and follow recognized principles of good governance." He asserted that there is a "vacuum" that needs to be filled in the realm of *education* on "basic standards and practices of good governance and accountability."

The TE/GE Commissioner, that day, made the best case that can be asserted for the intertwining of the matter of governance and nonprofit, tax-exempt organizations' compliance with the federal tax law. He said that a "well-governed organization is more likely to be compliant, while poor governance can easily lead an exempt organization into trouble." He spoke, for example, of an "engaged, informed, and independent board of directors accountable to the community [that the exempt organization] serves."

By the time the TE/GE Commissioner returned to this subject in a November 2007 speech, his attitude and tone had dramatically changed.[124] No more pondering, musing, and speculating. Rather, the Commissioner stated that "[w]hile a few continue to argue that governance is outside our jurisdiction, most now support an active IRS that is engaged in this area." He expressed his view that the IRS "contributes to a compliant, healthy charitable sector by expecting the tax-exempt community to adhere to commonly accepted standards of good governance." He said that IRS involvement in this area is "not new"; the agency has been "quietly but steadily promoting good governance for a long time." He noted that "[o]ur determination agents ask governance-related questions" and "our agents assess an organization's internal controls as the

---

123. The formal text of this speech is available at Bureau of Nat'l Affairs, *Daily Tax Report* (no. 81) TaxCore® (April 27, 2007).
124. The formal text of this speech is available at Bureau of Nat'l Affairs, *Daily Tax Report* (no. 222) TaxCore® (Nov. 19, 2007).

agents decide how to pursue an examination." He continued: "We are comfortable that we are well within our authority to act in these areas." And: "To more clearly put our weight behind good governance may represent a small step beyond our traditional sphere of influence, but we believe the subject is well within our core responsibilities."

When April 2008 rolled around, the TE/GE Commissioner had once again significantly evolved in his thinking on these points. In two speeches he made his view quite clear: (1) the IRS has a "robust role" to play in the realm of charitable governance, (2) the IRS does not even entertain the thought that involvement in governance matters is beyond the sphere of the agency's jurisdiction, and (3) he cannot be convinced that, "outside of very, very small organizations and perhaps family foundations, the gold standard should not be to have an active, independent and engaged board of directors overseeing the organization."[125] Thus, the "question is no longer whether the IRS has a role to play in this area, but rather, what that role will be." The governance section of the new annual information return, he said, will primarily dictate that role.

In the aftermath of these speeches, the director of the Exempt Organizations Division stated that the IRS is stepping back from recommending best practices as to governance and is focusing on education as to good governance.[126] On that occasion, she conceded that "not all IRS agents have gotten the message." Apparently this cadre of agents is not inconsequential in terms of size. The facts of a 2008 court opinion reflect the policy of some agents to demand changes in board composition, adoption of a conflict-of-interest policy, and adoption of other policies and procedures as a condition of recognition of tax exemption.[127]

The Commissioner of the IRS made his first public comments about nonprofit governance in November of 2008.[128] After expressing his admiration for the nonprofit sector, and its "diversity, its creativity, and its risk taking," he stated that the IRS "shouldn't supplant the business judgment of organizational leaders, and certainly shouldn't determine how a nonprofit fulfills its individual mission." He said that he "clearly see[s] our role as working with you and others to promote good governance, beginning with the proposition that an active, engaged, and independent board of directors helps assure that an organization is carrying out a tax-exempt purpose and acts as its best defense against abuse." The Commissioner concluded his remarks by saying that "[w]e want to arm you with information and guidance you need to help you comply."

---

125. The formal text of these speeches is available at Bureau of Nat'l Affairs, *Daily Tax Report* (no. 83) TaxCore® (April 30, 2008).
126. A summary of this speech is available at Bureau of Nat'l Affairs, *Daily Tax Report* (no. 119) G-6 (June 20, 2008).
127. Exploratory Research, Inc. v. Comm'r, 95 T.C.M. 1347 (2008).
128. The formal text of this speech is available at Bureau of Nat'l Affairs, 218 *Daily Tax Report* p. G-1, TaxCore® (Nov. 12, 2008).

A new TE/GE Commissioner took office in early 2009. In her first public address on nonprofit governance in June of that year, she said that the IRS "has a clear, unambiguous role to play in governance [of tax-exempt organizations]. Some have argued that we do not need to be involved, because we can count on the states to do their job and the sector to stay on the path of self-regulation. While both state regulation and sector self-regulation are important, and I welcome and respect them, they do not get the IRS off the hook. Congress gave us a job to do, and we cannot delegate to others our obligation to enforce the conditions of federal tax exemption. The federal tax law must be applied consistently across the country, and we will use both our education and outreach programs and a meaningful enforcement presence to accomplish this."[129]

These IRS speeches on nonprofit governance are inconsistent and are sending mixed messages to the nonprofit community. There is the message of militancy, stating that the IRS will robustly impose and enforce rules as to the governance of tax-exempt organizations, particularly public charities, while simultaneously conceding that these rules are not conditions of exemption. There is the message of the IRS as advisor, not an imposer of nonprofit governance requirements, focusing on educational efforts and other forms of guidance to assist organizations in complying with the federal tax laws.

*(o) IRS Ruling Policy (New)

The IRS has been actively issuing private letter rulings in the area of nonprofit governance, founded principally on an expansive (and incorrect) interpretation of the private benefit doctrine.[130] In the first of these rulings, the IRS ruled that an organization could not be exempt as a charitable entity, in part because it had two board members.[131] The IRS issued a private letter ruling holding that an organization could not be a tax-exempt, charitable entity, in part because it is "not operated by a community-based board of directors."[132] The IRS privately ruled that an organization that refused to adopt a conflict-of-interest policy and transform its board into an independent one could not qualify as a charitable entity.[133] The IRS privately ruled that an organization could not qualify as a tax-exempt charitable entity, in part because two individuals exercised "absolute control" over the organization and in part because it did not adopt a conflict-of-interest policy, did not have an executive compensation policy, and lacked an independent board.[134] Thereafter, the IRS privately ruled that an organization could not qualify as a tax-exempt,

---

* 129. The formal text of this speech is available at Bureau of Nat'l Affairs, 119 *Daily Tax Report*, p. G-6, TaxCore® (June 24, 2009).
* 130. See § 20.11(d).
* 131. Priv. Ltr. Rul. 200737044.
* 132. Priv. Ltr. Rul. 200828029.
* 133. Priv. Ltr. Rul. 200830028.
* 134. Priv. Ltr. Rul. 200843032.

charitable entity, in part because its three (unrelated) directors had "unfettered control" over the organization and its assets.[135]

In addition, the IRS ruled that an organization was not entitled to exemption as a charitable entity, in part because the entity is "governed by a board of directors that is controlled by members of the same family."[136]

These applications of the private benefit doctrine are flatly erroneous. There is absolutely no authority for the positions being taken by the IRS about board composition, independent boards, conflicts-of-interest policies, and other policies. Aside from the issue as to whether the IRS should be involved with nonprofit governance at all, it is certainly inappropriate to use the private benefit doctrine as a bolster for insertion of the agency into a realm as to which it lacks jurisdiction and competence. Moreover, these applications of the doctrine are based on speculation. The private benefit doctrine is to be applied where there has been unwarranted private benefit, not where there is some amorphous potential for private benefit. Indeed, in some of its rulings in the governance context, the agency has so stated. For example, in an instance where a small governing body controlled by an organization's founders was considered by the IRS, the agency did not find private benefit but instead observed that the facts created the need for the organization to be open and candid.[137] Likewise, the IRS, noting that an organization's board consists of three related individuals, wrote that this fact is "creating the potential for private control of" the entity.[138]

*(p) ACT Report on Role of IRS in Governance Issues (New)

The IRS's Advisory Committee on Tax Exempt and Government Entities (ACT), on June 11, 2008, issued a report on the appropriate role of the IRS with respect to tax-exempt organizations good governance issues. Noting that the IRS's rationale for inserting itself into nonprofit governance matters—that a well-governed charity is more likely to obey the tax laws, safeguard charitable

---

* 135. Priv. Ltr. Rul. 200845053.
* 136. Priv. Ltr. Rul. 200916035.
* 137. Priv. Ltr. Rul. 200846040.
* 138. Priv. Ltr. Rul. 200926037. Remarkably, this ruling was issued to an entity that was attempting to be a church. A commentary on the ruling observed that, in issuing it, the IRS took an "unusual step" (Kelderman, "IRS Denies Organization's Application as a Church," XXI *Chron. of Phil.* (no. 2) 69 (Oct. 30, 2008)). Nonetheless, the U.S. Tax Court held that an organization did not qualify as an exempt charitable entity, in part because it has only one board member (Ohio Disability Ass'n v. Comm'r, T.C. Memo. 2009-262 (Nov. 12, 2009)). The court noted that the organization has a prohibition in its articles of incorporation against private inurement and adopted a conflict-of-interest policy, yet "there are no procedures or personnel in place to ensure that either the stated policy will be followed or private inurement will not occur." Overall, wrote the court, the record "does not demonstrate that there is oversight to prevent the organization from being operated to benefit" its director.

assets, and serve charitable interests[139]—is "self-evident," the ACT observed that, at the same time, "efforts to promote good governance are fraught with complexity." Also noting that the IRS is a "powerful force that can drive behavior merely by asking about specific governance practices," the ACT expressed its belief that the IRS "should approach this area with caution."

The ACT stated that "there is little or no empirical evidence to date that supports the efficacy of any specific governance practices by nonprofit organizations, much less compliance with the requirements for maintaining tax exemption." It wrote that "we believe that respect for the diverse and evolving nature of the nonprofit sector requires that we continue to value flexibility in our expectations of the specific governance practices that may be essential to the health of the sector." Overall, the ACT observed, there is a greater need to tread lightly because of the burdens flowing from encouraging unnecessarily extensive governance reforms, the fact that the costs of adopting certain practices simply may not be worth the benefits, and the reality that the costs of governance will consume charitable assets that could otherwise be devoted to the organizations' programs."

The ACT noted that the IRS "may require specific governance practices on an ad hoc and inconsistent basis." It expressed its concern "about the IRS having this level of discretion in cajoling or requiring specific governance process, particularly in the determination phase, where there usually is no track record evidencing operational failures." The ACT, commenting on questions about governance in the new annual information return,[140] observed that inclusion of these questions "inherently (and intentionally) suggests that the IRS supports adoption of specific governance policies and practices." "The danger then," the ACT concluded, "is that organizations will take the path of least resistance and adopt the policies and practices whether or not they are appropriate for them, or effective in their context."

The ACT wrote: "We are very mindful of the fact that even the most modest level of prescription from a regulatory body such as the IRS regarding what constitutes 'good governance' can undermine the fundamental and wholly legitimate authority of the organization's governing board and can suggest a one-size-fits-all approach that can place undue burdens on an organization, divert the organization's attention from meaningful governance to policies and procedures, and do damage to the uniquely diverse and vibrant charitable sector in this country."

The ACT offered these recommendations to the IRS: (1) the agency should continue to work collaboratively with the tax-exempt community in connection with its governance initiatives; (2) specific governance practices should be mandated only in rare and limited circumstances; (3) the closer the nexus

---

* 139. See, e.g., § 5.6(n).
* 140. See, e.g., § 5.6(l).

to tax compliance, the more appropriate the governance inquiry or recommendation; (4) the IRS should explain the specific relationship between tax compliance and each governance practice about which it is inquiring or which it is addressing; (5) compliance questions or commentary are more appropriate than governance questions or commentary; (6) governance inquiries should be made and comments addressed in as neutral a manner as possible under the circumstances; (7) questions that ask about practices and approaches are typically better than questions that ask about policies; (8) the IRS should expressly acknowledge when governance practices about which it is inquiring or which it is addressing are not required; (9) the IRS should expressly acknowledge that governance practices about which it is inquiring or which it is addressing may be more appropriate for some types of organizations than for others and respect the role of the governing body in making these decisions; (10) taking into account the absence of certain governance practices in determining whether to audit or take other compliance actions may be appropriate in certain instances; (11) consistency and fair treatment are critical; and (12) education, thoughtfully implemented, is more appropriate than pressuring change.

*(q) College and University Compliance Questionnaire (New)

As part of its compliance check of a sampling of the nation's tax-exempt colleges and universities,[141] implemented by the mailing of a questionnaire,[142] the IRS asked private institutions whether they have a conflict-of-interest policy that governs members of the institutions' "ruling body" and their "top management" officials, whether they have such a policy that governs full-time faculty, and whether the institutions make their audited financial statements available to the public.

*(r) Exempt Organizations 2009 Annual Report (New)

The IRS announced in late 2008 that it is continuing its work in the tax-exempt organizations governance area by (1) development of a checklist to be used by agents in examinations of exempt organizations to determine whether the organizations' governance practices "impacted the tax compliance issues identified in the examination and to educate organizations about possible governance considerations;" (2) commencement of a training program to educate its employees about exempt organizations governance implications in the determinations, rulings and agreements, and education and outreach areas; and (3) identification of Form 990 governance questions that could be used in conjunction with other Form 990 information in possible compliance initiatives, such as those involving executive compensation, transactions with

---

* 141. See § 26.6(a)(ii), text accompanied by note 308.6.
* 142. Form 14018 (Sep. 2008).

interested persons, solicitations of noncash contributions, or diversion or misuse of exempt organizations' assets.[143]

*(s) Owens Letter to Treasury Department (New)

Noting that the IRS has "demonstrated a desire to increase its oversight" in the area of governance of nonprofit organizations and that there is "no precedential federal tax law guidance that prescribes the appropriate standards for nonprofit governance," the former director of the Exempt Organizations Division, Marcus Owens, wrote to the Department of the Treasury, on January 14, 2009, saying that "it would be helpful to have clear direction from the Treasury Department regarding the specific standards to which nonprofits will be held."[144]

Mr. Owens, now in private practice, observed that "this lack of guidance not only impairs taxpayer efforts at voluntary compliance but also creates a risk that similarly situated taxpayers may be subject to differing treatment" from the IRS. He stated that organizations that submit applications for recognition of exemption or ruling requests "may obtain disparate and subjective interpretations of the Service's policy, depending on the agent who happens to handle the matter." He continued: "Moreover, absent published guidance on this issue, a taxpayer under examination has no context or ability to challenge the Service's findings regarding its governance practices at the examination level or within the agency's Appeals function." Indeed, the Appeals Office "itself lacks the necessary standards by which to evaluate either the taxpayer's compliance or the revenue agent's analysis, which reduces the efficacy and undermines the purpose of the Appeals function."

To ensure "consistent, transparent enforcement of the federal tax laws," Mr. Owens requested Treasury to issue guidance regarding the standards for nonprofit governance, "with appropriate notice and opportunity for comment, as soon as possible."

*(t) IRS Training Materials (New)

The IRS released the materials that it has been using for the training of its agents in the field of nonprofit governance, for their edification in reviewing applications for recognition of exemption and annual information returns, and during examinations.[145] For the most part, these materials do not contain anything new in relation to what the IRS has been saying over the past few years

---

* 143. IRS Exempt Organizations 2008 Annual Report, at 20.
* 144. An article about and the text of this letter are available at Bureau of Nat'l Affairs, 10 *Daily Tax Report*, p. G-8, TaxCore® (Jan. 16, 2009).
* 145. An article about these training materials, which are available on the IRS's Web site, is at Bureau of Nat'l Affairs, 142 *Daily Tax Report*, p. G-1 (July 28, 2009).

about its position on governance issues pertaining to public charities. They reflect the inherent tension as to what the federal tax law requires, the IRS's lack of jurisdiction and competence in this area, and its positions on various governance matters.

Here (again) is the ultimate rationale the IRS uses to justify its involvement in nonprofit governance, particularly with respect to public charities: The agency "believes that a well-governed charity is more likely to obey the tax laws, safeguard charitable assets, and serve charitable interests than one with poor or lax governance."

These materials are replete with contradictory statements. For example, the IRS states that a charity that has "clearly articulated purposes that describe its mission, a knowledgeable and committed governing body and management team, and sound management practices is more likely to operate effectively and consistent with tax law requirements." Then, it writes that the tax law "generally does not mandate particular management structures, operational policies, or administrative practices."

The federal tax law "does not require charities to have governance and management policies." Then: The IRS "will review an organization's application for [recognition of] exemption and annual information returns to determine whether the organization has implemented policies relating to executive compensation, conflicts of interest, investments, fundraising, documenting governance decisions, document retention and destruction, and whistleblower claims." (In other words, despite the fact that the law does not require these policies, the IRS is going to look for (and probably demand) them anyway.)

There are lots of *shoulds* in these materials, even though there is no justification in law for any of them. For example, the IRS states that a governing board "should include independent members and should not be dominated by employees or others who are not, by their very nature, independent individuals because of family or business relationships." (Elsewhere the materials state that this is a suggestion and the IRS will not enforce the requirement.) The "nominating process" for members of the governing body "should reach out for candidates, actively recruiting individuals whose commitment, skills, life experience, background, perspective, and other characteristics will serve the public charity and its needs." "Attention should also be paid to the size of the board ensuring that it is the appropriate size. . . ." Governing boards "should be composed of persons who are informed and active in overseeing a charity's operations and finances." How about this one: "Term limits for board members are an effective way to ensure board vitality."

*(u) TIGTA Report on Tax-Exempt Organizations and Fraud (New)

The Treasury Inspector General for Tax Administration, in 2009, issued a report critical of the participation by the TE/GE Division in the agency's

National Fraud Program. According to the TIGTA, the five offices within the Division[146] have not been consistent in the implementation of this fraud program.[147] Management of the Division, however, agreed to develop and implement a centralized approach to the matter of fraud within the tax-exempt sector.

The TIGTA identified three reasons as to why it is easier today for tax-exempt organizations to be involved in fraudulent activities and more difficult for TE/GE management to identify and quantify the amount of fraud that exists. One of these reasons is that "[s]ome tax-exempt entities have not established independent, empowered, and active boards of directors to ensure that tax-exempt organizations serve public purposes and do not misuse or squander the resources and their trust."[148]

This report offered the following definition of the term *governance*: The "establishment of policies, and continuous monitoring of their proper implementation, by members of the governing body of an organization. It includes mechanisms required to balance the powers of the members (with the associated accountability) and their primary duty of enhancing the prosperity and viability of the organization."[149]

*(v) Senate Finance Committee Health-Care Legislation (New)

The Senate Finance Committee, on October 19, 2009, approved a health-care system reform bill.[150] This legislation includes authorization for a program to assist establishment and operation of nonprofit health insurance issuers that would be structured as cooperatives.[151] These entities, which would be tax-exempt under federal law,[152] would have to "incorporate ethics and conflict of interest standards protecting against insurance industry involvement and interference."[153]

*(w) IRS Governance Check Sheet (New)

The IRS, on December 10, 2009, made public the Governance Check Sheet that its examination agents will be using to gather data about the governance

---

* 146. See § 2.2(a).
* 147. TIGTA, "A Corporate Approach is Needed to Provide for a More Effective Tax-Exempt Fraud Program," 2009-10-096 (July 6, 2009).
* 148. *Id.* at 1.
* 149. *Id.* at 2.
* 150. America's Healthy Future Act of 2009 (S. 1796, 111th Cong., 1st Sess. (2009)).
* 151. *Id.* § 1401.
* 152. Prop. IRC § 501(c)(29).
* 153. In general, see Hopkins & Gross, *Nonprofit Governance: Law, Practices & Trends* (Hoboken, NJ: John Wiley & Sons, 2009).

practices of public charities (Form 14114), accompanied by a set of instructions. Here are some of the areas that will be explored:

(i) Governing Body and Management

- Whether the organization has a written mission statement that articulates its current exempt purposes
- Whether the organization's bylaws set forth information about its governing body, such as composition, duties, qualifications, and voting rights
- The extent to which copies of the organization's articles and bylaws have been distributed (e.g., to the board or the public).
- The frequency of meetings of voting board members with a quorum present

(ii) Compensation

- Whether compensation arrangements for all trustees, directors, officers, and key employees are approved in advance by an authorized body of the organization composed of individuals with no conflict of interest with respect to the arrangement
- Whether this body relies on comparability data in making compensation determinations
- Whether the basis for compensation determinations is contemporaneously documented

(iii) Organizational Control

- Whether any of the organization's voting board members have a family relationship and/or outside business relationship with any other voting or nonvoting trustee, director, officer, or key employee
- Whether effective control of the organization rests with a single or select few individuals

(iv) Conflicts of Interest

- Whether the organization has a written conflict-of-interest policy, and if so, whether its addresses recusals and requires annual written disclosures of conflicts
- If any actual or potential conflicts of interest were disclosed, whether the organization's policy was adhered to

(v) Financial Oversight

- Whether there are systems or procedures in place intended to ensure that assets are properly used, consistent with the organization's mission

- The frequency with which the organization provided its board members with written reports on its financial activities

- Whether, prior to filing, the organization's Form 990 was reviewed by the full board and/or a committee

- Whether an independent accountant's report was prepared, and if so, whether it was considered by the board and/or a committee

- Whether an independent accountant prepared a management letter, and if so, whether this letter was reviewed by the board and/or a committee and whether the organization adopted any of the recommendations in the letter

(vi) Document Retention

- Whether the organization has a written policy for document retention and destruction

- If so, whether the organization adheres to this policy

- Whether the board contemporaneously documents its meetings and retains this documentation

*(x) AGB/NACUBO College and University Governance Analysis (New)

In late 2008, the IRS sent a compliance questionnaire to approximately 400 colleges and universities, the majority of which were four-year public or independent degree-granting institutions. This questionnaire focused on governance, endowment management, employee compensation, and generation of unrelated business income.[154]

The Association of Governing Boards of Universities and Colleges and the National Association of College and University Business Officers, on December 17, 2009, unveiled publication, following a "parallel analysis" of data submitted to the IRS by colleges and universities, of their assessment of this information. The report analyzed the submitted responses of 146 institutions, representing over one-third of the entities that responded to the IRS questionnaire. Ernst & Young analyzed this data.

This analysis stated: "[I]t appears that, for the most part, the participating colleges and universities have adopted many governance best practices, provide strong oversight of endowment investments, set reasonable endowment

---

* 154. See § 8.3(a), text accompanied by notes 77.1–77.5.

spending rates, and follow a range of practices with regard to the realization and reporting of unrelated business income. Many of the participating private colleges and universities have meaningful policies for the review of executive compensation, but some have room for improvement."

This survey found that 98 percent of public institutions and 97 percent of private institutions have a written conflict-of-interest policy or are subject to a state statute governing conflicts. Seventy-five percent of public institutions and 78 percent of private institutions have a written or statutory conflicts policy for full-time faculty. Ninety-one percent of respondents make their audited financial statement available to the public.

PART THREE

Tax-Exempt Charitable Organizations

CHAPTER SIX

Concept of *Charitable*

§ 6.1 FEDERAL TAX LAW DEFINITION OF *CHARITABLE*

(b) Federal Tax Law Principles

p. 162, n. 41. Delete *(iii)* and insert *(iv)*.

§ 6.2 PUBLIC POLICY DOCTRINE

(a) General Principles

p. 166, *third complete paragraph.* Insert as last sentence:

Likewise, an organization formed by a violent sexual predator to sexually exploit children by promoting the repeal of child pornography and exploitation laws was found by the IRS to have a purpose that is "contrary to public policy to protect the sexual exploitation of children."[70.1]

p. 169, *last line.* Insert footnote following period:

[93.1]Priv. Ltr. Rul. 200909064.

(b) Race-Based Discrimination

(iii) Broader Policy Impact.

p. 173, n. 119. Delete *54* and insert *540*.

70.1. Priv. Ltr. Rul. 200826043.

*p. 174, *carryover paragraph.* Insert as second complete sentence:

Thus, the IRS ruled that a school could not be tax-exempt because of ineffective advertising, failure to reach out to the African American community, failure to have any African Americans on its scholarship committee or board of directors, and lack of full minority scholarships; the agency wrote that the school "failed to demonstrate that [it has] taken sufficient steps to overcome the inference of discrimination."[126.1]

§ 6.3   COLLATERAL CONCEPTS

(a)   Requirement of *Charitable* Class

p. 181, *carryover paragraph.* Insert as last sentence:

Current and former employees of a company can qualify as a charitable class for purposes of enabling a fund that provides emergency assistance to these beneficiaries to constitute a tax-exempt charitable entity.[178.1]

---

* 126.1. Priv. Ltr. Rul. 200909064.
   178.1. E.g., Priv. Ltr. Rul. 200839034.

CHAPTER SEVEN

Charitable Organizations

§ 7.2   RELIEF OF DISTRESSED

*p. 198, *last two lines*. **Delete (including footnote) and substitute:**

Tax-exempt charita-

*p. 199, *first three lines*. **Delete and substitute:**

ble status is available for an organization solely on the ground that it relieves individuals who are or were *distressed*. The IRS considered the tax treatment of a nonprofit hospice that op-

*p. 199, *first complete paragraph, second line*. **Delete** *being*.

*p. 200, *first complete paragraph, last line*. **Insert n. 51.1 at end of line, the text of which is in n. 63; delete reference to article.**

*p. 200, n. 53. **Delete text and substitute** *JCX-93-01*.

*pp. 200–201. **Delete last complete paragraph on p. 200, and paragraph that begins on p. 200 and carries over to p. 201 (including footnotes).**

*p. 201, *first complete paragraph, eighth line*. **Delete** *does* **and insert** *did*.

*p. 201, *second complete paragraph, first line*. **Delete** *offers* **and insert** *offered*.

*p. 201, *second complete paragraph, third line.* Delete *go* and insert *went.*

*p. 201, *second complete paragraph, eleventh line.* Delete *concludes* and insert *concluded.*

*p. 201. Delete last paragraph.

*pp. 202–203. Delete p. 202 and text of paragraph that carries over to p. 203 (including footnotes).

*p. 203. Insert following first complete paragraph, before heading:

The IRS inexplicably persists with the view that the standard for providing assistance in these contexts is that the potential beneficiaries be *needy*, rather than *distressed*. This approach to the analysis, which is clearly at odds with the applicable regulation, is rested on another regulation that defines the term *needy* in a wholly different statutory context—that pertaining to the charitable deduction for certain contributions of inventory.[66.1] In that setting, a *needy person* is an individual who lacks the necessities of life, involving physical, mental, or emotional wellbeing, as a result of poverty or temporary distress.[66.2] Examples of needy persons include an individual who (1) is financially impoverished as a result of low income and lack of financial resources, (2) temporarily lacks food or shelter (and the means to provide for it), (3) is the victim of a natural disaster (such as fire or flood), (4) is the victim of a civil disaster (such as a civil disturbance), (5) is temporarily not self-sufficient as a result of a sudden and severe personal or family crisis (such as an individual who is the victim of a crime of violence or who has been physically abused), (6) is a refuge or immigrant and who is experiencing language, cultural, or financial difficulties, and (7) is not self-sufficient as a result of previous institutionalization (such as a former prisoner or a former patient in a mental institution, as well as a minor child who is not self-sufficient and who is not cared for by a parent or guardian.[66.3] Certainly many if not all of the elements of what it means to be *distressed* are embraced by this expansive definition of the term *needy*, yet in a ruling the IRS noted that grants are made from a hardship fund "only to needy and distressed" individuals.[66.4]

*§ 7.2A DISASTER RELIEF PROGRAMS (NEW)

For many years, the IRS approved, as tax-exempt functions of charitable organizations, various types of disaster relief and hardship programs, including those where the beneficiaries were employees (and perhaps also former employees), and their families, of related companies or other organizations. In

---

* 66.1. IRC § 170(e)(3). See *Charitable Giving* § 9.3.
* 66.2. Reg. § 1.170A-4A(b)(2)(ii)(D).
* 66.3. *Id.*
* 66.4. Priv. Ltr. Rul. 200839034.

these situations, the group of potential beneficiaries, consisting of hundreds or perhaps thousands of employees and others, was characterized as a charitable class.[66.5] The emergency assistance provided is usually in the form of small grants, short-term loans, and the like. Any private benefit[66.6] conferred on the companies was deemed by the IRS to be incidental and thus to not adversely affect the grantor's exempt status.[66.7] If the grantor was a private foundation, the IRS dismissed any self-dealing[66.8] as also being incidental.

Beginning in the late 1990s, the IRS abruptly reversed this policy, concluding that company-sponsored disaster and emergency relief programs were not exempt charitable functions and that unwarranted private benefit was accruing to the companies in the form of promotion, establishment, and preservation of a loyal and stable employee base.[66.9] In the private foundation context, payments pursuant to these programs were not, according to the IRS, qualifying distributions[66.10] in that they were not made in advancement of charitable purposes, were forms of self-dealing, and were taxable expenditures.[66.11]

This was the status of the IRS's position with respect to disaster relief programs at the time of the terrorist attacks on September 11, 2001. As discussed, the IRS generated considerable confusion as to who was eligible for monetary relief and/or services provided by charities in the immediate aftermath of the attacks, with the agency proclaiming that, to qualify for assistance, an individual had to demonstrate a financial need, when in fact the proper standard in the federal tax law was whether an individual was distressed.[66.12] Legislation enacted in 2001 introduced rules for provision of assistance by charitable organizations to individuals who are victims of terrorism.[66.13]

An explanation of this legislation[66.14] addressed the provision of disaster relief assistance by a private foundation controlled by an employer where those who are assisted are employees of that employer. This explanation articulated this presumption: "If payments in connection with a qualified disaster are made by a private foundation to employees (and their family members) of an employer that controls the foundation, the presumption that the charity acts consistently with the requirements of section 501(c)(3) applies if the class of beneficiaries is large or indefinite and if recipients are selected based on an objective determination of need by an independent committee of the private

---

* 66.5. See § 6.3(a).
* 66.6. See § 20.11.
* 66.7. E.g., Priv. Ltr. Ruls. 9314058, 9516047. See § 20.11(a-1).
* 66.8. See § 12.4(a).
* 66.9. E.g., Priv. Ltr. Rul. 199917079, revoking Priv. Ltr. Rul. 9314058, Priv. Ltr. 199914040, revoking Priv. Ltr. Rul. 9516047.
* 66.10. See § 12.4(b).
* 66.11. See § 12.4(e).
* 66.12. See § 7.2, text accompanied by *supra* notes 49 and 50.
* 66.13. *Id.*, text accompanied by *supra* notes 52 and 53.
* 66.14. Joint Committee on Taxation, *Technical Explanation of the "Victims of Terrorism Tax Relief Act of 2001"* (JCX-93-01 (Dec. 21, 2001)).

foundation, a majority of the members of which are persons other than persons who are in a position to exercise substantial influence over the affairs of the controlling employer (determined under principles similar to those in effect under section 4958)."[66.15] This analysis stated that the IRS was expected to reconsider its ruling position in light of this new standard.

This explanation of the legislation also stated: "Providing assistance to relieve distress for individuals suffering the effects of a disaster generally serves a public rather than a private interest if the assistance benefits the community as a whole, or if the recipients otherwise lack the resources to meet their physical, mental and [should have been *or*] emotional needs."[66.16]

The IRS, in 2005, issued a publication concerning disaster relief programs provided by charitable organizations.[66.17] Disaster programs of company-sponsored charities may be treated as charitable activities where (1) the awards are paid to "needy and distressed persons" pursuant to appropriate standards; (2) the charitable organization's program does not relieve the company of any legal obligation, such as an obligation under a collective bargaining agreement or written plan to provide insurance benefits; and (3) the company does not use the program to recruit employees, induce employees to continue their employment, or otherwise follow a course of action sought by the company. The destruction of an employee's home by fire or medical emergency attributable to a health condition does not constitute an eligible disaster.

This publication stated that "providing aid to relieve human suffering that may be caused by a natural or civil disaster to relieve an emergency hardship is charity in its most basic form." Distributions may be made to "individuals who are financially or otherwise distressed." The publication states that "[p]ersons do not have to be totally destitute to be needy; they may merely lack the resources to obtain basic necessities." Thus, a private foundation may provide aid in the form of funds, services, and/or goods to ensure that persons have basic necessities, such as food, clothing, and shelter. Adequate records to support the basis on which assistance is provided must be maintained. A program to distribute forms of short-term emergency assistance requires less documentation concerning establishment of the need of disaster victims for assistance than the distribution of forms of long-term aid. Thus, in the face of an immediate disaster, the provision of "a drug rescue and telephone crisis center or recovery to a person lost at sea or trapped by a snow storm would not require a showing of financial need, since the individual requiring these services is distressed irrespective of the individual's financial condition."

---

* 66.15. *Id.* at 18. For these purposes, the term *qualified* disaster is a disaster that results from a terroristic or military action, a presidentially declared disaster, an accident involving a common carrier, and any other event that the IRS determines is catastrophic (IRC § 139(c)). The reference to "section 4958" is to the intermediate sanctions rules. See Chapter 21.
* 66.16. JCX-93-01, *supra* note 66.14, at 17.
* 66.17. *Disaster Relief: Providing Assistance Through Charitable Organizations* (Pub. 3833).

By contrast, individuals "may not require long-term assistance if they have adequate financial resources."

Thereafter, the IRS issued a favorable ruling to a health-care system, which began operating a fund to provide emergency assistance to eligible individuals who suffered an economic hardship due to accident, loss, or disaster.[66.18] The principal beneficiaries of this fund are employees of the system, who number about 5,000. To receive assistance from the fund, an individual must be *needy*.[66.19] The ruling suggests that this employee assistance program is in furtherance of the tax-exempt purpose of the system, which includes improving the overall health and wellbeing of individuals living in its community by providing excellence in health care. The IRS ruled that implementation and operation of this fund would not cause the exempt members of the system to lose their exempt status.

Yet, the IRS subsequently ruled that a financial assistance program was not a charitable undertaking, because a substantial portion of the charitable class to be aided consisted of employees of a related for-profit corporation, thus causing unwarranted private benefit and self-dealing involving the private foundation that would be conducting the program.[66.20] The principal purpose of this foundation was to provide financial assistance to families of private security professionals injured or killed during the course of employment. Assistance was to be provided on the basis of financial need and other "personal and subjective" information. About 20,000 professionals were to be among the potential beneficiaries; it was estimated that about 25 percent of this charitable class consisted of individuals employed by the corporation and their families.

In this case, the IRS ruled that this program would provide substantial private benefit to the for-profit corporation. This is because the program provides "contractors and their families with funds not otherwise available except by reason of their employment" with the corporation. The IRS explained that these individuals "realize a real and significant benefit because they have recourse to funds in times of financial hardship as a result of their employment when other avenues have been exhausted." Private security professionals will, the IRS wrote, find this program an "enhancement to financial security" and an "incentive to continue employment" with the corporation. The program was cast as one "akin to other employee benefit programs."

Thus, the state of the law with respect to employee hardship assistance programs is uncertain. The standard should be whether the members of the potential beneficiary charitable class are distressed, but the IRS is ruling that they must be needy. It is not clear whether, for these programs to be approved, the disaster involved must be a qualified one.

---

* 66.18. Priv. Ltr. Rul. 200839034.
* 66.19. See text accompanied by *supra* notes 66.2 and 66.3.
* 66.20. Priv. Ltr. Rul. 200926033.

§ 7.3   CREDIT COUNSELING

(c)   Contemporary IRS Policy

*p. 207, *first paragraph, last line.* **Insert footnote at end of line:**

> [85.1] The IRS's legal counsel thereafter issued (before enactment of the law summarized in § 7.3(e)) guidance as to when a credit counseling organization might qualify for tax exemption as an educational organization (see, e.g., § 8.4). Chief Counsel Adv. Mem. 200620001.

(d)   IRS Criteria for Exemption

p. 209. Insert as second complete paragraph, *before heading:*

In the first of the contemporary cases to be decided in the context of the IRS's new policy concerning tax exemption (or the lack thereof) for credit counseling organizations and before the effective date of the statutory criteria,[92.1] a court held that a nonprofit credit counseling organization did not qualify for exemption, either as a charitable or educational organization, principally because it was "primarily structured to market, determine eligibility for, and enroll individuals in DMPs."[92.2] This organization, wrote the court, "plans to inform consumers about the range of financial services it provides, not about understanding the cause of, and devising personal solutions to, consumers' financial problems."[92.3] It "does not plan to consider the particular knowledge of individual callers about managing their personal finances."[92.4] Rather, it "simply plans to collect data on the callers' debts as necessary to qualify them for a DMP or to determine whether they need other services that [it] provides."[92.5]

§ 7.5   DOWN-PAYMENT ASSISTANCE

p. 213, *third complete paragraph, third line.* **Insert** *(FHA)* **before** *home.*

p. 215. Insert as first and second complete paragraphs:

Despite the foregoing, the IRS thereafter issued a private letter ruling holding a type of down-payment assistance to be a charitable activity; this assistance, characterized as a "settlement assistance" program, comes in the form of a second mortgage, where the payment of interest and principal is deferred until the home involved is sold or ceases to be the borrower's principal residence.[139.1] The "charitable aspects" of this program were said to be reflected in the mortgages' payment deferral terms. The IRS, writing that the program

---

92.1. See § 7.3(e).
92.2. Solution Plus, Inc. v. Comm'r, 95 T.C.M. 1097, 1101 (2008).
92.3. *Id.*
92.4. *Id.*
92.5. *Id.*
139.1. Priv. Ltr. Rul. 200721025.

"structure and operations differ from those described in" the IRS's earlier guidance,[139.2] then wrote that the program is "operated in a manner similar" to one of the situations in that guidance.[139.3] In the facts of this private letter ruling, down-payment assistance was provided to moderate-income individuals.

The future of down-payment assistance programs and organizations was significantly imperiled when the Housing and Economic Recovery Act of 2008 was signed into law on July 30, 2008.[139.4] This legislation bans seller-funded down-payment assistance in connection with FHA-insured mortgages. This prohibition, encompassing funds provided by the "seller or any other person or entity that financially benefits from the transaction,"[139.5] took effect on October 1, 2008.

p. 215, n. 140, *first line.* **Delete** *200534021* **and insert** *200444024.*

§ 7.6   PROMOTION OF HEALTH

(a)   Hospitals

p. 217, n. 152. Insert following existing material:

The IRS, on July 19, 2007, released an interim report summarizing responses from about 500 tax-exempt hospitals to a May 2006 questionnaire as to how they provide and report benefits to the community (IR-2007-152). See *IRS Audits* § 4.5.

*p. 218. Insert as first complete paragraph, before heading:**

A four-entity reorganization resulted in formation of a *federally qualified health center* (as that term is defined in the Medicare and Medicaid statutes) (FQHC). A tax-exempt hospital transferred nine of its primary-care medical practices to a related supporting organization,[160.1] which thereafter is operating as an FQHC. A title-holding company[160.2] merged into the supporting organization. A for-profit company that provided certain support services to the hospital dissolved; the supporting organization absorbed its assets and liabilities. Noting that the FQHC will adopt a charity care policy and will have a board of directors that will be community controlled, the IRS ruled that the supporting organization remained tax-exempt as an organization that promotes health.[160.3]

139.2. See *supra* note 134.
139.3. See *supra* note 136.
139.4. Pub. L. No. 110-289, 110th Cong., 2d Sess. 2008 (title I of which is the FHA Modernization Act of 2008).
139.5. *Id.* § 2113.
* 160.1. See § 12.3(c).
* 160.2. See § 19.2(a).
* 160.3. Priv. Ltr. Rul. 200947064.

p. 218, n. 160, *third paragraph, first line*. Insert following first comma:

Zuckerman, "Nonprofit Hospitals: Operating for the Benefit of the Community," 54 *Exempt Org. Tax Rev.* (No. 1) 39 (Oct. 2006);

(i) Other Health Care Organizations

p. 231, n. 247. Insert following existing material:

In general, Elliott, "The Beginning of a New Era in Tax-Exempt Healthcare?," 49 *Exempt Org. Tax Rev.* (No. 1) 69 (July 2005).

*p. 231. Insert following second paragraph, before heading:

(j) Regional Health Information Organizations (New)

The IRS, in early 2009, began issuing exemption rulings to regional health information organizations (RHIOs), having gotten past concerns about the potential for unwarranted private benefit.[247.1] Several applications for recognition of exemption for RHIOs had been pending at the IRS, some for over three years.[247.2]

The essential purpose of an RHIO is to facilitate coordination of the exchange of electronic health records (EHRs). This information-sharing is and will be occurring among health-care providers, physicians, and insurers. The overall purpose of these records-exchange programs is promotion of health: improvement of the delivery of health-care services and patient outcomes. Nonetheless, for this tax exemption to be available, any resulting private benefit (to physicians, insurers, and other nonexempt entities) must be no more than incidental.

The federal government is promoting greater use of EHRs. This promotion was in President Bush's State of the Union address in 2006. The IRS, in 2007, issued a memorandum from the Director of the Exempt Organizations Division stating that the agency would not treat the benefits a tax-exempt hospital provides to its medical staff physicians, in the form of EHR software and technical support services, as impermissible private benefit or private inurement if these benefits fall within the range of the EHR items and services that are permissible under the Department of Health and Human Services (HHS) regulations promulgated in 2006.[247.3]

---

* 247.1. See § 20.11.
* 247.2. The first three of these entities to receive a favorable ruling were CareSpark, Inc. in Tennessee (Mar. 19, 2009), the Greater Rochester (N.Y.) RHIO (Mar. 30, 2009), and CalRHIO in California (Mar. 31, 2009).
* 247.3. See § 20.11(a-1), text accompanied by note 323.8.

Tax exemption for RHIOs was given a significant boost by language in the legislative history accompanying the stimulus legislation.[247.4] The conference committee report stated that, as a result of the incentives for health information technology provided in the legislation, it is expected that "nonprofit organizations may be formed to facilitate the electronic use and exchange of health-related information consistent with standards adopted by HHS, and that such organizations may seek exemption from income tax as organization described in IRC sec. 501(c)(3)."[247.5] Consequently, if a tax-exempt charitable organization "engages in activities to facilitate the electronic use or exchange of health-related information to advance the purposes of the bill, consistent with standards adopted by HHS, such activities will be considered activities that substantially further an exempt purpose under IRC sec. 501(c)(3), specifically the purpose of lessening the burdens of government."[247.6]

The conference report concluded with this observation: "Private benefit attributable to cost savings realized from the conduct of such activities will be viewed as incidental to the accomplishment of the nonprofit organization's exempt purpose."[247.7] That language was of considerable assistance to the IRS in enabling it to begin issuing favorable exemption rulings to qualified RHIOs.

The IRS, on April 6, published on its Web site the following frequently asked questions, and the agency's answers to them, about RHIOs:

- What are RHIOs? They are "organizations formed and operated to facilitate the exchange of electronic health records among hospitals, physicians, and others in the health care system."

- May RHIOs be tax-exempt charities? "For an organization to be granted tax-exempt status under section 501(c)(3) of the Internal Revenue Code, it must be organized and operated exclusively for one or more exempt purposes. Lessening the burdens of government is one of many exempt purposes under section 501(c)(3)."

- What triggered the recent increased public interest in RHIOs? Congress recently enacted the American Recovery and Reinvestment Act of 2009, which has as one of its purposes the promotion of "health information technology development and information exchange." Congress has "recognized that facilitating health information exchange and technology is important to improving the delivery of health care and reducing the costs of health care delivery and administration." The legislative

---

* 247.4. H. Rep. No. 111-16, 111th Cong., 1st Sess. (2009).
* 247.5. *Id*. at 106.
* 247.6. *Id*. See § 7.7.
* 247.7. *Id*.

history of this legislation "acknowledges" that certain nonprofit organizations that facilitate the exchange of health information qualify for tax exemption because they lessen the burdens of the federal government.

- How is the IRS handling exemption applications by RHIOs? The IRS, which has an "inventory" of these applications, is reviewing them "in light of the requirements of section 501(c)(3) along with the new legislation." Each of these determinations "is being made on a facts and circumstances basis." The IRS "expect[s] to process most of the remaining inventory over the next several months."

§ 7.7 LESSENING BURDENS OF GOVERNMENT

p. 233, line 6. Delete *and.*

p. 233, line 7. Delete period and insert semicolon; insert following footnote number:

an organization's program of arranging for pooled issuances of general obligation bonds for the benefit of its member governmental units;[263.1] an organization's operation of a health insurance plan for trainees associated with a government agency that it supports;[263.2] and an organization's provision of medication services to other entities to lower the costs of a state's program for providing services to the mentally ill.[263.3]

*p. 234. Insert as first complete paragraph:

An organization may operate facilities on behalf of a city, county, or other governmental unit, where the operations are not inherently charitable, yet nonetheless be found to be a tax-exempt charitable entity because it is lessening the burdens of the government. In some instances, the facilities being operated are used for sports activities;[276.1] it is common for a charitable organization to operate a convention center as a way of lessening a government's burden.[276.2] An organization operating a complex of facilities for a city, including an aquarium, horticulture conservatories, a theater, and a hotel, was ruled to be an exempt charitable entity because it lessened city burdens.[276.3]

*p. 234, *first complete paragraph.* **Insert as second sentence:**

In accordance with this position, the IRS ruled that an organization could not qualify as a charitable entity, in part because it may have engaged in an

---

263.1. Priv. Ltr. Rul. 200611033.
263.2. Priv. Ltr. Rul. 200724034.
263.3. Priv. Ltr. Rul. 200739012.
* 276.1. See, e.g., text accompanied by *supra* notes 262, 269.
* 276.2. E.g., Priv. Ltr. Rul. 200634036.
* 276.3. Priv. Ltr. Rul. 200727020.

illegal act (possible violation of state law concerning promotion of raffles) that may have increased the burden of the state.[277.1]

§ 7.8 ADVANCEMENT OF EDUCATION

p. 236, *last complete paragraph*. Insert as second sentence:

Likewise, a grant and loan program of an educational institution to enable fraternities and sororities on or near the campus to improve the safety of their housing was ruled to be advancement of education.[315.1]

§ 7.11 PROMOTION OF SOCIAL WELFARE

*p. 240, n. 359. Delete text following fifth period and substitute:

Also Rev. Rul. 76-408, 1976-2 C.B. 145 (nonprofit organization that provided interest-free home repair loans in a badly deteriorated urban residential area to low-income homeowners who are unable to obtain loans elsewhere was held to be charitable); Rev. Rul. 70-585, 1970-2 C.B. 115 (nonprofit housing organization created to aid low- and moderate-income families was ruled to be charitable).

*p. 240, *second complete paragraph*. Insert as penultimate sentence:

Likewise, a nonprofit organization formed to relieve poverty, eliminate prejudice, reduce neighborhood tensions, and combat community deterioration through a program of financial assistance in the form of low-cost or long-term loans to, or the purchase of equity interests in, various business enterprises in economically depressed areas was held to be an exempt charitable entity,[360.1] as was a nonprofit organization that purchased blighted land in an economically depressed community, converted the land into an industrial park, and encouraged industrial enterprises to locate facilities in the park to provide employment opportunities for low-income residents in the area.[360.2]

§ 7.14 INSTRUMENTALITIES OF GOVERNMENT

p. 255, n. 473, *first line*. Insert following second comma:

Blazek & Nelson, "When Can a Governmental Entity Qualify as a 501(c)(3) Organization and What is the Tax Reporting Consequence?," 53 *Exempt Org. Tax Rev.* (No. 3) 267 (Sep. 2006);

---

* 277.1. Priv. Ltr. Rul. 200929019.
  315.1. Priv. Ltr. Rul. 200839037.
* 360.1. Rev. Rul. 74-587, 1974-2 C.B. 162.
* 360.2. Rev. Rul. 76-419, 1976-2 C.B. 146. By contrast, an organization formed to increase business patronage in a deteriorated area by providing information on the area's shopping opportunities, local transportation, and accommodations was held to not be operated exclusively for charitable purposes (Rev. Rul. 77-111, 1977-1 C.B. 144).

§ 7.15 OTHER CATEGORIES OF CHARITY

(b) Promotion of Patriotism

p. 256, *second complete paragraph.* **Insert as last sentence:**

Where, however, the primary purpose of an organization is to promote recreational sports among adults, the entity provides no instruction to youth, it lacks a regular program of teaching a sport and does not have a sports trainer, and/or it expends most of its funds on travel and meals for a team comprised of individuals 18 years of age or older, the organization will not qualify for exemption as a charitable entity.[486.1]

486.1. Priv. Ltr. Rul. 200849018.

CHAPTER EIGHT

Educational Organizations

§ 8.2 *EDUCATION* CONTRASTED WITH *PROPAGANDA*

p. 267, n. 51. Insert following existing material:

In rejecting an organization's contention that it was an educational entity, a court, after characterizing the administrative record as consisting of "only irrelevant, unintelligible, and inflammatory statements, nonsensical distortions, and irrelevant photographs," concluded that the organization's activities "appear principally to involve the presentation to the public of unsupported opinions" and utilized the methodology test to deny exemption (Families Against Government Slavery v. Comm'r, 93 T.C.M. 958, 959, (2007)).

§ 8.3 EDUCATIONAL INSTITUTIONS

(a) Schools, Colleges, and Universities

*p. 270. Insert as second complete paragraph, before heading:

Launched by the mailing of a 33-page compliance questionnaire[77.1] containing 94 questions (many with sub-questions), the IRS began, in late 2008, examining various practices, with tax law implications, of the tax-exempt higher education community.[77.2] This college and university questionnaire focuses on unrelated business,[77.3] endowment funds,[77.4] and executive compensation.[77.5] The questionnaire was sent to a cross-section of small, mid-sized, and large

---

77.1. Form 14018 (Sep. 2008).
77.2. IR-2008-112.
77.3. See § 24.15.
77.4. See § 11.9(e).
77.5. See § 20.4(i).

private and public four-year colleges and universities (about 400 institutions). General information being solicited includes (as of 2006) the number of students (full-time equivalents) enrolled at the institution; the size of the faculty; the number of employees; the student/faculty ratio; the annual published full-time tuition rate for undergraduate students; the institution's gross assets, net assets, gross revenue, and total expenses; the conduct of any distance-learning activities; the conduct of educational programs internationally; the institution's five highest-paid employees; the five highest gross revenue–generating organizations that are related to the organization; various transactions with noncharitable organizations; and a description of how the institution determines pricing in its dealings with related organizations.

§ 8.6 EDUCATIONAL ACTIVITY AS COMMERCIAL BUSINESS

p. 281, note 203, *first line.* **Delete** *234* **and insert** *235.*

p. 284, n. 228. Insert following existing material:

Yet, the IRS ruled that the conduct of seminars for the public, without charge, is not an educational (nor charitable) activity (Priv. Ltr. Rul. 200844029).

*CHAPTER NINE

Scientific Organizations

§ 9.2   CONCEPT OF *RESEARCH*

*p. 289, *second line*. **Insert footnote at end of line:**

> [12.1] E.g., Priv. Ltr. Rul. 200852036.

CHAPTER TEN

Religious Organizations

§ 10.1 CONSTITUTIONAL LAW FRAMEWORK

(a) General Constitutional Law Principles

*p. 298, *first paragraph, first line.* **Insert,** *in part,* **following** *provides.*

*p. 298, *third paragraph, eighth line.* **Delete** *the* **and insert** *this aspect of* **following** *that;* **insert** *jurisprudence* **following** *Amendment.*

*p. 299, *second complete paragraph, fifth line.* **Delete** *to* **and insert** *of.*

*p. 299, *third complete paragraph, first line.* **Delete** *the.*

*p. 299, *third complete paragraph, fifth line.* **Delete** *principal* **and insert** *principle.*

*p. 299, **n. 21. Delete citation and substitute:**

> 544 U.S. 709, 719 (2005).

*p. 300, *second paragraph, first line.* **Delete** *case law* **and insert** *jurisprudence.*

*p. 300, **n. 34. Delete citation and substitute:**

> 536 U.S. 639, 652 (2002).

*p. 301, **n. 55. Delete** *Perr* **and insert** *Perry;* **delete citation and substitute:**

> 545 U.S. 677 (2005).

*p. 301, n. 56. Delete citation and substitute:

   545 U.S. 844 (2005).

*p. 302. Insert as third complete paragraph, before heading:

   Another case in this context involved *government speech*, which is not subject to conventional free speech considerations. (The First Amendment restricts government regulation of private speech.) A city maintaining a public park that contains a privately donated monument to the Ten Command-ments refused a contribution by a religious group of a monument devoted to the group's Seven Aphorisms. The Court, rejecting a public forum analy-sis, wrote that governments generally have the discretion to determine when to accept gifts of permanent monuments; the practice was said to be "selec-tive receptivity."[63.1] It was noted, however, that this case was litigated "in the shadow" of establishment-of-religion law, with the city "wary of associating itself too closely with the Ten Commandments monument displayed in the park, lest that be deemed a breach in the so-called wall of separation between church and State."[63.2]

*p. 316, *first complete paragraph, first line.* Delete *has since* and *the.*

*p. 317, n. 150. Insert as second paragraph:

   A court wrote that the criteria used by the IRS to determine church status bear a "striking similarity" to the topics of questions contained in a 1906 census of religious organizations. This resemblance, said the court, "strongly suggests" that these criteria are "time-conditioned and reflect institutional characteristics that no longer capture the variety of American religions and religious institutions in the twenty-first century." And: "The regime appears to favor some forms of religious expression over others in a manner in which, if not inconsistent with the letter of the Constitution, the court finds troubling when considered in light of the constitutional protections of the Establishment and Free Exercise Clauses." Foundation of Human Understanding v. United States, 88 Fed. Cl. 203 (U.S. Ct. Fed. Cl. (2009)).

*p. 318, *second complete paragraph, first line.* Delete text and substitute:

   A federal court of

§ 10.3   CHURCHES AND SIMILAR INSTITUTIONS

(a)   General Principles

*p. 320, *second complete paragraph.* Delete and substitute:

---

* 63.1. Pleasant Grove City, Utah v. Summum, 129 S. Ct. 1125, 1133 (2009).
* 63.2. *Id.* at 1139.

(b) Associational Test (New)

The IRS is adjusting its application of its criteria as to what constitutes a tax-exempt church. No longer is it the agency's position that only some of the criteria need be satisfied.[172] For example, the agency's lawyers stated that an exempt church must meet certain "minimum" standards, such as "regular religious services," a "body of believers or communicants that assembles regularly in order to worship," a "defined congregation of worshippers," and an "established place of worship."[173] The principal activity of this organization was religious broadcasting and publication; the IRS termed these *non-associational* activities, concluding that religious "programming" is not sufficient activity to enable an organization to constitute a church. (Yet, thereafter, the IRS ruled that an international ministry qualified as a church, writing that it satisfied "most" of the IRS church criteria; the entity, however, lacked a place of worship and a membership, and ordination of its clergy was not a requirement.[173.1])

Thereafter, the IRS ruled that a religious organization, which was said by the agency to meet "several" of the IRS criteria for a church, did not constitute a church in that the criteria it satisfied were not "distinctive characteristics" of a church but rather were "common to both churches and non-church religious organizations." The IRS said that the organization lacked a definite and distinct ecclesiastical government, and did not have a "regular congregation of its own that engages in regular worship services in an established place of worship." Further, the organization did not have a code of discipline; it did not operate programs for the religious instruction of the young; and it did not publicly identify itself as a church. Consequently, the IRS concluded that this entity could not qualify as a church.[173.2]

The IRS held that an online "seminary" did not qualify as a church, in that there was no regular place of worship[173.3] and it did not hold regular worship services; the agency wrote that this organization did not satisfy the IRS's criteria that are "considered the most important."[173.4] Other IRS rulings state that an organization could not qualify as a church because its conduct of religious services occurred in a room in a commercial resort hotel[173.5] and

---

* 172. See text accompanied by *supra* notes 145 and 146.
* 173. Tech. Adv. Mem. 200437040.
* 173.1. Priv. Ltr. Rul. 200530028.
* 173.2. Priv. Ltr. Rul. 200727021.
* 173.3. The IRS observed that the Internet "is not a building or a physical place."
* 173.4. Priv. Ltr. Rul. 200912039. On that occasion, the IRS wrote that its 14-point criteria are "helpful in deciding what constitutes a church for federal tax purposes, although they are not a definitive test."
* 173.5. Priv. Ltr. Rul. 200926036.

because an entity conducted its worship services only by teleconference and thus those participating in its activities did so in solitude.[173.6]

The U.S. Court of Federal Claims more formally articulated this associational test when it held that the test is a "threshold" standard that religious organizations "must satisfy in order to obtain church status."[173.7] The court quoted another court's observation that, to qualify as a church, an organization "must serve an associational role in accomplishing its religious purpose."[173.8] The court credited another court opinion as having created the associational standard as the "minimum" requirement necessary for a "religious organization to gain church status."[173.9]

In this case, the organization's primary activities were radio and Internet broadcasts, which the court declined to characterize as religious services. The court wrote that the "weight of persuasive authority" holds that broadcasts of this nature "lack critical associational aspects characteristic of religious services and are therefore instead properly regarded simply as broadcasting and publishing services insufficient to qualify a religious organization for church status."[173.10] Also, the organization's services in the form of Sunday meetings, weddings, and seminars were held to not be sufficiently frequent to be characterized as "regular." The U.S. Tax Court had previously concluded that this organization was a church;[173.11] at that time, the organization provided religious services to an established congregation and otherwise had considerable associational activities.

(c)   Perspective (New)

This opinion by the U.S. Court of Federal Claims nicely synthesized the federal tax law as to what constitutes a church.[173.12] The court observed that several courts have recognized that "there is very little guidance for courts to use in making decisions" as to church status.[173.13] Also, a

---

* 173.6. Priv. Ltr. Rul. 200926049.
* 173.7. Foundation of Human Understanding v. United States, 88 Fed. Cl. 203 (U.S. Ct. Fed. Cl. (2009)).
* 173.8. The Church of Eternal Life and Liberty, Inc. v. Comm'r, 86 T.C. 916, 924 (1986).
* 173.9. Foundation of Human Understanding v. United States, 88 Fed. Cl. 203 (U.S. Ct. Fed. Cl. (2009)), referencing American Guidance Foundation, Inc. v. United States, 490 F. Supp. 304, 306 (D.D.C. 1980).
* 173.10. Foundation of Human Understanding v. United States, 88 Fed. (U.S. Ct. Fed. Cl. 203 (2009)). The court quoted from another court's opinion that stated that the "permissible purpose may be accomplished individually and privately in the sense that oral manifestation is not necessary, but it may not be accomplished in physical solitude" (Chapman v. Comm'r, 48 T.C. 358, 367 (1967)).
* 173.11. Foundation of Human Understanding v. Comm'r, 88 T.C. 1341 (1987).
* 173.12. See *supra* note 173.7.
* 173.13. This quotation is from Spiritual Outreach Soc'y v. Comm'r, 927 F.2d 335, 338 (8th Cir. 1991).

"coherent definition [of the term *church* does not] emerge from reviewing ... the limited instances of judicial treatment."[173.14] Consequently, the court wrote, "[i]n the absence of Congressional guidance and without any guidance from within the [tax] regulations themselves, courts have developed at least three different approaches to determine whether" an organization qualifies as a church.[173.15]

The first approach is the "general or traditional understanding" of the term *church*, based on the "common meaning and usage of the word."[173.16] The court declined to adopt this approach, noting that "[t]here is no bright line beyond which certain organized activities undertaken for religious purposes coalesce into a 'church' structure ... [a]nd the range of 'church' structures extant in the United States is enormously diverse and confusing."[173.17]

The second approach is application of the IRS criteria. Despite the court's concern about the constitutionality and current applicability of these criteria,[173.18] and about a "mechanical application of rigid criteria to a diverse set of religious organizations,[173.19] the court applied the IRS criteria in this case, although not exclusively. In the case, the organization met some of these criteria, with the matter presenting a "close question" on that basis but the organization's failure to satisfy the third approach, the associational test, precluded it from qualifying as a church.[173.20]

§ 10.4 CONVENTIONS OR ASSOCIATIONS OF CHURCHES

p. 321. Insert as third complete paragraph:

It is the position of the IRS that a convention of churches is a statewide, regional, or national group of churches of the same denomination. These conventions typically carry out such activities as the operation of schools for ministers, teachers, and missionaries; support of missions; holding of annual

---

* 173.14. This quotation is from American Guidance Foundation, Inc. v. United States, 490 F. Supp. 304 (D.D.C. 1980).
* 173.15. Foundation of Human Understanding v. United States, 88 Fed. Cl. 203 (U.S. Ct. Fed. Cl. (2009)).
* 173.16. *Id.* The court opinion most associated with this approach is De La Salle Institute v. United States, 195 F. Supp. 891 (N.D. Cal. 1961).
* 173.17. This quotation is from American Guidance Foundation, Inc. v. United States, 490 F. Supp. 304, 306 (D.D.C. 1980).
* 173.18. See *supra* note 150, second paragraph.
* 173.19. Foundation of Human Understanding v. United States, 88 Fed. Cl. 203 (U.S. Ct. Fed. Cl. (2009)).
* 173.20. *Id.* This court observed that there are a few cases that fall outside this tripartite analytical framework because they involve organizations primarily engaging in "secular functions" (e.g., Junaluska Assembly Housing, Inc. v. Comm'r, 86 T.C. 1114 (1986)) or are "individual or single-family private religious enterprises" (e.g., Richardson v. Comm'r, 70 T.C.M. 14 (1995)).

sessions; the setting of minimum standards of belief; and the conduct of religious workshops. An association of churches is a group of churches organized on a level usually less than statewide; these associations normally carry out many of the same activities as conventions of churches.[179.1]

§ 10.7 APOSTOLIC ORGANIZATIONS

*p. 325, n. 204. *Insert following existing material:*

   A tax-exempt apostolic organization and its president were denied various tax deductions because the president, although a member of the organization, was not an employee of the organization; the faith-based nature of the relationship between the organization and its members was held to be inconsistent with the concept of an employer/employee arrangement (Stahl v. United States, 2009-2 U.S.T.C.¶ 50,785 (E.D. Wash. 2009)).

179.1. Priv. Ltr. Rul. 8309092.

CHAPTER ELEVEN

Other Charitable Organizations

§ 11.2   AMATEUR SPORTS ORGANIZATIONS

p. 332, *carryover paragraph*. Insert as last sentence:

Thus, an organization the primary activities of which are conducted on a local level and/or are for the benefit of adults cannot qualify for tax exemption pursuant to this body of law.[7.1]

§ 11.3   PUBLIC SAFETY TESTING ORGANIZATIONS

*p. 334, n. 29. Insert as first sentence:

An organization formed to provide carpool services for its members for a fee failed in its attempt to qualify as a tax-exempt organization that tests for public safety; the IRS observed that, although this organization conducts background checks on its prospective members to ascertain whether they are safe to ride with, these individuals are not *consumer products* (Priv. Ltr. Rul. 200910060).

§ 11.6   CHARITABLE RISK POOLS

*p. 339, n. 71. Insert following existing material:

A risk management pool for tax-exempt educational organizations failed to qualify as an exempt charitable risk pool because it did not receive the requisite startup capital (Priv. Ltr. Rul. 200941038).

7.1. E.g., Priv. Ltr. Rul. 200842055.

§ 11.8 DONOR-ADVISED FUND ENTITIES

(e) Statutory Criteria

p. 348, n. 135. Insert following existing material:

The Tax Technical Corrections Act added references to the donor-advised funds excise taxes to the definition of *qualified first tier taxes* (IRC § 4962) for purposes of tax abatement (Pub. L. No. 110-172, 110th Cong., 1st Sess. (2007) § 3(h)).

p. 349. Insert following existing material:

The IRS invited public comments in conjunction with this study.[144] In addition to comments on the foregoing four sets of issues, the IRS solicited comments as to (1) the advantages and disadvantages of donor-advised funds to the charitable sector, donors, and sponsoring organizations, compared to private foundations and other charitable giving arrangements; (2) the determination of the amount and availability of a charitable deduction for a transfer of assets to a donor-advised fund, and the tax-exempt or public charity status of the donee, if (a) the transferred assets are paid to or used for the benefit of the donor or related persons, (b) the donor has investment control over the transferred assets, (c) there is an expectation that the donor's advice will be followed, (d) the donor or the donee has option rights with respect to the transferred assets, and (e) the transferred assets are appreciated property that is not readily convertible to cash; (3) the effects or expected effects of this law on the practices and behavior of donors, donor-advised funds, and sponsoring organizations; and (4) the advantages and disadvantages of perpetual existence of donor-advised funds.

§ 11.9 ENDOWMENT FUNDS (NEW)

Interest in federal tax law issues surrounding endowment funds maintained by or for the benefit of public charities[145] (such as colleges, universities, hospitals, and museums) and certain other tax-exempt organizations, particularly social welfare organizations,[146] and associations and other business leagues,[147] is increasing.

(a) Definition of *Endowment Fund*

An *endowment fund* is a form of investment fund; money and property (usually derived from contributions or the organization's existing resources) are placed in and invested by means of the fund, some or all of the income of which

---

144. Notice 2007-21, 2007-9 I.R.B. 611.
145. See § 12.3.
146. See Chapter 13.
147. See Chapter 14.

is used by the organization to satisfy costs of operations, cover capital expenditures, and/or fund special projects or programs.[148] These funds are either part of the exempt organization or are held in a separate organization, such as a supporting organization,[149] which is either controlled by or independent of the organization that is the beneficiary of the fund. An endowment fund is an exempt organization, either as a fund within an exempt organization[150] or as an exempt entity itself, contributions to which are deductible as charitable gifts.[151]

(b) Focus on College and University Endowments

Endowment funds are, in general, growing in value and economic return. An analysis of the endowment assets for 765 colleges and universities totaled these assets at $340 billion in the fiscal year ended in June 2006, with income of $52 billion and earnings of 15.3 percent.[152] Endowment assets are heavily concentrated in a few institutions; the five institutions with the largest endowments accounted for 25 percent of endowment value, yet comprised less than 1 percent of these institutions of higher education; the top 20 universities accounted for almost one-half of all endowments yet less than 3 percent of the institutions.[153] According to this analysis, institutions with larger endowments are characterized by higher returns and a larger share of the growing investment in hedge funds and private equity funds, but tend to have the same payout rates as institutions with smaller endowments; the average payout rates frequently fell below 5 percent.[154] Among the 20 institutions with the largest endowments, the endowment on a per-undergraduate basis ranged from $2.8 million to $33,000.[155]

The principal criticism of endowment funds is that, despite tax-exempt status and the ability to attract deductible gifts, the payout rate is low. In a 2007 letter to the Secretary of the Treasury, the leadership of the Senate Finance Committee referenced charitable organizations maintaining endowments with "billions of dollars in the bank—or as is more common now, in investments offshore in places such as the Cayman Islands—[that provide] only pennies on the dollar to the charitable goals of the organization." This letter stated that the "public needs to understand clearer what is the endowment of the charity

---

148. E.g., Fund-Raising Forum, "Endowment Funds Go On Forever—An Endowment Campaign Should Not," www.raise-funds.com; www.bloomberg.com/invest/glossary. The IRS defined the various types of endowments in connection with the college and university compliance check questionnaire (see *infra* notes 170–172).
149. See §§ 12.3(c), 28.2.
150. See § 25.9(b).
151. See § 2.3.
152. Congressional Research Service, "Tax Issues and University Endowments" (M-082007 (Aug. 20, 2007)) ("University Endowment Analysis") at 1.
153. *Id*. For this period, the largest of the university endowments ($28.9 billion, at Harvard University) represented 8.5 percent of the total endowment at the 765 institutions.
154. University Endowment Analysis at 2.
155. *Id*.

(to include funds that are directly or indirectly under the control of the charity, such as a supporting organization); what those endowment funds are being spent on; the amount and percentage of the endowment being spent; how those endowment funds are being invested; the size of the endowment; what endowment funds are earmarked for specific purposes and what are those purposes; and the costs of the management of the endowment."[156]

In the higher education setting, the criticism concerning endowment fund payouts is inevitably correlated with tuition increases. The analysis of 765 colleges and universities reviewed the 62 institutions with more than $1 billion in endowments and reported that "earnings on endowments retained after payout significantly exceed[ed], on average, both tuition growth and undergraduate student aid."[157] This analysis concluded that, as to these 62 institutions, "increases in payouts could be used as a substitute for some or all tuition increases and could be used to increase student aid significantly, while endowments could continue to earn returns beyond those needed to maintain their real value."[158]

In its Exempt Organizations Implementing Guidelines for fiscal year 2008, the IRS announced that it will be conducting a "research/compliance initiative" involving colleges and universities, looking at various aspects of these institutions' operations, including how they invest and use their endowments.

(c) Form 990 Reporting

The redesigned annual information return[159] includes a section by which filing tax-exempt organizations report as to their endowment funds.[160] An organization is required to report the beginning-of-the-year balance in its

---

156. Letter to Secretary of the Treasury Henry Paulsen, dated May 29, 2007, from Senate Finance Committee Chairman Max Baucus (D-MT) and Ranking Member Charles Grassley. See 24 *Bruce R. Hopkins' Nonprofit Counsel* (no. 9) 5 (Sep. 2007). Sen. Grassley is further concerned about the practice of exempt colleges and universities maintaining large, untaxed endowments, while simultaneously borrowing money (bond financing) in the form of tax-exempt debt. On April 3, 2007, he requested a study of this matter by the Congressional Budget Office. See 24 *Bruce R. Hopkins' Nonprofit Counsel* (no. 6) 2 (June 2007).
157. University Endowment Analysis at 2. With each institution equally weighted, the payout rate was 4.6 percent, while tuition growth was 0.9 percent of the endowment, and student aid was 2.9 percent of the endowment (*id.*).
158. University Endowment Analysis at 2. This analysis observed that the "foregone revenue from not taxing these [endowment fund] returns probably exceeds the revenue loss from all income tax deductions for charitable contributions to higher education" (*id.* at 1). If that revenue were taxed at a 35-percent rate, the yield would be about $18 billion. The staff of the Joint Committee on Taxation reported that the total tax expenditure for the charitable contribution deduction for education for 2007–2011 is almost $37 billion (see § 1.2, note 38). One-fifth of $37 billion is $7.4 billion, so this observation was unnecessarily guarded.
159. See § 27.2A.
160. Form 990, Schedule D, Part V.

endowment fund, contributions to the fund during the reporting period, investment earnings or losses during the period, grants from the fund during the period, other expenditures for facilities and programs, administrative expenses during the period, and the end-of-the-year balance.

The filing organization is required to provide the estimated percentage of the year-end balances held as board-designated or quasi-endowment, permanent endowment, and/or term endowment. The organization must indicate whether there are endowment funds, not in the possession of the organization, which are held and administered for the organization by related or unrelated organizations. Also, the organization must describe the "intended uses" of its endowment fund(s).

(d) Policy Options to Increase Payout

The above-referenced analysis stated that there are a "number of approaches that might be used to encourage or require institutions with large tax-favored endowments to distribute endowments."[161] (Although these options are discussed in the higher education setting, they are generally applicable to public charities and other exempt organizations with endowment funds.) One approach is dissemination of "better information on what higher education institutions are doing with their endowments," thereby informing "contributors about where resources are being used and pressure higher education institutions to address issues of public concern such as high tuition rates."[162] Noting that this information is not always available or not available in an accessible form, this analysis suggested the possibility that this type of information be required to be reported to a central government agency (such as the IRS or the Department of Education) and posted on the Internet in an easily accessible form.[163]

Another suggested policy option, to be adopted instead of or in addition to the information-dissemination approach, is the use of "tax penalties ... to require institutions to distribute more of their endowment or to restrain growth in tuition, which might be accomplished with funds from the endowment."[164] A suggestion in this regard would be to require an annual payout rate, similar to the requirements imposed on private foundations,[165] as a criterion for qualification for exemption or to avoid an excise tax on the endowment; the rate could be based on a percentage or on earnings.[166] Another suggestion is

---

161. University Endowment Analysis at 14.
162. *Id.*
163. *Id.* at 15.
164. *Id.*
165. See § 12.4(b).
166. University Endowment Analysis at 15. Sen. Grassley, on October 29, 2007, stated that he wants pending higher education tax legislation to include a provision imposing a payout requirement on college and university endowments similar to the payout rules imposed on private foundations.

to impose taxes on endowments if institutions increased their tuition by more than an appropriate rate, such as inflation or consumer price index (plus an addition). Still another policy option (other than imposition of both sets of taxes simultaneously) is to apply a tax regime only to institutions that have endowments per undergraduate student (and/or graduate student) greater than a floor or tie the endowment distribution to undergraduate tuition.[167]

(e) College and University Questionnaire (New)

The compliance questionnaire sent by the IRS, in late 2008, to approximately 400 colleges and universities.[168] includes considerable insight as to the agency's contemporary thinking about endowment funds maintained by public charities and related federal tax law.[169] In that questionnaire, the IRS inquired whether (as of 2006) the institution had one or more endowment funds, another organization held or maintained one or more endowment funds on the institution's behalf, the institution has an investment policy for its endowment funds, the institution has an investment committee that oversees investment of endowment fund assets (and, if so, how many individuals serve on the committee), the institution engages an independent consultant for investment guidance, and compensation arrangements for internal and/or external investment managers were approved by a board committee or the full board. The IRS asked who manages the investments in the endowment funds, and how the institution compensates internal and external investment managers.

The IRS asked about the average amount of the endowment fund's investment assets per full-time student, the total year-end fair market value of the endowment's assets, the year-end value of quasi endowments,[170] the year-end value of term endowments,[171] and the year-end value of true endowments.[172] The IRS inquired into the holding by the institution (or a related party) of any life income funds (even if not in connection with an endowment fund), with questions directed at the percent of the endowment that was comprised of charitable gift annuities,[173] charitable remainder trusts,[174] and pooled income funds.[175]

The IRS asked about the percent of endowment assets that was invested in areas such as fixed income funds, equity funds, real estate, international

---

167. *Id.* at 15-16.
168. See §§ 8.3(a), notes 77.1–77.5, 26.6 (ii), text accompanied by note 308.6.
169. Form 14018, Part III.
170. The term *quasi endowment* is defined in the questionnaire as endowment pool investments of which the principal can be expended in the discretion of the institution's trustees.
171. The term *term endowment* is defined as endowment pool investments of which the principal can be expended after expiration of a defined term.
172. The term *true endowment* is defined as an endowment pool consisting of gifts of which only the return on principal investment can be expended. See § 11.9(a).
173. See *Charitable Giving*, Chapter 14.
174. *Id.*, Chapter 12.
175. *Id.*, Chapter 13.

funds, cash, and alternative investments (such as hedge and venture capital funds). The institutions were asked whether they made foreign investments of endowment funds through an investment entity, about the primary investment objective for the institution's portfolio for the next five years, whether the board or committee members placed restrictions on the purchase or sale of certain securities because of donor restrictions or special requests, about the top five restrictions (such as for fellowships or student aid) placed on endowments by donors or board or committee members, and whether they monitor endowment distributions to ensure that they were used for the donors' intended purposes. The IRS asked the institutions to provide information on distributions from endowment funds, such as for scholarships, research, general education support, general university operations, or chairs and professorships.

CHAPTER TWELVE

Public Charities and Private Foundations

§ 12.3 CATEGORIES OF PUBLIC CHARITIES

(b) Publicly Supported Charities

(i) Donative Publicly Supported Charities—In General.

p. 366, *second complete paragraph.* **Delete (including footnotes) and substitute:**

Calculation of the support fraction entails an assessment of the charitable organization's financial support that it has *normally* received. This means that the organization must satisfy the one-third support test during the course of a multiyear public support measuring period, in the aggregate. Prior to 2008, the measuring period was the four-year period immediately preceding the tax year involved (sometimes referred to as the *tested year*); where this was done, the organization was considered to have met the one-third support test for the current (tested) year and the year immediately succeeding it. Beginning in 2008,[154] however, the measuring period is the five-year period that includes the current tax year; again, an organization that meets this public support test for its current year is treated as a publicly supported entity for that year and the immediately succeeding tax year.[155] (A five-year computation period for meeting this support test is used for organizations in the initial years of their existence.[155.1])

---

154. Reg. § 1.170A-9T(k).
155. Reg. § 1.170A-9T(f)(4)(i).
155.1. See § 25.3(c).

For example, a calendar-year charitable organization that meets this public support test for 2011, based on the five-year computation period consisting of 2007–2011, is a publicly supported charity for 2011 and 2012. If this organization cannot meet a public support test for 2012, based on the computation period consisting of 2008–2012, it nonetheless will be a public charity for 2012 because it met a public support test for 2011, based on the computation period of 2007–2011. If, however, the organization cannot meet a public support test for 2013, based on the 2009–2013 computation period, the organization will become a private foundation as of January 1, 2013.

An organization may not be able to compute its public support for its current tax year until some time into the subsequent tax year. In the above example, 2013 may be underway (perhaps well so) by the time the organization has computed its public support for 2012. The organization may then realize that it is at risk of losing its public charity status as of January 1, 2013. Moreover, this organization may not know definitively that it is a private foundation for 2013 until some time in 2014, when it is able to calculate its public support.

Accordingly, the IRS will not assert private foundation excise taxes or penalties for all or part of the first tax year in which an organization is classified as a private foundation due to failure to satisfy a public support test in cases where the imposition of the taxes or penalties would lead to, in the words of the IRS's summary of these rules, "unfair or inequitable results," such as where the change in the organization's public support was "unforeseeable or due to circumstances beyond the organization's control." An organization that believes that the imposition on it of private foundation excise taxes and/or penalties for all or part of the first year in which it is classified as a private foundation is unfair or inequitable should contact the Rulings and Agreements unit of the Exempt Organizations Division, Washington, D.C.[155.2]

Previously, when an exempt charitable organization computed its public support, it was required to use the cash basis method of accounting to report its public support,[155.3] even if it used the accrual basis method of accounting in keeping its books and otherwise reporting on its annual information returns. Now, however, when a charitable entity computes its public support and reports the information on its annual information return, it must use the same accounting method that it uses in keeping its books and its annual information return reporting.[155.4]

An organization that generally uses the accrual method of accounting will not be able to use the support information reported on its annual information

---

155.2. In connection with publication of these temporary regulations, the IRS also issued proposed regulations (REG-142333-07); in that connection, the IRS sought comments regarding specific circumstances that may warrant this relief.

155.3. This support is reported on Form 990, Schedule A. See § 27.2A(b)(viii).

155.4. Reg. § 1.170A-9T(f)(13).

returns for prior years—because that support was reported using the cash method—in computing its public support ratio for the current year. Rather, it must revise its reporting for the prior years in the computation period so that it is reporting all support for the computation period on the accrual method.

(ii) Facts-and-Circumstances Test.

p. 367, *first paragraph, fifth line*. Delete *governmental and*.

p. 367, *first paragraph, seventh line*. Insert footnote following semicolon:

[156.1]The 10 percent public support element is calculated using the methodology of the general one-third support test (see § 25.3(b)(i)), including the rules that took effect in 2008 (Reg. § 1.170A-9T(f)(4)(ii)).

(iii) Community Foundations.

p. 368, n. 166. Insert hyphen following *508* and insert the following after existing material:

These tax regulations contained transition rules that became obsolete; temporary regulations issued in 2008 (T.D. 9423) deleted these rules.

(iv) Service Provider Publicly Supported Organizations.

pp. 369–370, *last paragraph on p. 369 that carries over to p. 370*. Delete (including footnote) all text other than last sentence and substitute:

Calculation of the support and investment income fractions entails an assessment of the charitable organization's financial support, including investment income, that it has *normally* received. This means that the organization must satisfy the one-third permitted sources support test and less-than-one-third gross investment income test during the course of a multiyear public support measuring period, in the aggregate. Prior to 2008, the measuring period was the four-year period immediately preceding the tax year involved (sometimes referred to as the *tested year*); where this was done, the organization was considered to have met the one-third public support test and the less-than-one-third gross investment income test for the current (tested) year and the year immediately succeeding it. Beginning in 2008,[180] however, the measuring period is the five-year period that includes the current tax year; again, an organization that meets these tests for its current year is treated as a publicly supported entity for that year and the immediately succeeding tax

---

180. Reg. § 1.509(a)-3T(o).

year.[180.1] (A five-year computation period for meeting these tests is used for organizations in the initial years of their existence.)[180.2]

p. 370. Insert as second and third complete paragraphs:

Previously, when an exempt charitable organization computed its public support and gross investment income, it was required to use the cash basis method of accounting to report its public support,[182.1] even if it used the accrual basis method of accounting in keeping its books and otherwise reporting on its annual information returns. Now, however, when a charitable entity computes its public support and reports the information on its annual information return, it must use the same accounting method that it uses in keeping its books and its annual information return reporting.[182.2]

An organization that generally uses the accrual method of accounting will not be able to use the support information reported on its annual information returns for prior years—because that support was reported using the cash method—in computing its public support ratio for the current year. Rather, it must revise its reporting for the prior years in the computation period so that it is reporting all support for the computation period on the accrual method.

(c) Supporting Organizations

*pp. 370–371. Delete last sentence that begins on p. 370 and carries over to p. 371 (including footnotes), and substitute:

A qualified supporting organization must satisfy an organizational test, an operational test, a relationship test,[187] and a disqualified person control test.

p. 371, n. 189. Delete sentence and insert:

The law is unclear as to the matter of substitution of supported organizations. In what may be the only private letter ruling on the point, the IRS allowed an organization to retain its status as a supporting organization, notwithstanding a transaction in which a supported organization will be substituted (although the IRS emphasized that the purposes and activities of the supporting organization will essentially remain the same) (Priv. Ltr. Rul. 200731034).

*p. 371, first complete paragraph. Insert as second and third sentences:

These organizations are referred to as Type I, Type II, or Type III supporting organizations, respectively.[190.1] Inasmuch as Type III supporting organizations

---

180.1. Reg. § 1.509(a)-3T(c)(1)(i). See the example and the appeals process summarized in § 12.3(b)(i).

180.2. See § 25.3(c).

182.1. This support is reported on Form 990, Schedule A. See § 27.2A(b)(viii).

182.2. Reg. § 1.509(a)-3T(k).

* 187. A supporting organization must support one or more qualified supported organizations (IRC § 509(f)(3)), which usually are institutions (see § 12.3(a)) and/or publicly supported organizations (see § 12.3(b)). Reg. § 1.509(a)-4(a)(5).

* 190.1. The Type III supporting organization is defined in IRC § 4943(f)(5)(A).

are classified as either functionally integrated Type III supporting organizations or non-functionally integrated Type III supporting organizations,[190.2] there are four types of supporting organizations.

*p. 371, n. 190. Delete sentences.

*p. 371, *second complete paragraph, fourth line.* Insert footnote following *organization(s):*

> [191.1] Prop. Reg. § 1.509(a)-4(i)(2).

*p. 371, n. 192. Insert following first period:

> Prop. Reg. § 1.509(a)-4(i)(10).

*p. 371. Delete n. 195.

*p. 371, *last paragraph, fifth line.* Insert following *organization:*

(other than a non–functionally integrated Type III supporting organization[195])

*p. 371, n. 191. Insert following existing material:

> A charitable organization failed to achieve status as a supporting organization, in part because disqualified persons controlled it (Polm Family Found., Inc. v. United States, 2009-2 U.S.T.C. ¶ 50,638 (D.D.C. 2009)).

*p. 372. Insert as first 16 complete paragraphs:

A supporting organization is *operated in connection with* one or more supported organizations (and thus is a Type III entity) only if it satisfies the notification requirement, the responsiveness test, and the integral part test.[197.1]

An organization is an *integral part* of a supported organization if it is "significantly involved in the operations of the supported organization and the supported organization is dependent upon the supporting organization for the type of support the supporting organization provides."[197.2] An organization is an integral part of a supported organization only if it satisfies the requirements for functionally integrated Type III supporting organizations or for non-functionally integrated Type III supporting organizations.[197.3]

A supporting organization meets the responsiveness test if it is "responsive to the needs or demands" of a supported organization.[197.4] This test is generally satisfied if (1) one or more trustees, directors, or officers of the supporting organization are elected or appointed by the supported organization; (2) one or

---

* 190.2. Prop. Reg. § 1.509(a)-4(i)(4), (5). See IRC § 4945(f)(5)(B).
* 195. See *supra* note 190.2.
* 197.1. Prop. Reg. § 1.509(a)-4(i)(1).
* 197.2. Prop. Reg. § 1.509(a)-4(i)(1)(iii).
* 197.3. *Id.*
* 197.4. Prop. Reg. § 1.509(a)-4(i)(3).

more members of the governing body of the supported organization are also trustees, directors, or officers of, or hold other important offices in, the supporting organization; or (3) the trustees, directors, or officers of the supporting organization maintain a "close and continuous" working relationship with the trustees, directors, or officers of the supported organization.

Also, by reason of one of these three elements, the trustees, directors, or officers of the supported organization must have a "significant voice" in the investment policies of the supporting organization, the timing of grants, the manner of making them, and the selection of recipients by the supporting organization, and in otherwise directing the use of the income or assets of the supporting organization.

A supporting organization meets the integral part test as a functionally integrated Type III supporting organization in one of two ways. One way to meet this test is to engage in activities (1) substantially all of which directly further the exempt purposes of the supported organization(s), by performing the functions of, or carrying out the purposes of, the supported organization(s); and (2) that, but for the involvement of the supporting organization, would normally be engaged in by the supported organization(s).[197.5] Fundraising, investing, and managing non-exempt use property, and making grants (to the supported organization or elsewhere), are *not* activities that meet the *directly further* standard.

The other way this test is met is for the supporting organization to be the parent of each of its supported organizations. This relationship exists where (1) the supporting organization exercises a "substantial degree of direction" over the policies, programs, and activities of the supported organization; and (2) a majority of the trustees, directors, or officers of the supported organization is appointed or elected by the supporting organization.[197.6]

A supporting organization meets the integral part test as a non-functionally integrated Type III supporting organization in one of two ways. One way to meet this test is to satisfy a distribution requirement and an attentiveness requirement.[197.7]

Pursuant to this *distribution requirement*, a supporting organization must distribute, for each of its years, to or for the use of one or more supported organizations, amounts equaling or exceeding its annual distributable amount on or before the last day of the year involved. Generally, the *annual distributable amount* is 5 percent of the excess of the aggregate fair market value of the

---

* 197.5. Prop. Reg. § 1.509(a)-4(i)(4)(i)(A).
* 197.6. Prop. Reg. § 1.509(a)-4(i)(4)(i)(B).
* 197.7. Prop. Reg. § 1.509(a)-4(i)(5)(i)(A). Congress mandated the promulgation of new regulations (see Reg. § 1.509(a)-4(i)(3)(iii)) requiring non-functionally integrated Type III supporting organizations to make distributions of a percentage of either income or assets to their supported organizations (Pension Protection Act of 2006, Pub. L. No. 109-280 § 1241(d)).

organization's non-exempt-use assets over the acquisition indebtedness with respect to the assets. This amount is increased by amounts received or accrued as repayments of amounts that were previously taken into account in meeting the distribution requirement. The amount is also increased by amounts received or accrued from the disposition of property to the extent that the acquisition of the property was taken into account in meeting the requirement. The distributable amount is reduced by the amount of any income taxes imposed on the supporting organization.[197.8]

Pursuant to this *attentiveness requirement*, a supporting organization must distribute at least one-third of its annual distributable amount to one or more supported organizations that are attentive to the operations of the supporting organization and to which the supporting organization is responsive (see above). Generally, a supported organization is *attentive* to the operations of a supporting organization if the supporting organization annually distributes to a supported organization an amount of support that represents a "sufficient part" of the supported organization's total support. The regulations provide three ways to demonstrate attentiveness. Nonetheless, a supported organization is *not* attentive to the operations of a supporting organization with respect to any amount received from the supporting organization that is held by the supported organization in a donor-advised fund.[197.9]

The second way to meet this test is to be a trust that, on November 20, 1970, met and continues to meet certain requirements if, for years beginning after October 16, 1972, the trustee makes annual written reports, containing certain information, to the supported organizations.[197.10]

For purposes of the distribution requirement, the amount of a distribution made to a supported organization is the fair market value of the property as of the date the distribution is made.[197.11] This amount is determined using the cash receipts and disbursements method of accounting. Distributions that count toward the distribution requirement include an amount (1) paid to a supported organization to accomplish its exempt purposes, (2) paid to acquire an asset used (or held for use) to carry out the exempt purposes of the supported organization(s), and (3) expended by the supporting organization for reasonable and necessary administrative expenses.

This proposed payout requirement is obviously framed in a fashion closely comparable to the private foundation payout rules.[197.12] One notable difference is that the proposed supporting organization payout rule does not accommodate set-asides.

---

* 197.8. Prop. Reg. § 1.509(a)-4(i)(5)(ii).
* 197.9. Prop. Reg. § 1.509(a)-4(i)(5)(iii).
* 197.10. Prop. Reg. §§ 1.509(a)-4(i)(5)(i)(B), 1.509(a)-4(i)(9).
* 197.11. Prop. Reg. § 1.509(a)-4(i)(6).
* 197.12. See § 12.4(b).

Generally, if with respect to a year, an excess distributed amount is created, the excess amount may be used to reduce the annual distributable amount in any of the 5 years immediately following the year in which the excess amount was created.[197.13] An *excess amount* is created where the total distributions made by a supporting organization to its supported organization(s) for a year exceed the supporting organization's annual distributable amount for the year.

The proposed regulations include extensive rules for ascertaining whether an asset is used or held for use to carry out exempt purposes of a supporting organization, determining the fair market value of various types of non-exempt-use assets of a supporting organization, and the timing of valuations.[197.14]

A Type III supporting organization that is in existence on the effective date of the regulations, that met and continues to meet the requirements of the existing *but for* test,[197.15] will be treated as meeting the integral part test for functionally integrated Type III supporting organizations until the first day of the organization's first year beginning after the date these regulations are published in final or temporary form.[197.16]

A Type III supporting organization in existence on the effective date of these regulations, that met and continues to meet the existing attentiveness test,[197.17] will be treated as meeting the integral part test for non-functionally integrated Type III supporting organizations until the first day of its second year beginning after the effective date of these regulations.[197.18]

*p. 372, *first complete paragraph.* **Delete second sentence (including footnotes).**

p. 372. Insert as last complete paragraph:

The IRS invited public comments in conjunction with this study.[207.1] In addition to comments on the foregoing two sets of issues, the IRS solicited comments as to (1) the advantages and disadvantages of supporting organizations to the charitable sector, donors, and supported organizations, compared to private foundations and other charitable giving arrangements; (2) the determination of the amount and availability of a charitable deduction for a transfer of assets to a supporting organization if (a) the transferred assets are paid to or used for the benefit of the donor or related persons, (b) the donor has investment control over the transferred assets, (c) the donor or the donee has option rights with respect to the transferred assets, and (d) the transferred

---

* 197.13. Prop. Reg. § 1.509(a)-4(i)(7).
* 197.14. Prop. Reg. § 1.509(a)-4(i)(8).
* 197.15. Reg. § 1.509(a)-4(i)(3)(ii).
* 197.16. Prop. Reg. § 1.509(a)-4(i)(11)(i).
* 197.17. Reg. § 1.509(a)-4(i)(3)(iii).
* 197.18. Prop. Reg. § 1.509(a)-4(i)(11)(ii).
  207.1. Notice 2007-21, 2007-9 I.R.B. 611.

assets are appreciated property that is not readily convertible to cash; (3) the effects or expected effects of this law on the practices and behavior of donors, supporting organizations, and supported organizations; and (4) the advantages and disadvantages of perpetual existence of supporting organizations.

*p. 372, n. 201. Insert following existing text:

The contours of this definition are, however, evolving. The IRS, on August 1, 2007, announced that it is expected that all Type III supporting organizations will be required to meet the present-day *responsiveness test* (Reg. § 1.509(a)-4(i)(2)(ii)). Also, the agency announced that it is anticipating proposing rules concerning Type III supporting organizations, including a requirement that these organizations that are functionally integrated with one or more supported organizations meet (1) the existing *but for test* in the regulations (Reg. § 1.509(a)-4(i)(3)(ii)), (2) an expenditure test that will resemble the qualifying distributions test for private operating foundations (see § 12.1(b), text accompanied by *supra* notes 10–21), and (3) an assets test that will resemble the alternative assets test for operating foundations (*id.*, text accompanied by *supra* notes 22, 25–28) (REG-155929-06). It is also expected that a Type III supporting organization that is not functionally integrated will be required to meet a payout requirement equal to the qualifying distribution requirement imposed on standard grantmaking private foundations (see § 12.4(b)). The proposed regulations may be expected to provide that certain Type III supporting organizations that oversee or facilitate the operation of an integrated system that includes one or more charitable organizations and that may be unable to satisfy certain requirements of the operating foundations' expenditure and assets tests, such as certain hospital systems, will nonetheless be classified as functionally integrated entities in the proposed regulations if they satisfy the existing but for test. The IRS reiterated these proposed regulations on September 28, 2007 (Ann. 2007-87, 2007-40 I.R.B. 753). The IRS, on December 21, 2007, announced transitional relief and filing procedures for certain charitable trusts that may, as of August 17, 2007, no longer qualify as Type III supporting organizations because of elimination of the *charitable trust test* of the responsiveness test (Reg. § 1.509(a)-4(i)(2)(iii)) by enactment of § 1241(c) of the Pension Protection Act of 2006 (Notice 2008-6, 2008-3 I.R.B. 275).

These regulations have, as discussed, been promulgated in proposed form (see text accompanied by *supra* notes 197.1–197.18).

The IRS, on December 6, 2006, issued interim guidance concerning supporting organizations and private foundation grants to them, including a definition of a functionally integrated Type III supporting organization on which foundation grantors may rely for purposes of pregrant due diligence (Notice 2006-109, 2006-51 I.R.B. 1121). The agency announced, on February 22, 2007, that it had suspended issuance of determination letters where organizations are seeking recognition as a functionally integrated Type III supporting organization, pending issuance of guidance as to the meaning of that phrase (memorandum for the Manager, Exempt Organizations (EO) Determinations, from the Acting Director, EO Rulings and Agreements). As a consequence of the announcement of these proposed rules on August 1, 2007, the IRS announced, on September 24, 2007, that it lifted the suspension of issuance of determination letters in cases of functionally integrated Type III supporting organizations (memorandum for the Manager, EO Determinations, from the Director, EO Rulings and Agreements).

*p. 373, n. 211, *second paragraph*. Insert as last sentence:

The IRS updated these procedures (Ann. 2009-62, 2009-33 I.R.B. 247), principally to bring them into conformity with the new public support computation rules (see text accompanied by *supra* notes 155 and 180) and new rules concerning the accounting method for determining that support (see text accompanied by *supra* notes 155.4 and 182.2).

p. 373, n. 211. Insert as third paragraph:

A court held that an organization that had as its sole activity the rental of unrelated debt-financed commercial real estate and payment of its profits to a public charity was a feeder organization, rather than a tax-exempt charitable organization, notwithstanding the organization's claim to be a supporting organization (CRSO v. Comm'r, 128 T.C. 153 (2007), on appeal to U.S. Court of Appeals for Ninth Circuit).

§ 12.4   PRIVATE FOUNDATION RULES

(f)   Other Provisions

p. 385, *first paragraph.* Insert as second sentence:

Capital gains from appreciation are included in this tax base.[337.1]

337.1.   IRC § 4940(c)(4)(A). Congress attempted to broaden this tax base in this regard when it enacted the Pension Protection Act of 2006 (§ 1221) but the statutory language did not suffice. This matter was remedied by enactment of the Tax Technical Corrections Act of 2007 (Pub. L. No. 110-172, 110th Cong., 1st Sess. (2007) § 3(f)).

PART FOUR

Other Tax-Exempt Organizations

CHAPTER THIRTEEN

Social Welfare Organizations

§ 13.1 CONCEPT OF *SOCIAL WELFARE*

(b) Benefits to Members

p. 393, n. 40. Insert following existing material:

Using this rationale, the IRS denied recognition of exemption to an organization that had the primary activity of negotiating contracts with vendors, receiving rebates, and passing them on to its members (Priv. Ltr. Rul. 200742022). As the IRS stated in this ruling, an organization that "primarily benefits a private group of citizens cannot qualify for exemption."

§ 13.2 REQUIREMENT OF *COMMUNITY*

(a) Community and Condominium Associations

p. 396, *last paragraph, seventh line*. Insert footnote following period:

[73.1]These and other machinations of the IRS in this context are the subject of Priv. Ltr. Rul. 200706014 (exclusion of public from a development by means of security gates).

p. 397, n. 77. Delete text and insert:

Id. at 133.

p. 397, n. 78. Delete text and insert:

Id.

∗p. 398, n. 88. Insert before final period:

, *aff'd*, 2008-1 U.S.T.C. ¶ 50,173 (9th Cir. 2008), *cert. den.*, 129 S. Ct. 898 (2009)

(b) Broader Requirement of Community

p. 400, *second paragraph*. Delete last sentence.

p. 400. Insert following second paragraph, before heading:

Nonetheless, the IRS subsequently has adopted a far more expansive view of the concept of a *community* in this context, equating it essentially to the entirety of the nation's public. This position is largely rested on a federal court of appeals decision issued in 1962.[101.1] The court rejected the claim that a nonprofit organization operated to provide low-cost housing for veterans was a tax-exempt social welfare entity, portraying it as merely an "economic and private cooperative undertaking."[101.2] This appellate court wrote that an exempt social welfare organization must "offer a service or program for the direct betterment or improvement of the community as a whole"; these organizations must, added the court, function on a "community basis."[101.3] The IRS's lawyers characterized this opinion as meaning that *social welfare* is the "well-being of persons of a community" and that the "benefits provided by a social welfare organization must be municipal or public."[101.4]

The IRS also relies on an appellate court decision rendered in 1964.[101.5] In this case, the court characterized the promotion of social welfare as involving the serving of "purposes beneficial to the community as a whole" or the promotion of the "welfare of mankind."[101.6] The IRS portrayed this decision as follows: The court "explained that since the exemption granted to social welfare and like organizations is made in recognition of the benefit which the public derives from their social welfare activities, it is only fair to determine a particular organization's right to an exemption largely on the basis of the effect its operations have on the public."[101.7]

The IRS ruled that a state-approved discharge cleanup organization that worked to prevent oil spills and had pollution control programs was a tax-exempt social welfare organization.[101.8] Certain members of the organization could meet part of the state's licensing requirements for their facilities.

101.1. Comm'r v. Lake Forest, Inc., 305 F.2d 814 (4th Cir. 1962), *rev'g and rem'g* 36 T.C. 510 (1962).
101.2. *Id.* 305 F.2d at 820.
101.3. *Id.* at 818.
101.4. Tech. Adv. Mem. 200829029.
101.5. People's Educ. Camp Soc'y, Inc. v. Comm'r, 331 F.2d 923 (2d Cir. 1964, *aff'g* 39 T.C. 756 (1963), *cert. den.*, 379 U.S. 839 (1964).
101.6. *Id.* 331 F.2d at 933.
101.7. Tech. Adv. Mem. 200829029.
101.8. Rev. Rul. 79-316, 1979-2 C.B. 228.

The IRS concluded that, by cleaning up spills of members and nonmembers, however, the organization acted to prevent deterioration of a port community and not merely to prevent damage to its members' facilities. The agency thus ruled that this organization was primarily engaged in activities designed to benefit all inhabitants of the community served by it.[101.9] In reliance on this ruling, the IRS held that an organization that promoted uniform codes and otherwise provided programs concerning hazardous situations supported the "public sector" and generally worked to "ensure the public safety," and therefore qualified as an exempt social welfare organization because it benefited the "community as a whole."[101.10]

§ 13.3 ADVOCACY ORGANIZATIONS

p. 400, *third paragraph.* Delete last sentence.

101.9. In this instance, the community involved was a discrete local community, rather than the public.

101.10. Tech. Adv. Mem. 200829029.

CHAPTER FOURTEEN

Business Leagues and Like Organizations

§ 14.1 CONCEPT OF *BUSINESS LEAGUE*

(c) Line-of-Business Requirement

(iii) Other Developments.

p. 413, *first complete paragraph.* **Insert as last two sentences:**

Similarly, an organization had its exempt status revoked because it was operating "solely as a leads/referrals group which only benefits uncommon business members," and its activities were "providing a direct benefit to the members rather than for the improvement of business conditions as a whole."[60.1] Likewise, a court held that the Bluetooth specification and accompanying trademark, created as marketed by an association, is a brand being sold by the association in a "garden variety" business rather than an effort to promote a common business interest.[60.2]

p. 413, *first complete paragraph.* **Insert as last sentence:**

A classic example of violation of the line-of-business requirement was provided when the IRS ruled that an organization, serving as an association for

---

60.1. Priv. Ltr. Rul. 200709070.
60.2. Bluetooth SIG, Inc. v. United States, 2008-1 U.S.T.C. ¶ 50,177 (W.D. Wash. 2008).

the independent restaurant industry, had as its primary activity the marketing of an "identifiable brand" as a way of public promotion of the member restaurants; the IRS held that this marketing effort was intended to provide the association's members a competitive advantage over other independent restaurants.[60.3]

(d) Membership Services

p. 414, *first complete paragraph, last line*. Delete period and insert:

and a self-regulatory organization with authority to promulgate and enforce business conduct and certain ethical rules with respect to an industry.[82.1]

§ 14.2 DISQUALIFYING ACTIVITIES

(a) Line-of-Business Requirement

p. 419, *second paragraph*. Insert as last sentence:

The IRS, from time to time, issues private letter rulings holding that an organization cannot qualify as a tax-exempt business league because it does not represent a line of business.[115.1]

(b) For-Profit Business Activities

(i) General Rule.

p. 420. Insert as second complete paragraph:

The Bluetooth (a radio-based technology that supports wireless communications) specification and accompanying trademark, created and marketed by an association, was held by a court to be a brand being sold by the association in a "garden variety" business, thus precluding the association from tax-exempt status.[124.1] As the court viewed the matter, while an exempt business league can advance a common and *preexisting* interest among its members, the association at issue was formed to *create* a common business interest among its members. The court wrote that the "collective enterprise of the [a]ssociation derives from the fact that it has created a thing of value, which its members can then use to enhance the value of the products they sell."[124.2]

60.3. Priv. Ltr. Rul. 200837035.
82.1. Priv. Ltr. Rul. 200723029.
115.1. E.g., Priv. Ltr. Ruls. 200837035 (promotion of a brand name for an organization's members to provide them with a competitive advantage in the industry), 200843035 (association of shopping center merchants), and 200845054 (organization with membership of a limited group of franchisees).
124.1. Bluetooth SIG, Inc. v. United States, 2008-1 U.S.T.C. ¶ 50,177 (W.D. Wash. 2008).
124.2. *Id.*

(c)   Performance of Particular Services

(i) Particular Services.

p. 421. Insert as third complete paragraph:

In the case referenced above concerning the Bluetooth technology,[135.1] the court also found that the association was providing particular services for individual persons, thereby not qualifying as an exempt business league on that basis. The court wrote: "It is undisputed that use of the Bluetooth trademark is absolutely limited to members who pay the appropriate listing fee."[135.2] Also: "[S]omething of value is offered to all comers on the condition that they pay for it, and the benefits are in proportion to the contribution," and "[f]rom the standpoint of manufacturers, Bluetooth quite simply benefits those who use it, which is why it is for sale."[135.3]

(ii) General Rule.

p. 425, n. 167. Insert following existing material:

The IRS denied recognition of exemption, as a business league, to an organization that had the primary activity of negotiating contracts with vendors, receiving rebates, and passing them on to its members, on the ground that the negotiating activity was the performance of particular services for its members (Priv. Ltr. Rul. 200742022).

p. 427. Insert as first complete paragraph:

The IRS, from time to time, issues private letter rulings holding that an organization cannot qualify as a tax-exempt business league because it provides particular services to some or all of its members.[182.1]

(d)   Private Inurement

*p. 427, n. 188. Delete and substitute:

See § 20.9.

§ 14.3   CHAMBERS OF COMMERCE

p. 428, n. 192, *last line*. Insert period at end of line.

135.1. Bluetooth SIG, Inc. v. United States, 2008-1 U.S.T.C. ¶ 50,177 (W.D. Wash. 2008). See *supra* note 124.1.

135.2. *Id*.

135.3. *Id*.

182.1. E.g., Priv. Ltr. Rul. 200742022.

CHAPTER FIFTEEN

Social Clubs

§ 15.1   SOCIAL CLUBS IN GENERAL

(b)   Club Functions

*p. 436, *first complete paragraph.* **Insert as last sentence:**

The IRS ruled that an exempt club's practice of allowing certain unaccompanied guests and "full privilege guests" to use its golf course and clubhouse facilities gave rise to *member use,* exempt function income.[22.1]

§ 15.3   INVESTMENT INCOME LIMITATION

p. 440, *third paragraph, sixth line.* **Insert footnote following period:**

[67.1]E.g., Priv. Ltr. Rul. 200534023.

§ 15.6   SALE OF CLUB ASSETS

p. 448, *last paragraph.* **Insert as last sentence:**

The IRS applied this body of law in an instance where an exempt social club terminated and relinquished a parcel of long-termed leased property in exchange for a larger acreage of land to be used in furtherance of its exempt purposes.[128.1]

---

* 22.1. Priv. Ltr. Rul. 200915053.
  128.1. Priv. Ltr. Rul. 200826038.

CHAPTER SIXTEEN

Labor, Agricultural, and Horticultural Organizations

§ 16.2 AGRICULTURAL ORGANIZATIONS

p. 459, *second complete paragraph.* **Insert as third sentence:**

Thus, an organization operating a certification and marketing program for high-quality, branded, value-added products of its members did not qualify as an exempt agricultural entity because it did not benefit the producers in the particular field generally; indeed, the IRS concluded that this organization was merely a "sales agent" for its members.[71.1]

71.1. Priv. Ltr. Rul. 200644043.

CHAPTER SEVENTEEN

Political Organizations

§ 17.6   TAXATION OF OTHER EXEMPT ORGANIZATIONS

p. 473, n. 77. Delete sentence.

§ 17.8   INDEPENDENT POLITICAL ACTION COMMITTEES

p. 477, n. 104, *first line*. Insert following first comma:

Mayer, "The Much Maligned 527 and Institutional Choice," 58 *Exempt Org. Tax Rev.* (No. 1) 21 (Oct. 2007);

CHAPTER EIGHTEEN

Employee Benefit Funds

§ 18.3   VOLUNTARY EMPLOYEES' BENEFICIARY
ASSOCIATIONS

*p. 492, n. 51. Insert following existing material:

> Certain health insurance (IRC § 35) may be provided under an employee benefit plan funded by a VEBA, in the case of eligible coverage months beginning before January 1, 2011, where the VEBA was established pursuant to an order of a bankruptcy court or by agreement with an authorized representative (IRC § 35(e)(1)(K)). This rule was enacted by § 1899G of the American Recovery and Investment Act of 2009 (Pub. L. No. 111-5).

*p. 492, *carryover paragraph*. Insert as fourth sentence on page:

A VEBA may provide identity theft insurance to its participants and their dependents.[51.1]

p. 492, *last paragraph*. Insert as first two sentences:

Often, application of the private inurement doctrine occurs in the context of assessing the reasonableness of compensation.[55.1] Thus, the IRS ruled that the transfer, by the trustee of a VEBA, of the trust's administration business to a for-profit company will not result in private inurement as long as the fees paid by the trustee to the company do not exceed the administrative fees paid by other entities to the company for comparable services.[55.2]

---

*   51.1. Priv. Ltr. Rul. 200911037.
    55.1. See § 20.4.
    55.2. Priv. Ltr. Rul. 200503027.

p. 494, n. 78. Delete second and third sentences, and insert:

The U.S. Court of Federal Claims held that this limitation on exempt function income cannot be avoided by allocating investment income to the payment of welfare benefits during the year involved (that is, by spending rather than accumulating) (CNG Transmission Management VEBA v. United States, 84 Fed. Cl. 327 (Ct. Fed. Cl. 2008) *aff'd*, U.S. Ct. App. for Fed Cir., Dec. 14, 2009), while the U.S. Court of Appeals for the Sixth Circuit held that the limitation is applicable only to income actually accumulated during the course of a VEBA's year (Sherwin-Williams Co. Employee Health Plan Trust v. Comm'r, 330 F.3d 449 (6th Cir. 2003), *rev'g*, 115 T.C. 440 (2001), IRS nonacquiescence in AOD 2005-02, 2005-35 I.R.B. 422).

CHAPTER NINETEEN

Other Tax-Exempt Organizations

§ 19.5   BENEVOLENT OR MUTUAL ORGANIZATIONS

(b)   Mutual Organizations

p. 514, n. 131. Insert following existing material:

A tax-exempt rural electric cooperative developed a new line of business, consisting of the sale of natural gas to its members; the IRS ruled that this service "clearly" is a public utility-type service and thus "fits squarely" within the definition of a *like organization* (Priv. Ltr. Rul. 200717020).

§ 19.9   INSURANCE COMPANIES AND ASSOCIATIONS

(a)   Present Law

*p. 524, *second complete paragraph, fourth line.* Insert footnote following period:

[212.1]E.g., Priv. Ltr. Rul. 200830025.

§ 19.11 VETERANS' ORGANIZATIONS

(a) General Rules

*p. 527, n. 241. Insert as first sentence:

The IRS's legal counsel concluded, on the basis of federal tax law in the social club context (see Chapter 15), that a veterans' organization is operating to provide social and recreational activities to its members when it provides these services to "nonmembers who are guests or dependents" but if a "substantial amount" of the services are provided to other categories of nonmembers the veterans' organization would not qualify for exemption (Chief Couns. Adv. Mem. 200936027).

§ 19.12 FARMERS' COOPERATIVES

p. 531, *second paragraph, fifth line*. Delete *and*.

p. 531, *second paragraph, sixth line*. Change the period to a comma and insert thereafter:

and a cooperative that processed and marketed brine shrimp cysts where the harvesting of the shrimp was in a publicly owned lake.[285.1]

§ 19.17 QUALIFIED TUITION PROGRAMS

(a) State-Sponsored Programs

*p. 541, n. 382. Insert following existing material:

The concept of these expenses was expanded to include, with respect to expenses paid or incurred in 2009 or 2010, outlays for the purchase of computer technology or equipment (IRC § 170(e)(6)(F)(i)) or Internet access and related services, if the technology, equipment, or services are to be used by the beneficiary and the beneficiary's family during any of the years the beneficiary is enrolled at an eligible educational institution (IRC § 529(e)(3)(A)(iii)). This rule, which was enacted by § 1005 of the American Recovery and Investment Act of 2009 (Pub. L. No. 111-5), does not embrace expenses for "computer software designed for sports, games, or hobbies unless the software is predominantly educational in nature."

*p. 541, n. 384. Delete and substitute:

IRC § 529(b)(4). A program does not violate this investment restriction if it permits a change in the investment strategy selected for a section 529 account twice per calendar year for 2009, as well as a change in the designated beneficiary of the account (Notice 2009-1, 2009-1 C.B. 250) subject to program requirements stated in 2001 (Notice 2001-55, 2001-2 C.B. 299).

285.1. Priv. Ltr. Rul. 200841038. This organization differed from the one referenced in *supra* note 271 inasmuch as, in the facts of the 1964 ruling, the fishing was in privately owned waters (i.e., a fish farm).

*p. 541, n. 385. Delete and substitute:

IRC § 529(b)(3).

*p. 542, n. 389. Delete and substitute:

IRC § 529(b)(5).

*p. 542, n. 390. Delete and substitute:

IRC § 529(b)(6).

(c)   Other Rules

p. 543, n. 401. Insert following existing material:

Thereafter, the IRS issued an advance notice of proposed rulemaking on transfer tax provisions that apply to these accounts (REG-127127-05) and sought public comment on these proposed rules (Ann. 2008-17, 2008-9 I.R.B. 512).

§ 19.22   PROPOSED EXEMPT ORGANIZATIONS

p. 554, *item no. 33, second line*. Insert *H.R. 1840 (2007)*, following opening parenthesis.

p. 555, *seventh line*. Insert *(2006)* following bill number.

*p. 555. Insert following seventh line, before heading:

41. To provide tax-exempt status for nonprofit health insurance issuers that are structured as cooperatives (proposed IRC § 501(c)(29)) (S. 1796 (2009)).

PART FIVE

Principal Exempt Organization Laws

CHAPTER TWENTY

Private Inurement and Private Benefit

§ 20.1　CONCEPT OF *PRIVATE INUREMENT*

p. 561, n. 24. Insert following existing material:

An individual who was the founder, president, chief executive officer, and executive director of a tax-exempt school caused the school to have its exemption revoked because she had "control . . . over the entity's funds, assets, and disbursements; use of entity moneys for personal expenses; payment of salary or rent to [her] without any accompanying evidence or analysis of the reasonableness of the amounts; and purported loans to [her] showing a ready private source of credit" (Rameses School of San Antonio, Texas v. Comm'r, 93 T.C.M. 1092, 1097 (2007)).

§ 20.4　COMPENSATION ISSUES

(b)　Determining Reasonableness of Compensation

*p. 571, n. 93. Convert existing material to second paragraph of note and insert as first paragraph:

The IRS wrote that "exemption from federal income tax of an organization is not jeopardized where agreements on compensation [with insiders] are entered into through negotiations conducted at arm's length and are not considered to be excessive based on persons having similar responsibilities and comparable duties"; the governing board of the organization involved adopted a "Policy Against Inurement," which the IRS referenced with approval (Priv. Ltr. Rul. 200944055).

p. 573, n. 109, *last line.* **Insert ¶ before** *50,493* **and insert** *aff'd, 2008-1 U.S.T.C.* **¶** *50,244 (9th Cir. 2008)* **before final closing parenthesis.**

(e)   Role of Board

p. 576, *last line.* **Insert footnote following period:**

135.1See § 5.6.

p. 578. Insert following second complete paragraph, before heading:

(i)   IRS College and University Questionnaire (New)

The compliance questionnaire sent by the IRS, in late 2008, to approximately 400 colleges and universities[142.1] includes considerable insight as to the agency's contemporary thinking about executive compensation paid by tax-exempt organizations, particularly public charities, and related federal tax law.[142.2] In that questionnaire, the IRS focused on the six highest-paid trustees, directors, officers, and key employees of these institutions. There is no particular significance to be given to the number *six* in this context, other than that it may be the IRS's level of concentration in connection with the compensation practices of any exempt organization, such as when reviewing an annual information return or conducting an examination. Also, it is notable that the IRS is also looking at compensation paid to these individuals by related organizations.

With this questionnaire, the IRS is inquiring into the following types of remuneration: base salary; bonus; contributions to employee benefit plans (e.g., health benefit), incentives; contributions for life, disability, and/or long-term care insurance coverage; split-dollar life insurance (where the premiums are paid by the organization); loans or other extensions of credit (including forgone interest or debt forgiveness arrangements); stock or stock options (forms of equity-based compensation); severance or change-of-control payments; personal use of an organization credit card (where there is no reimbursement); personal use of organization vehicle; personal travel for the individual or spouse or other family member (where there is no reimbursement); expense reimbursements (other than from an accountable plan); value of housing and utilities provided by organization; value of organization-provided vacation home; personal services provided at individual's residence (e.g., housekeeper, lawn service, and/or maintenance or repair services); other personal services (e.g., legal, financial, and/or retirement); health or social club dues; personal use of organization aircraft or boat; first-class travel;[142.3] taxable scholarship

---

142.1.   See §§ 8.3(a), notes 77.1–77.5, 26.6(ii), text accompanied by note 308.6.

142.2.   Form 14018, Part IV.

142.3.   Payment for first-class travel is not a form of remuneration or other compensation.

or fellowship grants; other executive fringe benefits (other than these benefits excluded from gross income); and other forms of compensation.

The IRS also inquired into contributions to deferred compensation plans, namely, the organization's contributions to a 401(a) plan; the participant's contributions to a 401(a) plan; organization's contributions to a 403(b) plan; the participant's contributions to a 403(b) plan; the organization's contributions to a 457(b) plan; the participant's contributions to a 457(b) plan; the organization's contributions to a 457(f) plan; the participant's contributions to a 457(f) plan; the organization's contributions to 415(m) qualified governmental excess benefit arrangements; the participant's contributions to 415(m) qualified governmental excess benefit arrangements; and other deferred compensation arrangements, whether qualified or unqualified.

This questionnaire asks whether the tax-exempt organization has a formal written compensation policy that governs compensation of at least some of its trustees, directors, officers, or key employees. The IRS asks whether the organization hired an outside (independent) executive compensation consultant to provide comparable compensation data to determine the compensation of any of these individuals; the IRS also asks, if a consultant was hired, whether the consultant provided other services to the organization. The IRS requests information as to who in the institution sets compensation for the positions, such as the organization's board, its officers, or a compensation committee.

As to these highest compensated individuals, the IRS wants to know whether the individual has an employment agreement or independent contractor agreement with the organization. The IRS asks whether, in determining these compensation arrangements, the organization used a process that was intended to satisfy the intermediate sanctions' rebuttable presumption of reasonableness procedure.[142.4] The IRS inquires as to whether the organization documented the basis for setting the individual's compensation before the compensation was provided. The IRS asks whether payments to these individuals were made pursuant to the intermediate sanctions' initial contract exception.[142.5] The IRS asks whether the compensated person was a disqualified person with respect to the organization[142.6] immediately prior to entering into the employment or independent contractor arrangement.

The IRS, by means of this questionnaire, asks whether the organization's board of directors or other authorized governing body (that did not have a conflict of interest) approved the individual's compensation. Other questions are whether the individual recused himself or herself from the discussion about and/or the voting on his or her compensation, and whether the organization obtained an independent compensation comparability survey that was used in setting the individual's compensation. If the answer to the foregoing question

---

142.4. See § 21.9.
142.5. See § 21.8.
142.6. See, e.g., § 21.3.

is yes, the IRS inquires as to whether the individual's compensation was set within the range of the comparability survey data. If the answer to that question is yes, the IRS asks about the percentage from the comparability survey data that was used to determine the individual's compensation.

This questionnaire makes clear what the IRS believes are the factors that should be taken into account by a tax-exempt organization and/or a compensation consultant in setting executive compensation.[142.7] These factors include compensation levels paid by similar organizations (tax-exempt and taxable), the level of the individual's education and experience, the specific responsibilities of the position, the individual's previous salary or compensation package, similar services in the same geographic or metropolitan area, similar number of employees, and the organization's annual budget and/or gross revenue/assets.

The questionnaire requires the institution to indicate the sources used to obtain comparability data for each of these individuals' compensation, such as published surveys of compensation at similar institutions, Internet research on compensation at similar institutions, telephone surveys of compensation at similar institutions, an outside expert hired to provide comparable compensation data and a report, a report prepared by a compensation analyst employed by the institution, written offers of employment from similar institutions, annual information returns filed by similar institutions, and the annual budget or gross revenue/assets.

The questionnaire probes into the matter of loans and other extensions of credit to the institutions' highest compensated individuals. Questions include whether the organization maintains documents detailing terms, payments, and interest rates for these transactions; the transactions were approved by the organization's board; the beneficiary made cash payments in accordance with a repayment schedule; the loan agreement's interest rates met the applicable federal rate standards;[142.8] collateral was provided for the loan or other extension of credit; any portion of the loan or credit extension was considered compensation for services performed; and the organization forgave any of these loans or indebtedness.

p. 578. Insert following second full paragraph, before heading:

(j) Illegal Payments (New)

Also, aside from the matter of reasonableness, private inurement can arise where the payment of compensation is contrary to law. In one instance, the

---

142.7. See § 20.4(b).
142.8. IRC § 6621.

IRS revoked the tax-exempt status of an organization, which is subject to the private inurement doctrine, where state law requires workers in the particular field to be volunteers and the organization nonetheless compensated them.[142.9]

§ 20.7 INCIDENTAL PRIVATE INUREMENT

*p. 596, *first paragraph, first line*. Insert *the concept of* following *is*.

*p. 596, *first paragraph*. Insert as last sentence, prior to note number:

Regulations promulgated by the IRS illustrate when the existence of private inurement only has the consequence of application of the intermediate sanctions penalties.

*p. 596, n. 264. Delete and substitute:

See § 21.16.

§ 20.9 PRIVATE INUREMENT AND BUSINESS LEAGUES

*p. 596, *fourth paragraph*. Insert as last sentences:

By contrast, private inurement was not found in connection with a payment by a business league to its members, where the source of the funding was a publicly traded company that paid the money in satisfaction of a condition, which was a change in the business league's governance structure, to a merger transaction.[272.1]

Likewise, the IRS ruled that a return of contributions by an exempt business league, on a pro rata basis, where the funds were given to finance litigation, following a lucrative settlement, was not private inurement.[272.2]

§ 20.11 PRIVATE BENEFIT DOCTRINE

(a) General Rules

*p. 600, n. 306. Delete and substitute:

See § 20.11(a-1). Cf. § 20.7.

142.9. Priv. Ltr. Rul. 200842051. It was not clear in this instance, however, that the workers were insiders.
272.1. Priv. Ltr. Rul. 200723029.
* 272.2. Priv. Ltr. Rul. 200917042.

p. 600, *first paragraph.* **Insert as last sentence:**

As the IRS characterized the point, the private benefit doctrine applies to "all kinds of persons and groups."[309.1]

*p. 601. **Delete third paragraph (including footnotes) and substitute:**

(a.1) Incidental Private Benefit

As noted, the federal tax law recognizes the concept of *incidental* private benefit, that is, private benefit that does not jeopardize or preclude a charitable organization's tax exemption.[322]

As an illustration, a tax-exempt charitable organization that allocated Medicaid patients to physicians in private practice was held to provide qualitatively and quantitatively incidental private benefit to the physicians, including some on the organization's board of directors, inasmuch as it was "impossible" for this organization to accomplish its exempt purposes without providing some measure of benefit to these physicians.[323] Likewise, an exempt hospital received a ruling that it, having constructed new facilities, had the only economically viable alternative of transferring its prior facilities to an unrelated, for-profit organization, at a below-market price, for the purpose of leasing space in the renovated facility to community businesses; the IRS held that this rental activity would create new jobs in the hospital's economically depressed community[323.1] and entail only incidental economic benefit to the for-profit company.[323.2] Similarly, the IRS ruled that an exempt hospital's investment in a for-profit medical malpractice insurance company, using funds paid by its staff physicians, furthered charitable purposes[323.3] and was deemed to not extend impermissible private benefit, because the investment was required for the writing of insurance for the physicians, the physicians needed the insurance to practice at the hospital, and the hospital needed the physicians to provide health-care services in its communities.[323.4]

Likewise, the IRS held that a supporting organization operating for the benefit of a tax-exempt college[323.5] may make grants to a capital fund for advancement of a business incubator program, with the business thus created contributing importantly to the college's teaching program; the benefit

---

309.1. Priv. Ltr. Rul. 200635018.

* 322. See text accompanied by *supra* note 306. On occasion, a private benefit is disregarded for tax exemption purposes as being *unavoidable.* See § 6.3(b).

* 323. Priv. Ltr. Rul. 9615030.

* 323.1. See §§ 7.11, 7.15(e).

* 323.2. Priv. Ltr. Rul. 200103083.

* 323.3. See § 7.6.

* 323.4. Priv. Ltr. Rul. 200606042.

* 323.5. See § 12.3(a), (c), respectively.

conferred to the companies by the incubator investments was considered incidental to the advancement of the college's educational purposes.[323.6] A public
charity that educated the public about the history and architecture of a cemetery was allowed to participate in a burial lot exchange with a donor, with the
IRS observing that "any benefit to the donor in connection with the exchange
will not lessen the public benefits" flowing from the organization's operations,
and dismissing any adverse application of the private benefit doctrine.[323.7] The
IRS announced that it does not treat the benefits an exempt hospital provides to
its medical staff physicians—in the form of electronic health records software
and technical support services—as impermissible private benefit if the benefits fall within the range of electronic health records items and services that are
allowable under Department of Health and Human Services regulations, and
if the hospital operates in a certain manner.[323.8]

Also, a research agreement between an exempt scientific organization and
a for-profit business was held to not jeopardize this tax exemption because
the resulting private benefit, to overlapping directors involving the exempt
organization and another for-profit business, was considered by the IRS to be
incidental in relation to the benefit accruing to the scientific organization.[323.9]
The IRS began issuing favorable ruling letters to regional health information organizations after being reassured by Congress that the private benefit
involved was incidental.[323.10]

By contrast, a nonprofit organization was formed to generate community
interest in retaining classical music programming on a commercial radio station, by seeking sponsors for the programs, urging listeners to patronize the
sponsors, and soliciting listener subscriptions to promote the programs; the IRS
ruled that the organization could not qualify for tax exemption as a charitable
and educational entity because these activities increased the station's revenues
and thus benefited it in more than an insubstantial manner.[323.11] Likewise, an
inventor was ruled to receive unwarranted private benefit when he licensed a
patent on one of his inventions to a would-be charitable organization, which
would then employ him; the organization was seen by the IRS as merely a vehicle to enable him to complete his work on the patent and thereafter be "richly
compensated."[323.12] Similarly, an organization formed to improve the quality

---

* 323.6.   Priv. Ltr. Rul. 200614030.
* 323.7.   Priv. Ltr. Rul. 200708087.
* 323.8.   Memorandum dated May 11, 2007, from the Director, Exempt Organizations Division
        to the Directors, EO Examinations and Rulings and Agreements. The Department of
        Health and Human Services earlier promulgated regulations permitting hospitals to
        provide, within certain parameters, such electronic health records services to their
        medical staff physicians without violating the federal anti-kickback and physician self-
        referral laws.
* 323.9.   Priv. Ltr. Rul. 200905033.
* 323.10. See § 7.6(j).
* 323.11. Rev. Rul. 77-206, 1977-1 C.B. 149.
* 323.12. Priv. Ltr. 200849017.

of health care available to consumers, with its first priority being promotion of adoption of standardized performance measures of health-care quality and efficiency, was ruled by the IRS to not constitute an exempt charitable and educational entity in part because it was characterized as a "cooperative enterprise" that primarily benefited its members, who were large for-profit businesses and health-care insurance companies.[323.13]

The private benefit doctrine is nearly boundless.[323.14] The doctrine's use by the IRS is pliant; the IRS can be generous in dismissing private benefit as incidental. Yet when the agency embarks on a massive campaign to eradicate tax exemption in a particular field, such as exemption for employee hardship assistance funds,[323.15] credit counseling organizations,[323.16] housing provider entities,[323.17] or down payment assistance organizations,[323.18] the IRS will swiftly and strictly apply the private benefit doctrine. The IRS was paralyzed as to its ruling policy with respect to regional health information organizations, until it was directed by Congress to treat the private benefit involved as being incidental.[323.19]

(b) Joint Venture Law

p. 604, *third complete paragraph*. Insert as last sentences:

As an example of application of this opinion, an organization providing healthcare services was denied recognition of exemption because it was "effectively controlled" by two for-profit medical practices and because the provision of the services "enhances these businesses [the medical practices] and improves their reputation in the community."[341.1] In another illustration, an organization was denied recognition of exemption because it was "totally dependent" on its for-profit creator for material and operations, the two entities are "functionally inseparable," and the organization "ceded control to a for-profit [organization] that has an independent financial interest in your activities and no obligation to operate for exempt purposes."[341.2]

p. 605, *second complete paragraph*. Insert as last sentence:

In application of this decision, the IRS refused to recognize exemption in a case of a nonprofit corporation with four directors who were also the directors of a for-profit entity; the IRS ruled that the nonprofit entity was

* 323.13. Priv. Ltr. Rul. 200944053.
* 323.14. See § 20.11(c).
* 323.15. See § 7.2A.
* 323.16. See § 7.3.
* 323.17. See § 7.4.
* 323.18. See § 7.5.
* 323.19. See § 7.6(j).
  341.1. Priv. Ltr. Rul. 200635018.
  341.2. Priv. Ltr. Rul. 200702042.

"totally dependent upon your for-profit creator" and that it "ceded control" to the for-profit company.[347.1]

(c)   Perspective

p. 606, *second paragraph, first line.* **Delete** *proposed* **and insert** *promulgated.*

p. 606, n. 351. Delete text and insert:

> T.D. 9390.

p. 606, n. 352. Delete *Prop.*

p. 606, n. 353, *first line.* **Delete** *Id.* **and substitute:**

> Reg. § 1.501(c)(3)-1(d)(1)(iii).

p. 606. Insert following existing material in fn. 374:

> This approach of the IRS is reflected in the facts in Exploratory Research, Inc. v. Comm'r, 95 T.C.M. 1347 (2008).

p. 607, n. 354, *first line.* **Delete** *Id.* **and substitute:**

> Reg. § 1.501(c)(3)-1(d)(1)(iii).

*pp. 607–608. Delete last paragraph (including footnotes) on p. 607 and its carryover on p. 608.

*p. 608. *Insert following existing material:*

(d)   Doctrine and IRS Governance Enforcement (New)

The IRS is becoming heavily involved in governance issues with respect to tax-exempt organizations, particularly public charities, as manifested in policy statements and private letter rulings.[368] This insertion by the agency into nonprofit organization governance matters entails a variety of new (ostensible) requirements as a condition of exemption, including an independent board, adoption of a conflict-of-interest policy, and adoption of other policies, procedures, and protocols. Generally, however, neither federal nor state law requires any of these conditions to exemption being asserted by the IRS. Thus, the IRS is relying on a strained interpretation of the private benefit doctrine to buttress its ruling policy.

347.1. Priv. Ltr. Rul. 200702042.
368. See § 5.6(m), (n).

The private benefit doctrine, like the private inurement doctrine,[369] the excess benefit transactions rules,[370] and the self-dealing rules,[371] is triggered when a transaction occurs or arrangement is put into place that entails the provision of an unwarranted private benefit. These rules of law do not come into play solely because of a potential of private benefit. (It is a rare tax-exempt organization that does not have the opportunity to convey a private benefit.) Nonetheless, the IRS, in an effort to sustain its ruling policies in the governance context, is now asserting that the private benefit doctrine is implicated when private benefit might occur. Also, the IRS often denies recognition of exemption because the applicant organization cannot prove the proverbial negative by showing that private benefit will not occur.

For example, the IRS ruled that the composition of a board of directors of an organization seeking to qualify as a tax-exempt charitable entity automatically gave rise to private benefit.[372] In that ruling, the sheer fact of control of the organization by one individual was found to be private benefit. The IRS wrote that, inasmuch as the entity is controlled by one individual, who is its founder, sole donor, one of two related trustees, and one of two related officers, "taking into account your structure, governance, and operations, your activities result in the provision of more than an incidental level of private benefit to [this individual] and his family."[373]

In another ruling, the IRS concluded that an organization could not qualify as a tax-exempt charitable entity, in part because it did not adopt a conflict-of-interest policy and lacked an independent board.[374] The board of this organization consisted of four related individuals, one of which was the organization's founder. The IRS considered this lack of an independent board in light of the private benefit doctrine. Noting that this family exercised "complete control" over the organization, its assets, the IRS wrote, "could be used to benefit the family." The agency concluded: "The structure of your organization indicates that it can be used to benefit private individuals, such as [the founder] and his family, and you lack safeguards that would help to prevent such use." In addition, the IRS said, "you have provided no evidence that the organization will not be used for the benefit of private individuals."[375]

---

369. See § 20.1.
370. See Chapter 21.
371. See § 12.4(a).
372. Priv. Ltr. Rul. 200736037, reissued as Priv. Ltr. Rul. 200737044.
* 373. Thereafter, the IRS denied recognition of exempt status to an organization, in part because the entity was "governed by a board of directors that is controlled by members of the same family." Priv. Ltr. Rul. 200916035. It would be the rare family private foundation that could remain tax-exempt were this standard the law.
374. Priv. Ltr. Rul. 200830028.
375. Thousands of tax-exempt charitable organizations would lose their exempt status were this standard the law.

In another instance, the IRS found private benefit where three unrelated individuals, comprising an organization's board of directors, had "unfettered control" over the entity and its assets.[376]

---

* 376. Priv. Ltr. Rul. 200845053. It is not clear where, if control is not to be with the board of a tax-exempt organization, the control is supposed to be.

CHAPTER TWENTY-ONE

Intermediate Sanctions

§ 21.2　TAX-EXEMPT ORGANIZATIONS INVOLVED

p. 611, *third paragraph, first line.* **Delete** *proposed* **and insert** *promulgated.*

p. 611, *fourth paragraph, first line.* **Delete** *proposed.*

p. 611, *fourth paragraph, last line.* **Delete** *penalties* **and insert** *taxes.*

p. 611, n. 12. Delete text and substitute:

T.D. 9390.

p. 611, n. 14. Delete *Prop.* **and insert the following after existing material:**

Also Reg. § 1.501(c)(3)-1(f)(1).

p. 611, n. 16. Delete *Prop.*

§ 21.3　DISQUALIFIED PERSONS

*p. 612, n. 24. Delete sentences and substitute:**

An individual is a *highly compensated employee* with respect to a year if he or she received compensation in excess of a dollar limitation, which is indexed for inflation, in the immediately prior year. This limitation for 2010 is $110,000 (IR-2009-94), for determinations made in 2011.

§ 21.4   TRANSACTIONS INVOLVED

(d)   Automatic Excess Benefit Transactions and Supporting Organizations

p. 617, *first complete paragraph, last line.* **Insert footnote at end of line:**

[66.1] These rules generally do not apply to a transaction between a supporting organization and a supported organization with respect to it. When this exception was originally written, as part of the Pension Protection Act of 2006 (§ 1242), supported organizations that are exempt social welfare, labor, agricultural or horticultural entities, or business leagues, were inadvertently omitted from the scope of the exception. This matter was rectified on enactment of the Tax Technical Corrections Act of 2007 (§ 3(i)), by revision of IRC § 4958(c)(3)(C)(ii) (Pub. L. No. 110-172, 110th Cong., 1st Sess. (2007)).

*p. 617. **Insert following fourth complete paragraph, before heading:**

(f)   Scholarships and Similar Grants

A scholarship, fellowship, or similar grant[70.1] may be an excess benefit transaction, if the grantor is an applicable tax-exempt organization[70.2] and the grantee is a disqualified person.[70.3] There is little law directly pertaining to grantmaking to individuals by public charities; the IRS states that charitable organizations may distribute funds to individuals, as long as the distributions are made on a charitable basis in furtherance of exempt purposes and adequate records and case histories are maintained.[70.4] Private foundations are more restricted in their ability to make grants to individuals, largely because of the rules concerning taxable expenditures.[70.5]

For purposes of scholarship awards granted by a private foundation to be used for study at an educational institution, the grants must be awarded on an "objective and nondiscriminatory basis" pursuant to a procedure approved in advance by the IRS.[70.6] Although public charities are not subject to these requirements, the IRS stated that a "scholarship program conducted by a public charity which conforms to these standards for objectivity and educational character will ordinarily be considered to be in furtherance of exempt purposes."[70.7]

In this context, for grants to be considered awarded on an objective and nondiscriminatory basis, the grantees must be selected from a group of individuals who are chosen on the basis of criteria that reasonably relate to the purpose of the grant and generally are from a group that is sufficiently broad

---

* 70.1. See § 7.8.
* 70.2. See § 21.2.
* 70.3. See § 21.3.
* 70.4. Rev. Rul. 56-304, 1956-2 C.B. 306.
* 70.5. See § 12.4(e). See *Private Foundations* § 9.3.
* 70.6. IRC § 4945(g). See *Private Foundations* § 9.3(g).
* 70.7. Priv. Ltr. Rul. 200332018.

to constitute a charitable class.[70.8] Furthermore, the group must be sufficiently broad so that the making of grants to the group would be considered in fulfillment of a charitable purpose.[70.9] Selection from a group, however, is not necessary where, taking into account the purposes of the grant, one or several individuals are selected because they are exceptionally qualified to carry out the organization's purposes or it is otherwise evident that the selection is particularly calculated to effectuate the purpose of the grant rather than to benefit particular persons or a particular class of persons.[70.10]

As noted, the criteria used in selecting the grantees must be related to the purpose of the grant.[70.11] For example, in granting academic scholarships, an organization's selection criteria might include prior academic performance, performance on aptitude tests, recommendations from instructors, financial need, and the conclusion a selection committee has drawn from a personal interview as to the prospective grantee's motivation, character, ability, and potential.[70.12] Moreover, the persons or group of persons who select recipients of the grants should not be in a position to derive a private benefit, directly or indirectly, if certain potential grantees are selected instead of others.[70.13]

The IRS's lawyers determined that educational grants are not awarded on an objective and nondiscriminatory basis if preference in awarding the grants is accorded to relatives of the charitable organization's grant-makers.[70.14] In this determination, IRS counsel referenced the history of the private foundation taxable expenditures regulations, stating that it was "intended that grantees could not be selected for personal reasons but rather that the selection process, including the preliminary matter of determining the composition of the class of 'candidates' for grants from which the recipients are chosen, must be based on criteria which related to the 'educational' purpose of the grant."

As to the intermediate sanctions rules, the standard is whether scholarship grants are excess benefit transactions. Where the scholarship amounts are reasonable, the grants of them are not excess benefit transactions (even if paid to or for the benefit of disqualified persons). In the scholarships setting, the IRS, in determining whether payments were reasonable, determines whether the payments were made in accordance with objective and nondiscriminatory criteria.

---

* 70.8. Reg. 53.4945-4(b)(2).
* 70.9. *Id.*
* 70.10. *Id.*
* 70.11. Reg. § 53.4945-4(b)(3).
* 70.12. *Id.*
* 70.13. Reg. § 53.4945-4(b)(4).
* 70.14. Gen. Coun. Mem. 38954.

§ 21.14 RETURN FOR PAYMENT OF EXCISE TAXES

p. 632, n. 185. Insert following existing material:

It is the view of the IRS that interest begins to accrue on intermediate sanctions excise taxes on the date the return reporting the tax was due (Chief Couns. Adv. Mem. 200819017); this position is based on the conclusion that these taxes are indeed taxes and not penalties (where interest starts accruing following notice and demand for payment by the IRS), following Latterman v. United States, 872 F.2d 564 (3rd Cir. 1989).

§ 21.15 STATUTE OF LIMITATIONS

p. 632. Delete third complete paragraph and substitute:

In general, the statute of limitations for assessment by the IRS of an intermediate sanctions excise tax is the same as the general statute of limitations rules with respect to the assessment of taxes,[186] that is, three years.[187] The general rule in this regard is that the statute of limitations begins to run as of the date the return involved was filed or the due date of the return, whichever is later, and ends three years after that date. Thus, in the intermediate sanctions context, the statute begins to run on the later of the date the applicable tax-exempt organization filed its annual information return[188] or the due date of the return.

The intermediate sanctions taxes are excise taxes. In the case of a return involving an excise tax, if the return omits an amount of tax properly includible on the return that exceeds 25 percent of the amount of the reported tax, the tax may be assessed (or a court proceeding commenced) at any time within six years after the return is filed.[189] The tax-exempt organizations annual information return, however, does not provide for the payment of any tax.[189.1] Thus, in determining the amount of tax "omitted" on the return, an intermediate sanctions tax is not taken into account if the excess benefit transaction that gave rise to the tax is disclosed in the return in a manner adequate to apprise the IRS of the existence and nature of the transaction.[189.2] The IRS has the burden of proving that the disclosure of information on an exempt organization's annual information return was insufficient to apprise it of the existence and nature of the excess benefit transaction involved.[189.3]

---

186. IRC § 6501(a); Reg. § 301.6501(a)-1(a).
187. Reg. § 53.4958-1(e)(3).
188. See § 27.2.
189. IRC § 6501(e)(3); Reg. § 301.6501(e)-1(c)(3)(ii).
189.1. See IRC §§ 6501(b)(4), 6501(l)(1); Reg. § 301.6501(n)-1(a)(1), (c).
189.2. Id.
189.3. Rev. Rul. 69-247, 1969-1 C.B. 303.

§ 21.16 INTERRELATIONSHIP WITH PRIVATE INUREMENT DOCTRINE

p. 633, *third paragraph, first line.* **Delete** *Proposed regulations* **and insert** *Regulations.*

p. 633, *third paragraph, ninth line.* **Delete** *repeated* **and insert** *multiple.*

p. 633, *fourth paragraph, first line.* **Delete** *strongly* **and insert** *heavily.*

p. 633, *fourth paragraph, fourth and fifth lines.* **Delete** *, according to the proposal,.*

p. 633, n. 192, *last line.* **Insert following first closing parenthesis:**

; also Reg. § 1.501(c)(3)-1(f)(2)(i)

p. 633, n. 194. Delete text and substitute:

T.D. 9390. These regulations are applicable with respect to excess benefit transactions occurring after March 28, 2008 (Reg. § 1.501(c)(3)-1(f)(3).

p. 633, n. 195. Delete text and substitute:

Reg. § 1.501(c)(3)-1(f)(2)(ii).

p. 633, n. 196. Delete text and substitute:

Reg. § 1.501(c)(3)-1(f)(2)(iii).

p. 634, *first complete paragraph, third line.* **Insert** *promptly* **following** *museum.*

p. 634, n. 197. Delete text and substitute:

Reg. § 1.501(c)(3)-1(f)(2)(iv), Example 1.

p. 634, *third complete paragraph.* **Delete (including footnote) and substitute:**

In a third example, a public charity uses several buildings in the conduct of its exempt activities. This charitable organization sold one of its buildings for an amount that was substantially below fair market value; the sale was a significant event in relation to the entity's other activities. The building was sold to a company that is wholly owned by the charity's CEO. At the time of the transaction, the governing board of the charity did not undertake due diligence that could have made it aware that the sales price was below fair value. Nonetheless, prior to an IRS examination of the charity, the board determined that the company underpaid for the property. Realizing that an excess benefit transaction (and a private inurement transaction) occurred, the board promptly terminated the employment of the CEO, hired legal counsel to recover the excess benefit, and adopted a conflict-of-interest policy and new contract review procedures. This organization continues to be tax-exempt.[200]

p. 634. Insert as last paragraph:

A public charity, with substantial assets and revenues, furthers its exempt purposes by providing social services in a geographical area. The organization's board of directors adopted written procedures for setting of executive compensation, modeled on the procedures for establishing the rebuttable presumption of reasonableness.[201.1] On the basis of recommendations from its compensation committee, the board approved compensation packages for the organization's top executives and timely documented the basis for its decision in board meeting minutes. The IRS, on examination, determined that the requirements of the presumption were not met and that the executives' compensation packages in a year were excessive. The board thereafter appointed additional members to the compensation committee, amended its procedures, and renegotiated the executives' compensation on a going-forward basis. The compensation payments as to the year involved thus were excess benefit and private inurement transactions. In part because the size and scope of the excess benefit transactions were not significant in relation to the size and scope of the organization's charitable functions, the organization continued to be tax-exempt, even though it engaged in multiple excess benefit transactions, did not void the compensation contracts for the year, and did not seek correction from the top executives for the excessive compensation.[201.2]

p. 635, n. 203, *first line*. Insert following semicolon:

Lowe, "Applying Section 4958 to Qualified Retirement Plans," 53 *Exempt Org. Tax Rev.* (No. 3) 275 (Sep. 2006);

---

200. *Id.*, Example 4.
201.1. See § 21.9.
201.2. Reg. § 1.501(c)(3)-1(f)(2)(iv), Example 6.

Legislative Activities by Tax-Exempt Organizations

*p. 637, n. 1. Insert following existing material:

These rules are principally applicable to public charities (see § 12.3); private foundations are governed by somewhat more restrictive rules (see § 12.4(e)). As to the latter, see *Private Foundations* § 9.1.

§ 22.3 LOBBYING BY CHARITABLE ORGANIZATIONS

(d) Expenditure Test

*p. 650. Insert as second complete paragraph:

(iii-a) Non-Earmarked Grants. The federal tax lobbying rules concerning non-earmarked grants by private foundations[116.1] are applicable to like grants by public charities that have elected the expenditure test.[116.2] Thus, a general support grant by an electing public charity to another public charity may be treated as a non-lobbying expenditure as long as it is not earmarked for lobbying, even if some or all of the funds are expended by the grantee for lobbying. Likewise, an electing public charity's grant restricted for use for a specific project of a grantee public charity will not, solely by reason of the restriction, be considered earmarked for lobbying. Grants to a public charity for a specific purpose will not be considered earmarked for lobbying as long

---

* 116.1. Reg. § 53.4945-2(a)(6)(i). See *Private Foundations* § 9.1(c).
* 116.2. Priv. Ltr. Rul. 200943042.

as all the grants by the grantor during the year involved do not exceed the amounts budgeted for non-lobbying activities. If, however, the public charity's grants exceed the amount budgeted for non-lobbying activities, the amount in excess of the non-lobbying activities amount will be considered a lobbying expenditure.

§ 22.6 LEGISLATIVE ACTIVITIES OF BUSINESS LEAGUES

(a) Business Expense Deduction Disallowance Rules

*p. 658, n. 196, *third sentence.* Delete and substitute:

This $50 amount is indexed for inflation; for tax years beginning in 2010, the amount is $101 (Rev. Proc. 2009-50, 2009-45 I.R.B. 1 § 3.32).

CHAPTER TWENTY-THREE

Political Campaign Activities by Tax-Exempt Organizations

*p. 677, n. 2. Insert following existing material:

These rules are aimed primarily at public charities (see § 12.3); private foundations are also governed by more specific rules (see § 12.4(e)). As to the latter, also see *Private Foundations* § 9.2.

§ 23.2 PROHIBITION ON CHARITABLE ORGANIZATIONS

(b) *Participation* or *Intervention*

*p. 680, *carryover paragraph, last sentence*. Delete (including footnotes) and substitute:

This state of affairs has dramatically changed in recent years, however, with the launch by the IRS of its Political Activities Compliance Initiative (PACI).[20] The PACI was commenced in response to allegations of participation by charitable organizations, including churches, in the 2004 political campaign.[21] This

---

* 20. A memorandum from the Director, Exempt Organizations Division, dated April 17, 2008, referred to the PACI as deployment by the IRS of a "focused approach" as to enforcement of the political campaign intervention rules.

* 21. The IRS issued, in April 2004, a news release summarizing the political campaign intervention rules (IR-2004-59) and sent, in June 2004, a letter explaining these rules to national political parties (IR-2004-79). The PACI, as applied with respect to the 2004 election cycle,

initiative was repeated in connection with the 2006 elections[21.1] and the 2008 elections.[21.2]

*p. 680, n. 22. Delete text and substitute:

The federal election law specifically applicable to tax-exempt organizations is summarized in Appendix H.

(iii) Ascertaining Intervention.

p. 681. Insert as third complete paragraph:

Thereafter, the IRS issued more formal guidance on this subject, indicating whether, in 21 factual situations, a tax-exempt charitable organization violated the federal income tax law proscription on participation or intervention in a political campaign on behalf of or in opposition to a candidate for public office.[27.1] The agency observed that, in each of these situations, "all the facts and circumstances are considered in determining whether an organization's activities result in political campaign intervention." (This guidance addresses voter education and registration, action by organizations' leaders, candidate appearances, issue advocacy, and activity on Web sites.)

---

entailed, according to the IRS, examination of 132 organizations, leading to, for the most part, issuance of advisory letters (IR-2006-36). The Treasury Inspector General for Tax Administration (TIGTA) concluded, in 2009, that the IRS overstated its inventory of these cases (due to coding errors); as of November 2008, the IRS had completed 107 of 110 examinations in this area, with revocation of exemption in six instances (TIGTA report 2009-10-080).

* 21.1. In early 2006, facing the election cycle for that year and armed with what it learned during the 2004 election cycle (see *supra* note 21), the IRS announced that it was distributing and making widely available expanded educational materials, starting monitoring earlier in the election year to ensure consistent and timely case referral selections and examinations, publicizing this project in advance so charitable organizations will not be "surprised," and augmenting the PACI team that had been assembled to assure prompt handling of these case (FS-2006-17).

A TIGTA report, released on June 30, 2008, concluded that the TE/GE Division did not always meet its timeliness standards established for evaluating referrals of cases in the context of the PACI and that not all of the IRS employees involved in this initiative understood the referral process (TIGTA report 2008-10-117).

* 21.2. The memorandum from the Director, Exempt Organizations Division (see *supra* note 20) outlined the goals of the IRS with respect to the PACI for the 2008 election cycle. This memorandum stated that the goals of this program for 2008 were to continue to be to (1) educate the public and the relevant community, and provide guidance, on the political campaign prohibition rules, and (2) maintain a "meaningful enforcement presence" in this area. As of the close of 2009, the IRS had not reported its experiences with respect to the 2008 election cycle.

27.1. Rev. Rul. 2007-41, 2007-2 C.B. 1421.

(d) Requirement of Candidate

*p. 690, n. 83. Insert follow existing material:

The federal election campaign law (see Appendix H) defines the term *candidate* to mean an individual who seeks nomination for election, or election, to federal office; an individual is deemed to seek nomination or election if he or she has received contributions or made expenditures in excess of $5,000 or given his or her consent to another person to receive contributions or make expenditures on behalf of him or her in those amounts. 2 U.S.C. § 431(2). See, however, the admonition in *infra* note 185.

*p. 690, *third complete paragraph, last line*. Insert footnote following line:

[84.1] The federal election law (see Appendix H) defines the term *election* to mean a general, special, primary, or runoff election; a convention or caucus of a political party that has authority to nominate a candidate; a primary election held for the selection of delegates to a national nominating convention of a political party; and a primary election held for the expression of a preference for the nomination of individuals for election to the office of President. 2 U.S.C. § 431(1). See, however, the admonition in *infra* note 185.

(g) Activist Organizations

p. 696, n. 118, *first line*. Insert following second comma:

Owens & Fay, "Penalizing Instigators of Political Campaign Intervention," 54 *Exempt Org. Tax Rev.* (No. 3) 265 (Dec. 2006); Siegel, "The Wild, the Innocent, and the K Street Shuffle: The Tax System's Role in Policing Interactions Between Charities and Politicians," 54 *Exempt Org. Tax Rev.* (No. 2) 117 (Nov. 2006); Hill, "Auditing the NAACP: Misadventures in Tax Administration," 49 *Exempt Org. Tax Rev.* (No. 2) 205 (Aug. 2005);

p. 696, n. 118, *second line*. Insert *Exempt Org. Tax Rev.* following 46.

p. 696, n. 118, *third line*. Insert *Exempt Org. Tax Rev.* following 46.

§ 23.3 POLITICAL CAMPAIGN EXPENDITURES AND TAX SANCTIONS

*p. 699, n. 134. Insert following existing material:

The IRS, in one instance, assessed this tax, then abated and refunded it, yet refused to expressly concede that political campaign activity did not occur; a complaint filed by the organization to force the agency to make that concession was dismissed on the ground that the tax refund mooted the case (Catholic Answers, Inc. v. United States, 104 AFTR 2d 2009-6894 (S.D. Cal. 2009)).

§ 23.5 POLITICAL ACTIVITIES OF SOCIAL WELFARE ORGANIZATIONS

(a) Allowable Campaign Activity

p. 700, *last paragraph, fifth line*. Insert footnote following period:

[150.1] E.g., Priv. Ltr. Rul. 200833021.

(b) Political Campaign Activities

p. 701, *second complete paragraph.* **Insert as last sentence:**

The IRS also denied recognition of exemption as a social welfare organization to an entity the principal functions of which were the recruitment of individuals to become active in politics at the precinct level and the distribution of voter guides that were not nonpartisan educational materials.[155.1]

§ 23.10 INTERNET COMMUNICATIONS

*p. 705. Insert as third and fourth complete paragraphs, before heading:

The IRS concluded that a public charity intervened in political campaigns where its Web site included candidate questionnaires and endorsements. This came about because the material on the site of an affiliated social welfare organization, that permissibly contained these items, was integrated with the public charity's site. It was argued to the IRS that this was a "shared site" with the Web pages containing the political campaign material "separate," by reason of a previous reimbursement arrangement. This assertion was unconvincing to the IRS, which observed that the Web site pages were "virtually indistinguishable."[179]

The Director of Exempt Organizations Examinations, on July 28, 2008, sent a memorandum to exempt organizations revenue agents concerning the examination of public charities in instances of political campaign activities by means of the Internet. The underlying issue prompting this memorandum was whether material on a linked website is to be attributable to a charitable organization for federal tax law purposes. The IRS is focusing on links between charitable organizations and unrelated organizations (whether or not tax-exempt). The IRS will pursue a case where the facts and circumstances indicate that the charitable organization is "promoting, encouraging, recommending or otherwise urging viewers to use the link to get information about specific candidates and their positions on specific issues." Also, where the facts and circumstances suggest that a charitable organization is using a link (other than to a related social welfare organization's site to "indirectly communicate a message that could well be a violation of the law were it done directly, [the Examinations office] will pursue the case."

*p. 705. Convert note 179 in text to note 179.1 and move note to end of last line of newly created fourth complete paragraph.

§ 23.11 FEDERAL ELECTION LAW

*pp. 705–717. Delete § 23.11.

155.1. Priv. Ltr. Rul. 200833021.
* 179. Tech. Adv. Mem. 200908050.

CHAPTER TWENTY-FOUR

Unrelated Business Activities

p. 719, *left column, in reference to § 24.5(e), change "leagues" to "Leagues."*

§ 24.1 INTRODUCTION TO UNRELATED BUSINESS RULES

p. 721, n. 7. Insert following existing material:

In general, Gelblum, "*Hattem v. Schwarzenegger*: Terminating Preemption Challenges to State Taxation of ERISA Plans' Unrelated Business Taxable Income," 60 *Tax Law* (No. 1) 215 (Fall 2006).

§ 24.2   DEFINITION OF *TRADE* OR *BUSINESS*

(b)   Requirement of Profit Motive

p. 726, *second paragraph.* **Insert as last sentence:**

The IRS ruled that a tax-exempt university is not engaged in unrelated business if it enables charitable remainder trusts,[59.1] as to which it is trustee and remainder interest beneficiary, to participate in the investment return generated by the university's endowment fund, because the university is not receiving any economic return by reason of the arrangement.[59.2]

(g)   Nonbusiness Activities

*p. 731, *carryover paragraph.* **Insert as last sentence:**

The IRS ruled that the sale of grantmaking services by a community foundation[93.1] to charitable organizations (principally small private foundations) in its community is a related business, while the sales of administrative and clerical services to them are unrelated businesses.[93.2]

(h)   Real Estate Development Activities

p. 733, *first paragraph, sixth line.* **Insert footnote following investor:**

[108.1] E.g., Farley v. Comm'r, 7 T.C. 198 (1946); Rymer v. Comm'r, 52 T.C.M. 964 (1986).

p. 733, *first paragraph, seventh line.* **Insert footnote following period:**

[108.2] E.g., Brown v. Comm'r, 143 F.2d 468 (5th Cir. 1944); Rev. Rul. 55-449, 1955-2 C.B. 599.

p. 733, *second paragraph, last line.* **Insert footnote at end of line:**

[108.3] E.g., Adam v. Comm'r, 60 T.C. 996 (1973). Also Houston Endowment, Inc. v. United States, 606 F.2d 77 (5th Cir. 1979); Biedenharn Realty Co., Inc. v. United States, 526 F.2d 409 (5th Cir. 1976); Buono v. Comm'r, 74 T.C. 187 (1980).

p. 733, *last paragraph.* **Insert as last sentence:**

The IRS reached the same conclusion in connection with a "liquidity challenged" charitable trust, that wanted to sell leased fee interests in three

---

59.1. See *Charitable Giving*, Chapter 12.
59.2. Priv. Ltr. Rul. 200703037. These arrangements also do not give rise to unrelated business income because they entail transactions between related organizations (see § 25.5(j)).
* 93.1. See § 12.3(b)(iii).
* 93.2. Priv. Ltr. Rul. 200832027.

condominium properties; the underlying land was acquired by gift nearly 100 years ago, and most of it has been maintained to produce rental income in support of its exempt activities.[113.1]

§ 24.4 DEFINITION OF *SUBSTANTIALLY RELATED*

(a) General Principles

*p. 741. Insert as first complete paragraph, before heading:

In a series of technical advice memoranda, the IRS entered the ongoing fray over whether tax-exempt credit unions should retain their exempt status or lose it because of competition with commercial banks,[172.1] by holding that various insurance products and financial services provided by exempt credit unions to their members constituted unrelated businesses (and thus are not exempt functions but rather are businesses directly competing with for-profit banks). These unrelated products and services included the sale of accidental death and dismemberment, dental, cancer, guaranteed automobile protection, and credit disability insurance.[172.2] Thereafter, the agency's lawyers concluded that funds in the form of nonmember automated teller machine fees also are unrelated business income.[172.3]

Nonetheless, thereafter, in a jury trial, a court concluded that the sales, by an exempt credit union, of credit life and credit disability insurance, and guaranteed automobile protection insurance, were related businesses, in that they improved the social and economic life of the credit union's members.[172.4] The IRS's ruling policy is continuing, however, as illustrated by a determination that the sales of financial management services, and credit life and credit disability insurance, were unrelated businesses.[172.5]

(f) Related Business Activities

p. 748, *carryover paragraph, penultimate line.* Delete *and*.

113.1. Priv. Ltr. Rul. 200728044.
172.1. See § 19.7.
172.2. Tech. Adv. Mem. 200709072. The sale of checks to members was held to be a related business.
172.3. Tech. Adv. Mem. 200717031.
* 172.4. Community First Credit Union v. United States, 2009-2 U.S.T.C. ¶ 50,496 (E.D. Wis. 2009).
* 172.5. Tech. Adv. Mem. 200931064.

p. 748, *carryover paragraph, last line.* **Delete period and insert comma; insert following footnote number:**

The conduct of public outreach events by a charitable organization in cooperation with exempt and nonexempt sponsoring organizations.[276.1]

§ 24.5 CONTEMPORARY APPLICATIONS OF UNRELATED BUSINESS RULES

(a) Educational Institutions

p. 752, n. 312. Insert following existing text:

Income derived by an exempt educational institution from rental of living quarters to its faculty, and rental of temporary living quarters to family members of students and faculty, potential students and their family members, and guest speakers, was ruled to be related business income (Priv. Ltr. Rul. 200625035). In the last of these rulings, the IRS ruled that income received by this educational institution from rental of living quarters to its students is not unrelated business income because the income is protected from taxation by the convenience doctrine (see § 24.7(b)); this ruling is incorrect on the point because this type of income is exempt function revenue.

∗p. 754, n. 334. Insert as second paragraph:

Recent years have brought controversy about the relationship between collegiate sports and the federal tax law (in the form of tax exemption, deductible charitable giving, and tax-exempt bond financing). The Congressional Budget Office (CBO), in a report issued in May 2009 (and reproduced in the *Daily Tax Report*, May 20, 2009, TaxCore®), stated that "sports in many universities have become highly commercialized" (see § 4.11) and "[s]uccessful athletic programs are very rewarding financially." This CBO report concluded that the "large sums" colleges and universities derive from their sports programs raise questions, such as whether these programs have become "side businesses for schools" and, if so, whether the "same tax preferences should apply to them as to schools in general." Observing that an option for Congress is to treat collegiate sports revenue as unrelated business income, the CBO report stated that "highly competitive college sports teams with large-capacity stadiums and prime-time television events with advertising are more reasonably considered participants in the market for entertainment" and these teams have professional sports leagues as their "direct competitors."

(b) Health Care Providers

(ii) Sales of Pharmaceuticals.

p. 756. Insert as fourth paragraph:

The IRS ruled that the operation by a public charity of a national Internet-based specialty pharmacy that sells prescription pharmaceuticals, durable medical equipment, and nonprescription vitamins and other supplements, all

---

276.1. Priv. Ltr. Rul. 200733030.

related to a disease, is a substantially related business.[360.1] Commercial pharmacies do not stock these products because they must be refrigerated, delivered in cold packages, and thus are too expensive to purchase and hold in inventory. This organization also provides free medication to certain individuals, offers financial assistance to individuals with this disease, and sponsors an annual conference on ways to treat and cure the disease.

(e) Business Leagues

(ii) Insurance Programs.

p. 766, n. 439, *first line.* **Delete second period.**

(j) Provision of Services

*∗**p. 789,** *first complete paragraph.* **Insert as last sentence:**

Similarly, the IRS ruled that charitable purposes were being served when a community foundation sold grantmaking services to charitable organizations in its community.[621.1]

p. 791. Insert following second complete paragraph, before heading:

(j.1) Sales of Merchandise (New)

Generally, the sale of merchandise to the public is a commercial enterprise and, thus from the standpoint of the law of tax-exempt organizations, usually is an unrelated business.[632.1] On occasion, nonetheless, sales of merchandise can be related activities, such as in the museum and fundraising contexts.[632.2] The facts and circumstances of each case will determine whether merchandise sales is a related or unrelated business.

In one instance, a public charity had as its tax-exempt purpose the eradication of breast cancer by funding research, educating the public, and sponsoring screening and treatment programs. This organization and its affiliates sell merchandise, almost all of which bears a symbol that is universally known as the image for breast cancer awareness, to the public. The charitable organization's toll-free number and Web site address accompany the merchandise, enabling purchasers to obtain information on the need for early detection of breast cancer and the practice of positive breast health. The IRS ruled that the sale of this merchandise "reminds and encourages those who wear, display or

---

360.1. Priv. Ltr. Rul. 200723030.
∗ 621.1. Priv. Ltr. Rul. 200832027.
632.1. See § 4.11.
632.2. See §§ 5.5(c), 5.5(h)(i).

see the images" about breast cancer and encourages the organization's message that early detection of breast cancer and the practice of positive breast health save lives, and thus that this sales activity is substantially related to the organization's exempt purpose.[632.3]

(k) Share-Crop Leasing

p. 791, n. 635, *second line*. Insert closing parenthesis before period.

(o) Other Organizations' Exempt Functions

p. 800, n. 697. Insert, *e.g.*, following *See*.

§ 24.6 MODIFICATIONS

(h) Rent

(iii) Related Rental Activities.

p. 805, *second complete paragraph*. Insert as last sentence:

Also, the leasing of a medical office building by a partnership involving a supporting organization was ruled by the IRS to be related to the organization's exempt purpose.[742.1]

(i) Other Investment Income

p. 806, n. 746. Delete first hyphen.

(o) Brownfield Sites Gain

*p. 809, first line. Delete *a five-year* and insert *the*.

*p. 809, second line. Insert footnote following comma:

[772.1] The Tax Extenders Act of 2009 (H.R. 4213), which passed the House of Representatives on December 9, 2009, would extend this provision through 2010 (Act § 137); this measure is pending in the Senate.

632.3. Priv. Ltr. Rul. 200722028.
742.1. Priv. Ltr. Rul. 200717019.

§ 24.7 EXCEPTIONS

(f) Trade Shows

p. 817. Insert as third paragraph:

A tax-exempt association entered into an agreement with a for-profit company that owned and operated annual trade shows for the industry involved, by which the association was the sponsor of two of the company's trade shows. The association publicized the show, its activities in this regard were directed toward educating its members and the public about the industry, and its activities stimulated an interest in and a demand for products provided by the industry. The support services provided by the association help bring its members together with suppliers and potential customers. The IRS ruled that these convention and trade show activities qualified for this exception, and that the fact that this sponsorship of and participation in "commercial trade shows" with a for-profit entity did not change their nature as qualified activities.[860.1]

(j) Low-Cost Articles

*p. 819, n. 881. Delete sentence and insert:

The IRS calculated that the low-cost article threshold for tax years beginning in 2010 is $9.60 (Rev. Proc. 2009-50, 1 § 3.25(1)).

(l) Associate Member Dues

p. 820, n. 891. Delete sentence and insert:

For tax years beginning in 2009, this threshold is $145 (Rev. Proc. 2008-66, 2008-45 I.R.B. 1 § 3.24).

§ 24.8 CORPORATE SPONSORSHIPS

p. 825, n. 937. Insert following existing material:

In general, Stone, "Halos, Billboards, and the Taxation of Charitable Sponsorships," 82 *Ind. L. J.* (no. 2) 213 (Spring 2007).

§ 24.10 SPECIAL RULES

*p. 828. Insert as first complete paragraph, before heading:

Generally, income received by a tax-exempt parent organization from a controlled subsidiary is regarded as unrelated business income.[966.1] A special

---

860.1. Priv. Ltr. Rul. 200713024.
* 966.1. See § 29.7(b). Also § 28.6.

rule, however, excludes certain forms of this type of income from unrelated business income taxation.[966.2]

§ 24.11 COMMERCIAL-TYPE INSURANCE

*p. 828, *first complete paragraph.* **Insert as last sentence:**

This term does not, however, include conventional charitable gift annuities.[971.1]

§ 24.12 UNRELATED DEBT-FINANCED INCOME

(b) Debt-Financed Property

p. 830. Insert as last sentence of carryover paragraph:

Further, the IRS held that rental income to be derived by a public charity that assists individuals with disabilities from the lease of a portion of a tax-exempt bond financed building to another public charity with similar purposes will not be treated as unrelated debt-financed income in that the rental of the property is in furtherance of the lessor's charitable purposes.[986.1]

*p. 835, n. 1034, *second line.* **Insert before third period:**

, *cert. den.,* 531 U.S. 978 (2000)

*p. 835, n. 1034, *second line.* **Insert following third period:**

Also, Henry E. & Nancy Horton Bartels Trust for the Benefit of Cornell Univ., The v. United States, 2009-2 U.S.T.C. ¶ 50,745 (U.S. Ct. Fed. Cl. 2009).

p. 837. Insert following existing material:

§ 24.15 COLLEGE AND UNIVERSITY COMPLIANCE QUESTIONNAIRE (NEW)

The compliance questionnaire sent by the IRS, in late 2008, to approximately 400 colleges and universities[1054] includes considerable insight as to the agency's contemporary thinking about unrelated business issues.[1055] In this document, the IRS evinces interest in advertising, corporate sponsorships, rental activities, Internet sales, travel tours, broadcasting, affinity card programs, royalty

---

* 966.2. See § 29.7(d).
* 971.1. IRC § 501(m)(3)(E), (5). See § 24.12(c), text accompanied by *infra* note 1002.
986.1. Priv. Ltr. Rul. 200843036.
1054. See § 26.6(ii), text accompanied by note 308.6.
1055. Form 14018, Part II.

arrangements, commercial research, hotel and restaurant operations, conference center operations, parking lot operations, operation of bookstores, and operation of golf courses.

By means of this questionnaire, institutions are asked to identify which activities generate entirely unrelated business income, some unrelated business income, or no unrelated business income; whether there was any debt-financing; whether the activity was managed by another party; whether there were losses from each activity in three out of five years; to identify similar information concerning activities conducted in a partnership, S corporation, or controlled entity in which the institution has an ownership share; to identify the five largest activities, by gross revenue, that were not treated as unrelated businesses (conducted directly and by means of joint ventures); and to identify other activities that generated more than $50,000 in gross revenue.

The organization is asked whether it filed an unrelated business income tax return. It is asked to identify the bases for allocation of expenses in connection with unrelated businesses. For all activities reported on the income tax return, the organization is asked to provide a percentage breakdown of direct and indirect expenses (or do so on the questionnaire). The organization is asked to identify the five unrelated businesses that resulted in the largest losses. For all activities reported on the return, the organization is asked to provide a percentage breakdown of "inter-company" expenses and other expenses (or do so on the questionnaire).

The IRS poses this intriguing question: Did the institution rely on one or more independent accountants or legal counsel for advice as to whether its activities were related or unrelated, allocation of expenses between unrelated and exempt activities, and/or pricing between the institution and its related organizations for expenses incurred in unrelated activities?

PART SIX

Acquisition and Maintenance of Tax Exemption

CHAPTER TWENTY-FIVE

Exemption Recognition and Notice Processes

§ 25.1 RECOGNITION APPLICATION PROCEDURE

p. 842, *second complete paragraph, penultimate line.* **Insert
(EO Determinations) before semicolon.**

p. 842, *second complete paragraph, last line.* **Insert (EO Technical) before
period.**

*p. 842, n. 7, *first line.* **Delete citation and substitute:**

> Rev. Proc. 2009-9, 2009-1 C.B. 256 (updated annually).

p. 842, n. 7, *second sentence.* **Delete on and substitute in.**

*p. 842, n. 7. **Delete last sentence and substitute:**

> Rev. Proc. 80-27, 1980-1 C.B. 677, sets forth procedures under which tax exemption may
be recognized on a group basis (see § 25.6). Rev. Proc. 2009-6, 2009-1 C.B. 189, currently applies in
instances involving the tax exemption of funds underlying pension, profit-sharing, stock bonus,
annuity, and employee stock ownership plans. User fees for requests for a determination letter
(see § 25.1(d)) are currently set forth in Rev. Proc. 2009-8, 2009-1 C.B. 229.

*p. 842, n. 8. Insert following existing material:

More technically, a *determination letter* is a written statement issued by the Exempt Organizations (EO) Determinations office (see § 2.2(b), text accompanied by note 72) or an Appeals Office in response to the filing of such an application (Rev. Proc. 2009-9, 2009-1 C.B. 256 § 1.01(6)).

*p. 842, n. 9. Insert following existing material:

More technically, a *ruling* is a written statement issued by EO Technical (see § 2.2(b), text accompanied by note 72.1) in response to the filing of an application for recognition of exemption (Rev. Proc. 2009-9, 2009-1 C.B. 256 § 1.01(7)).

*p. 842, n. 10. Insert before existing material:

Rev. Proc. 2009-9, 2009-1 C.B. 256 § 3.03.

*p. 842, n. 12. Insert before existing material:

Rev. Proc. 2009-9, 2009-1 C.B. 256 § 3.04.

*p. 842, n. 13. Insert before existing material:

Rev. Proc. 2009-9, 2009-1 C.B. 256 § 3.06.

*p. 842, n. 14. Insert before existing material:

Rev. Proc. 2009-9, 2009-1 C.B. 256 § 3.05.

(a) General Procedures

*p. 843, n. 17. Insert before final period:

; Rev. Proc. 2009-9, 2009-1 C.B. 256 § 4.01

p. 843, *second paragraph*. Insert as second sentence:

A determination letter or ruling as to exempt status is issued solely on the basis of the facts and representations contained in the administrative record; the applicant is responsible for the accuracy of the factual representations contained in the application.[17.1]

*p. 843, n. 18. Delete text and substitute:

Rev. Proc. 2009-9, 2009-1 C.B. 256 § 4.02(2)).

p. 843, *second paragraph*. Insert as last sentence:

The failure to disclose a material fact or misrepresentation of a material fact on the application may adversely affect the reliance that would otherwise be obtained through issuance by the IRS of a favorable determination letter or ruling.[18.1]

---

* 17.1. Rev. Proc. 2009-9, 2009-1 C.B. 256 §§ 4.02, 4.02(1).
* 18.1. Rev. Proc. 2009-9, 2009-1 C.B. 256 § 4.02(3).

(i) Required Information.

p. 843, *fourth paragraph.* **Insert as second sentence:**

The IRS may deny an application for recognition of exemption for failure on the part of the applicant organization to establish compliance with one or more of the statutory requirements for exemption; in the case of an organization seeking qualification as a charitable entity, compliance with the private benefit doctrine[22.1] is also required.[22.2]

*p. 843, n. 19. Delete second citation and substitute:

Rev. Proc. 2009-9, 2009-1 C.B. 256 § 4.03.

p. 843, *last paragraph.* **Insert as second sentence:**

Where an applicant organization cannot demonstrate to the satisfaction of the IRS that it qualifies for exemption pursuant to the exemption category under which exemption is claimed, the agency generally will issue a proposed adverse determination letter or ruling.[22.3]

*p. 844, *second paragraph, first sentence.* **Delete (including footnote) and substitute:**

The IRS refuses to grant recognition of tax exemption when the application, in the agency's view, provides "only general information," lacks "sufficient detail," does not "fully describe" the organization's programs and other activities, and otherwise is "vague."[27] Matters can worsen when the information submitted to the IRS in response to follow-up queries is "contradictory."[27.1]

*p. 844, *second paragraph, fourth line.* **Delete** *another* **and insert** *one.*

*p. 844. Insert as last paragraph:

Irrespective of the content of an application for recognition of exemption, the IRS is likely to visit the applicant's Web site in search of additional (or, worse, inconsistent or contradictory) information.[31.1]

p. 844, n. 28, *last line.* **Delete** *in* **and substitute** *is.*

*p. 844, n. 29. Delete text and substitute:

Rev. Proc. 2009-9, 2009-1 C.B. 256 § 4.03.

22.1. See § 20.11.
22.2. Reg. § 1.501(c)(3)-1(f)(1).
* 22.3. Rev. Proc. 2009-9, 2009-1 C.B. 256 § 4.03(3).
* 27. E.g., Priv. Ltr. Rul. 200536021.
* 27.1. E.g., Priv. Ltr. Rul. 200851033.
* 31.1. E.g., Priv. Ltr. Rul. 200815035.

(ii) Other Procedural Elements.

p. 845, *second paragraph.* **Delete second sentence (and footnote) and combine first sentence with third paragraph.**

p. 845, *third paragraph.* **Delete first sentence (and footnote) and substitute:**

If an application for recognition of tax exemption does not contain the requisite information,[36] the IRS may return the application to the applicant for completion or may retain it and request the necessary additional information.[37]

＊p. 845, n. 38. Insert before third period:

; Rev. Proc. 2009-9, 2009-1 C.B. 256 § 4.05(2).

p. 845, *fourth paragraph, last line.* **Delete** *or* **and insert a comma.**

p. 845, *fourth paragraph, last line.* **Delete period and substitute:**

, or if issuance of a determination letter or ruling is not in the "interest of sound tax administration."

＊p. 845, n. 39. Delete second citation and substitute:

Rev. Proc. 2009-9, 2009-1 C.B. 256 § 4.04.

p. 845, *fifth paragraph, third line.* **Delete** *an initial adverse* **and substitute** *a.*

p. 845, *fifth paragraph.* **Insert as second sentence:**

Therefore, an application may not be withdrawn after the issuance of a proposed adverse determination letter or ruling.[39.1]

＊p. 845, n. 40. Delete text and substitute:

Rev. Proc. 2009-9, 2009-1 C.B. 256 § 6.01(1). The IRS may consider the information submitted in connection with the withdrawn request in a subsequent examination of the organization (*id.*).

p. 846. Insert as third paragraph:

An applicant organization may request expedited handling of an application for recognition of tax exemption; this request may be approved where there is a "compelling reason for processing the application ahead of others," such as (1) a grant to the applicant is pending and the failure to secure the grant (because of absence of recognition of exemption) may have an adverse impact on the organization's ability to continue operations; (2) the purpose of the newly created organization is to provide disaster relief to victims of emergencies, such as flood and hurricane; and (3) undue delays in issuing a determination letter or ruling caused by an IRS error.[45.1]

---

36. See § 25.1(b).
＊ 37. Rev. Proc. 2009-9, 2009-1 C.B. 256 § 4.05.
＊ 39.1. Rev. Proc. 2009-9, 2009-1 C.B. 256 § 6.01.
＊ 45.1. Rev. Proc. 2009-9, 2009-1 C.B. 256 § 4.07.

(b)   *Substantially Completed* Application

*p. 847, n. 47. Delete text and substitute:

> Rev. Proc. 2009-9, 2009-1 C.B. 256 § 3.01.

*p. 847, n. 50. Delete text and substitute:

> Rev. Proc. 2009-9, 2009-1 C.B. 256 § 4.05(2).

p. 847, *second complete paragraph.* Delete third bullet item.

p. 847, *second complete paragraph, fourth bullet item, fifth line.* Delete *full.*

p. 847, *second complete paragraph, fifth bullet item, first line.* Insert *detailed* after first *a* and insert *(including each of the fundraising activities of a charitable organization)* before *and.*

p. 848, *carryover paragraph, second bullet item, second line.* Insert following the comma:

> which need not be signed if submitted as an attachment to the application; otherwise, the bylaws must be

*p. 848, n. 55. Delete citation and substitute:

> Rev. Proc. 2009-9, 2009-1 C.B. 256 § 3.08.

p. 848, *first complete paragraph, second line.* Delete *significant.*

*p. 848, n. 56. Change footnote number from *58* to *56;* delete citation and substitute:

> Rev. Proc. 2009-9, 2009-1 C.B. 256 § 4.06(1).

*p. 848, n. 58. Delete first citation and substitute:

> Rev. Proc. 2009-9, 2009-1 C.B. 256 § 4.06.

*p. 848, n. 59. Delete citation and substitute:

> Rev. Proc. 2009-9, 2009-1 C.B. 256 § 4.05(2).

(c)   Issuance of Determinations and Rulings

p. 848, *fifth complete paragraph, second line.* Insert *(EO Determinations)* before period.

*p. 848, n. 60. Delete second citation and substitute:

> Rev. Proc. 2009-9, 2009-1 C.B. 256 § 5.01.

p. 848, *fifth complete paragraph, third line.* Insert *(EO Technical)* following *IRS.*

p. 848, *last paragraph, first line.* **Delete** *An IRS representative* **and substitute** *EO Determinations;* **delete** *the National Office of the IRS* **and substitute** *EO Technical.*

p. 848, *last paragraph, second line.* **Delete** *questions the answers to* **and substitute** *issues.*

p. 848, *last paragraph, third line.* **Delete** *which* **and insert** *that.*

p. 849, *carryover paragraph, third line.* **Delete** *and/or* **Internal Revenue Manual and substitute** *or by other IRS;* **delete** *the* **and substitute** *EO Technical.*

p. 849, *carryover paragraph, fourth line.* **Delete** *National Office.*

p. 849, *carryover paragraph, last sentence.* **Delete and substitute:**

In this instance, EO Technical will notify the applicant organization on receipt of a referred application, consider the application, and issue a ruling to the organization.

∗p. 849, n. 62. Delete second citation and substitute:

Rev. Proc. 2009-9, 2009-1 C.B. 256 § 5.02.

p. 849, *first complete paragraph, second line.* **Insert** *EO Determinations* **before the comma.**

p. 849, *first complete paragraph, third line.* **Insert** *or there has been non-uniformity in the IRS's handling of similar cases* **before the comma; delete** *the IRS to* **and substitute** *that EO Determinations refer the application to EO Technical or.*

p. 849, *first complete paragraph, fourth line.* **Delete** *the IRS National Office* **and substitute** *EO Technical;* **delete** *the IRS* **and substitute** *EO Determinations.*

∗p. 849, n. 64. Delete second citation and substitute:

Rev. Proc. 2009-9, 2009-1 C.B. 256 § 5.03.

p. 849, *first complete paragraph, fifth line.* **Delete** *the National Office* **and substitute** *EO Technical.*

p. 849, *first complete paragraph, seventh line.* **Delete** *the IRS representative* **and substitute** *EO Determinations;* **delete** *the Na-* **and substitute** *EO Technical.*

p. 849, *first complete paragraph, last line.* **Delete** *tional Office.*

p. 849, n. 65. Delete *6.04* **and insert** *5.04.*

p. 849, n. 65. Insert following existing material:

This rule does not apply, however, where EO Technical issued an adverse ruling and the organization subsequently made changes to its purposes, activities, or operations to remove the basis for which recognition of exempt status was denied (*id.*).

p. 849, *second complete paragraph, first line.* **Delete** *Some determination* **and substitute** *Determination;* **delete** *the IRS are* **and substitute** *EO Determinations may be;* **delete** *in the IRS Na-.*

p. 849, *second complete paragraph, second line.* **Delete** *tional Office* **and substitute** *by EO Technical.*

p. 849, *second complete paragraph, fourth line.* **Delete** *the IRS National Office* **and substitute** *EO Technical;* **insert** *issued by EO Determinations* **before the comma; delete** *IRS.*

p. 849, *fifth line.* **Delete** *representative* **and insert** *manager of EO Determinations.*

p. 849, *sixth line.* **Delete** *the National Office* **and substitute** *EO Technical.*

p. 849, n. 66. Delete *8.01* **and insert** *9.01.*

p. 849, n. 67. Delete *8.02* **and insert** *9.02.*

p. 849, *last complete paragraph, fifth line.* **Insert** *by the IRS* **prior to first** *to.*

*∗**p. 849, n. 69,** *first line.* **Delete second citation and insert:**

Rev. Proc. 2009-9, 2009-1 C.B. 256 § 11.01.

p. 849, n. 69, *second line.* **Insert before period:**

and for certain types of employee benefit plans (see § 25.5).

*∗**p. 849, n. 70. Delete citation and insert:**

Rev. Proc. 2009-9, 2009-1 C.B. 256 § 11.01(1), (2).

p. 849, n. 70, *last line.* **Insert** *§ 11.01(2)* **following first period.**

*∗**p. 850, n. 71. Delete second citation and insert:**

Rev. Proc. 2009-9, 2009-1 C.B. 256 § 11.02.

p. 850, *first paragraph.* **Insert as last sentence:**

Also, a determination letter or ruling may not be relied on if it was based on any inaccurate material factual misrepresentations.[71.1]

∗ 71.1. Rev. Proc. 2009-9, 2009-1 C.B. 256 § 11.02.

(d) User Fees

p. 850, *second paragraph*. Insert as second sentence:

Submission of an application for recognition of exemption must be accompanied by the correct user fee.[72.1]

§ 25.2 REQUIREMENTS FOR CHARITABLE ORGANIZATIONS

(a) General Rules

*p. 856, n. 110. Delete citation and substitute:

> Rev. Proc. 2009-9, 2009-1 C.B. 256 § 11.01(2). See *supra* note 70.

p. 857, n. 118. Convert existing material to second paragraph of note and insert the following as the first paragraph of note:

> The Director of Exempt Organizations Rulings and Agreements, by memorandum dated March 13, 2008, to the Determinations office, transmitted guidelines IRS personnel are to use in processing applications for recognition of exemption filed by entities seeking qualification as supporting organizations (see § 12.3(c)); the Director, by memorandum dated July 31, 2008, transmitted guidance to the Determinations office for processing applications for recognition of exemption submitted by supporting organizations that maintain donor-advised funds (see § 11.8).

p. 859. Insert as second paragraph, before heading:

(d) Application Processing Backlog (New)

With annual receipt of over 90,000 applications for recognition of exemption (most of them Form 1023), the IRS, unable to timely process them, is strenuously endeavoring to reduce this backlog of applications (what the agency terms its inventory) and decrease the applications' processing time. The IRS separates these applications into three groups. The first group consists of applications that, based on their completeness, can be processed immediately. The second group is the batch of applications that need a minor amount of additional information to be resolved. The third group of applications is those that require additional substantive development.

According to the IRS, this triage approach is working. During fiscal year 2007, the agency was able to reduce the unassigned inventory of applications for recognition of exemption from 8,693 to 5,625. The assigned inventory was reduced by 27 percent (6,544). The average time to assign an application case

---

* 72.1. Rev. Proc. 2009-9, 2009-1 C.B. 256 § 3.02. Generally, the user fee will not be refunded if an application is withdrawn (*id*. § 6.01(2)).

has been reduced from 7 to 3 months. The average application processing time has been reduced by 12 days.[132.1]

The IRS is in the process of developing an electronic determinations case processing and tracking system that is intended to shorten the time it takes the agency to process applications for recognition of exemption (the TE/GE Determination System (TEDS)). The agency stated that TEDS will give the agency the "ability to store, assign, and eventually process application files in a totally online environment, making paper files a thing of the past." In fiscal year 2008, TEDS will "pilot the scanning of incoming applications and paper case files to create electronic case files that are processed by technical screeners." The TEDS process is intended to "simplify the generation of determination letters and expedite the closing of [application] cases."[132.2]

The IRS is also developing a computer program that will guide users through the application process and generate a completed application (the Cyber Assistant). This program is a "web-based tool that will guide an applicant through the application [for recognition of exemption] process while educating the applicant about the duties and responsibilities that go along with tax-exempt status." This program "solicits information about the applicant and builds an exemption [recognition] application based on the user's responses," and it "alerts the user to errors in the application and prompts the user to supply missing information." The final product will be a completed application that can be printed and mailed to the IRS, along with printed barcodes that will help in processing the application in TEDS. The Cyber Assistant is expected to be introduced in 2010.[132.3]

§ 25.3 NONPRIVATE FOUNDATION STATUS

(a) Notice Requirement

p. 859, *second paragraph, first line*. **Insert semicolon following** *foundation.*

*p. 860, n. 142. **Delete citation and substitute:**

> Rev. Proc. 2009-9, 2009-1 C.B. 256.

132.1. These data are from the IRS' Exempt Organizations Fiscal Year 2008 Implementing Guidelines.

132.2. *Id.* The IRS is struggling with the TEDS. In a report issued on December. 11, 2007, the Treasury Inspector General for Tax Administration (TIGTA) presented the results of its review of the system, observing that by the time the system is completed "its cost may far outweigh its benefits" (Report No. 2008-10-025). Delicately referencing $17 million in "inefficient use of resources," the TIGTA report stated: "The high cost of the TEDS compared to the benefits it will deliver brings into question whether sound investment decisions were made during development of the System and whether this was the best use of Federal Government funds."

132.3. These quotes are from the IRS' Exempt Organizations Fiscal Year 2008 Implementing Guidelines.

p. 862. Insert following first paragraph, before heading:

(c) New Rules for Publicly Supported Charities (New)

For tax years beginning on or after January 1, 2008, new rules applicable to charitable organizations that seek classification as publicly supported entities went into effect.[152.1] These rules eliminated the advance ruling process (including the Form 8734 filing requirement). Pursuant to this new approach, an organization will be classified as a publicly supported charity if, as part of the process for seeking recognition of tax exemption, it can show that (in addition to qualification for tax exemption) it can reasonably be expected to be publicly supported during its first five years.[152.2] The organization has public charity status for this five-year period irrespective of the amount of public support it received.

Beginning with the organization's sixth year, it must establish (if it can) that it meets the applicable public support test by showing that it is publicly supported; this is evidenced on Form 990, Schedule A.[152.3] The organization will not owe a private foundation investment income tax[152.4] or private foundation termination tax[152.5] with respect to its first five years. Beginning with the organization's sixth year, for every year where it cannot establish that it is a public charity, it will be liable for the private foundation taxes.

§ 25.6 GROUP EXEMPTION RULES

*p. 863, *last paragraph, eighth line*. Delete *not*.

*p. 863, n. 168. Delete citation and substitute:

Rev. Proc. 2009-9, 2009-1 C.B. 256.

*p. 866, *carryover paragraph*. Delete last sentence, including footnote.

*p. 866. Insert as second complete paragraph:

The IRS is subtly attempting to narrow utilization of the group exemption procedure. The Internal Revenue Manual states that group exemption letters are "typically limited to organizations that are basically identical in form and function" to the central organization.[178.1] The IRS observes, in a form letter, that the group exemption "is not appropriate when the activities of the subordinate

---

152.1. Reg. §§ 1.170A-9T(k), 1.509(a)-3T(o).
152.2. Reg. §§ 1.170A-9T(f)(4)(v), 1.509(a)-3T(d)(1).
152.3. Reg. §§ 1.170A-9T(f)(4)(i)-(iii), 1.509(a)-3T(c)(1). See §§ 12.3(b)(i), 12.3(b)(iv).
152.4. See § 12.4(f).
152.5. See IRC § 507. See *Private Foundations*, Chapter 13.
* 178.1. IRM Exhibit 7.20.4-4. This statement is not entirely accurate, in that the tax-exempt status of the central organization can be different from the exempt status of the subordinates, so there can be differing functions.

organizations present special issues for consideration," that is, where the tax exemptions of the ostensible subordinates are based on differing rationales (even though these exemptions are based on the same paragraph of the general exemption rules). Examples provided of qualifying subordinates are fraternal organizations, labor unions, and churches. The IRM adds that "[a]ctivities may be too broad to make a determination as to whether every subordinate will meet the requirements."[178.2] There is, however, nothing in the IRS's procedures that requires this identity of form and function (although often that is the case, as with, for example, chapters and lodges); all that is basically required is the requisite affiliation and supervision or control, and same category of exemption as among the subordinates.[178.3]

§ 25.7 SUSPENSION OF TAX EXEMPTION

*p. 866, n. 181. Insert following existing material:

Rev. Proc. 2009-9, 2009-1 C.B. 256 § 3.09.

§ 25.8 NOTICE REQUIREMENTS FOR POLITICAL ORGANIZATIONS

*p. 867, n. 193. Insert following existing material:

Rev. Proc. 2009-9, 2009-1 C.B. 256 § 3.07.

---

* 178.2. *Id.*
* 178.3. Thus, pursuant to this position, a group exemption is available to, e.g., a cluster of churches, but not to, e.g., a group of charitable organizations where the exemption of one of them is based on relief of the poor (see § 7.1), the exemption of another is based on promotion of health (see § 7.6), the exemption of another is based on lessening the burdens of government (see § 7.7), the exemption of another is based on advancement of education (see § 7.8), and the like.

CHAPTER TWENTY-SIX

Administrative and Litigation Procedures

§ 26.1 ADMINISTRATIVE PROCEDURES WHERE RECOGNITION DENIED

p. 875, *sixth line.* **Insert** *adverse determination* **following fourth** *the.*

p. 875, *eighth line.* **Insert** *an* **appeal** *or* **following opening parenthesis.**

***p. 875, n. 3. Delete citation and substitute:**

> Rev. Proc. 2009-9, 2009-1 C.B. 256 § 7.01.

***p. 875, n. 4. Delete citation and substitute:**

> Rev. Proc. 2009-9, 2009-1 C.B. 256 § 7.01(2).

p. 876, *second line.* **Delete** *a hearing* **and substitute** *an appeals office conference.*

∗p. 876, *carryover paragraph.* Insert as last sentences:

A determination letter issued on the basis of technical advice from EO Technical may not be appealed to the appeals office on issues that were the subject of the technical advice.[5] A proposed adverse ruling issued by EO Technical will advise the organization of its opportunity to file a protest within 30 days and request a conference.[6]

p. 876, *first–sixth complete paragraphs.* Delete (including footnotes) and substitute:

If an organization does not timely appeal a proposed adverse determination letter issued by EO Determinations, or timely file a protest of a proposed adverse ruling issued by EO Technical, a final adverse determination letter or ruling will be issued to the organization. This final adverse letter or ruling will provide information about the filing of tax returns and the disclosure of the proposed and final adverse letters or rulings.[7] If an organization submits an appeal of a proposed adverse determination letter, EO Determinations will review the appeal; if it determines that the organization qualifies for tax-exempt status, it will issue a favorable determination letter. If EO Determinations maintains its adverse position after reviewing the appeal, it will forward the appeal and the application case file to the appeals office.[8]

If the appeals office, having considered the organization's appeal, agrees with the proposed adverse determination, it will issue a final adverse determination or, if a conference was requested, contact the organization to schedule a conference. At the end of the conference process, which may entail the submission of additional information, the appeals office will issue a final adverse determination letter or a favorable determination letter. If the appeals office believes that an exemption or public charity/private foundation status issue is not covered by published precedent or that nonuniformity exists, the appeals office must request technical advice from EO Technical.[9]

If an organization submits a protest of a proposed adverse tax-exempt status ruling, EO Technical will review the protest. If the protest convinces EO Technical that the organization qualifies for exempt status, a favorable ruling will be issued. If EO Technical maintains its adverse position, it will issue a final adverse ruling or, if a conference was requested, contact the organization to schedule a conference. At the end of the conference process, which may

---

∗ 5. Rev. Proc. 2009-9, 2009-1 C.B. 256 § 7.02. Technically, an *appeal* is what is taken of a proposed adverse determination letter and a *protest* is what is made of a proposed adverse letter; in practice, the term *protest* is often used in either instance.
6. *Id.* § 7.03.
7. *Id.* § 7.04.
8. *Id.* § 7.05.
9. *Id.* § 7.06.

entail the submission of additional information, EO Technical will issue a final adverse or favorable ruling.[10]

An organization may withdraw its appeal or protest before the IRS issues a final adverse determination letter or ruling. On receipt of the withdrawal request, the agency will complete the processing of the case in the same manner as if an appeal or protest was not received.[11] The opportunity to appeal or protest a proposed adverse determination letter or ruling, and the conference rights, are not available in instances of matters where delay would be prejudicial to the interests of the IRS (such as in cases involving fraud, jeopardy, the imminence of expiration of a statute of limitations, or where immediate action is necessary to protect the interests of the federal government).[12]

p. 877, n. 13. Delete *14.01* and insert *12*.

*****p. 877, n. 16. Delete citation and substitute:**

> Rev. Proc. 2009-9, 2009-1 C.B. 256 § 12.01.

§ 26.2   REVOCATION OF TAX-EXEMPT STATUS: LITIGATION PROCEDURES

*****p. 878, n. 30, *first line*. Delete citation and substitute:**

> Rev. Proc. 2009-9, 2009-1 C.B. 256 § 12.02.

p. 878, n. 30, *last line*. Delete citation and insert *id*.

(b)   Declaratory Judgment Rules

*****p. 880, *second complete paragraph, fourth and fifth lines*. Delete *tax status of charitable organizations* and substitute:**

initial or continuing qualification or classification of an organization as a charitable entity,[43.1] a public charity,[43.2] a private operating foundation,[43.3] or an organization eligible to receive deductible charitable contributions.[43.4]

*****p. 880, n. 44, *first line*. Insert before existing material:**

> Rev. Proc. 2009-9, 2009-1 C.B. 256 § 10.01.

(i) General Requirements.

p. 881, *first complete paragraph, second line*. Insert *, as noted*, following *to*.

---

10. *Id*. § 7.07.
11. *Id*. § 7.08.
12. *Id*. § 7.09.
43.1. See Part Three.
43.2. See § 12.3.
43.3. See § 12.1(b).
* 43.4. See § 2.3. Rev. Proc. 2009-9, 2009-1 C.B. 256 § 10.01.

*p. 881, n. 53. Delete citation and substitute:

Rev. Proc. 2009-9, 2009-1 C.B. 256 § 10.05.

*p. 883, n. 68, *first line*. Insert before existing material:

Exhaustion of remedies includes (1) filing of a substantially completed application for recognition of exemption (see § 25.1(b)), a group exemption request (see § 25.6), or a request for a determination of public charity/private foundation status (see § 25.2); (2) in appropriate circumstances, requesting relief with respect to an extension of time for making an election or application for relief from tax; (3) the timely submission of all additional information requested by the IRS necessary to perfect an application for recognition of exemption or request for determination of public charity or private foundation status; and (4) exhaustion of all appeals within the IRS (Rev. Proc. 2009-9, 2009-1 C.B. 256 § 10.02).

*p. 883, n. 70, *second line*. Delete citation and substitute:

Rev. Proc. 2009-9, 2009-1 C.B. 256 § 6.02.

*p. 885, n. 84. Delete citation and substitute:

Rev. Proc. 2009-9, 2009-1 C.B. 256 § 10.03.

(ii) Exhaustion of Administrative Remedies.

p. 886, *first three lines*. Insert period following *IRS* and delete text (including footnote) beginning with *as*.

p. 886, *first complete paragraph, fifth line*. Delete *notice of*.

p. 886, *second complete paragraph, second line*. Delete second *the* and substitute *an*.

p. 886, *second complete paragraph, third line*. Delete first comma.

*p. 886, n. 89, *first line*. Delete citation and substitute:

Rev. Proc. 2009-9, 2009-1 C.B. 256 §§ 7, 10.02(4).

*p. 886, n. 91. Delete text and substitute:

Rev. Proc. 2009-9, 2009-1 C.B. 256 § 10.03.

p. 886, n. 92, *first line*. Delete *12.03* and insert *10.04*.

(iii) Deductibility of Contributions.

*p. 887, *first complete paragraph, third sentence.* Delete *inevitably.*

*p. 887, *first complete paragraph, fifth line.* Insert footnote following period:

> [97.1]Traditionally, this publication has been in the Internal Revenue Bulletin (IRB); it will instead be on the IRS Web site, although there will be initial notices of this changeover in practice in the IRB, along with advisories as to when this electronic list of revoked organizations is updated (Program Manager Tech. Adv. (PMTA) 2009-156).

§ 26.3 RETROACTIVE REVOCATION OF TAX-EXEMPT STATUS

*p. 893, n. 140. Insert before last period:

> ; Rev. Proc. 2009-9, 2009-1 C.B. 256 § 12.01.

p. 893. Insert as second complete paragraph:

The IRS revoked the tax-exempt status of a supporting organization, retroactive to the date of its inception, on the grounds of material misstatements in the application for recognition of exemption, and tax avoidance and prohibited transactions, such as noncollateralized, interest-only loans to donors, and use of grant funds to pay the tuition of the donors' children and to satisfy their tithing obligations.[143.1] A similar retroactive revocation occurred, with the individuals who formed the organization agreeing with the IRS that the arrangement constituted an "abusive trust" and a "sham."[143.2] Likewise, the exempt status of a supporting organization was retroactively revoked where several loans, made on terms that an independent lender would not agree to, were made to the donor and grants to the public charity involved were made, accompanied by her "wish," which was to use funds for her private purposes and to which the charity always acceded.[143.3]

p. 894, *third complete paragraph, first line.* Delete *In the principal case* and insert *In one of two principal cases.*

p. 895. Insert as first complete paragraph, before heading:

In the second case, a court ruled that the IRS abused its discretion in retroactively revoking the tax-exempt status of an organization that, over the years, engaged in activities and policies that were materially similar to those stated in its application for recognition of exemption.[162.1] The IRS, in 2002, attempted to revoke the exempt status of the organization, formed in 1985, for its years

---

143.1. Priv. Ltr. Rul. 200844022.
143.2. Priv. Ltr. Rul. 200810025.
143.3. Priv. Ltr. Rul. 200752043.
162.1. Democratic Leadership Council, Inc. v. United States, 542 F. Supp. 2d 63 (D.D.C. 2008).

1997–1999. The court found that this organization did not omit or misstate a material fact or operate in a manner materially different in the three years at issue from that originally represented. Thus, the court concluded that, once the IRS made its determination as to this entity's exemption, the IRS was bound to follow it (without retroactivity) as long as the organization continued to operate in the manner originally described to the IRS.[162.2]

§ 26.6   IRS EXAMINATION PROCEDURES AND PRACTICES

(a)   General IRS Exempt Organizations Audit Procedures and Practices

(i) General Procedures.

p. 911, *second complete paragraph.* **Insert as last sentence:**

The IRS has become quite aggressive in revoking the exempt status of organizations that fail to respond to its requests for information.[296.1]

p. 911, n. 298. **Insert following existing material:**

> The IRS subsequently described the audit process in the tax-exempt organizations context (FS-2008-14), including guidance on the process to be followed in filing a complaint involving an exempt organization (FS-2008-13).

(ii) Types of Examinations.

*p. 913, *third complete paragraph, second sentence.* **Delete and insert:**

Examples of these projects are the agency's inquiries into (1) the levels and types of compensation provided by tax-exempt organizations, particularly public charities;[308.1] (2) involvement by public charities in political campaign activities;[308.2] (3) the provision of community benefits by tax-exempt hospitals;[308.3] (4) the extent to which exempt organizations engaged in tax-exempt bond financing are complying with certain recordkeeping requirements;[308.4] (5) successor member interest contributions;[308.5] (6) capital gain avoidance using charitable remainder trusts;[308.6] (7) unrelated business activities, use of endowment funds, and executive compensation practices of exempt

---

* 162.2. The government appealed this decision to the U.S. Court of Appeals for the District of Columbia Circuit, then, in early 2009, dropped the appeal.
  296.1. E.g., Priv. Ltr. Rul. 200634040.
  308.1. See § 20.4(b); *IRS Audits* § 4.3.
  308.2. See Chapter 23; *IRS Audits* § 4.4. Also IRS Exempt Organizations 2008 Annual Report, at 22.
  308.3. See § 7.6(a); *Healthcare Organizations*, Chapter 6; *IRS Audits* § 4.5. Also IRS Exempt Organizations 2008 Annual Report, at 22.
  308.4. See *IRS Audits* § 4.8.
  308.5. See *Charitable Giving* § 10.15; *IRS Audits* § 4.9.
* 308.6. Notice 2008-99, 2008-2 C.B. 1194.

colleges and universities;[308.7] (8) the operations of community foundations;[308.8] (9) gaming;[308.9] (10) employment tax payment and reporting;[308.10] (11) Form 990 non-filers;[308.11] (12) compliance with the commensurate test;[308.12] (13) various noncash gifts issues;[308.13] (14) governance;[308.14] (15) compliance with the 85-percent member-income test by mutual organizations;[308.15] and (16) the executive compensation and for-profit subsidiary practices of exempt student loan organizations.[308.16]

p. 913, n. 309. Insert following existing material:

The IRS subsequently described the compliance-check process in the tax-exempt organizations context (FS-2008-14).

(iv) Coping with Examination.

p. 914, n. 314, *first line*. Insert *IRS Audits;* following first comma.

(b)   IRS Exempt Organizations Examination Guidelines

p. 915, n. 347. Insert following existing material:

In general, *IRS Audits*, Chapter 7.

(c)   Church Audits

p. 916, second paragraph, lines 2–3. Delete *the appropriate IRS regional commissioner (or higher official)* and insert the following:

an appropriate high-level Treasury official[350.1]

---

* 308.7. See §§ 24.15, 11.9(e), 20.4(i). This compliance check project, which elevated the questionnaire involved into a formal IRS form (Form 14018), involved the sending by the IRS of a 33-page compliance questionnaire, containing 94 questions (many with sub-questions), to about 400 exempt four-year colleges and universities (IR-2008-112). Also IRS Exempt Organizations 2009 Annual Report, at 21.
* 308.8. See § 12.3(b)(iii). Also IRS Exempt Organizations 2009 Annual Report, at 22-23.
* 308.9. IRS Exempt Organizations 2009 Annual Report, at 23.
  308.10. *Id.*
  308.11. *Id.*
* 308.12. See § 4.7. Also IRS Exempt Organizations 2009 Annual Report, at 20.
* 308.13. IRS Exempt Organizations 2009 Annual Report, at 20.
* 308.14. See § 5.6(p). Also IRS Exempt Organizations 2009 Annual Report, at 20.
* 308.15. See § 19.5(b). Also IRS Exempt Organizations 2009 Annual Report, at 20-21.
* 308.16. IRS Exempt Organizations 2009 Annual Report, at 21.
* 350.1. That phrase is defined to mean the Secretary of the Treasury "or any delegate of the Secretary whose rank is no lower than that of a principal Internal Revenue officer for an internal revenue region" (IRC § 7611(h)(7)). Prior to its reorganization (see § 2.2(a)), the IRS identified the appropriate Regional Commissioner (or higher Treasury official) as this appropriate high-level official (Reg. § 301.7611-1T, Q & A (1)). The

p. 917, fourth paragraph, first line. Delete *IRS regional commissioner* **and insert** *high-level Treasury official.*

p. 920, n. 390, *second paragraph, first line.* **Insert following first comma:**

> *IRS Audits*, Chapter 6; Garthwaite, "An End to Politically Motivated Audits of Churches? How Amendment to Section 7217 Can Preserve Integrity of the Tax Investigation of Churches Under Section 7611," 60 *Tax Law.* (No. 2) 503 (Winter 2007);.

*p. 920. Insert following existing material:

§ 26.6A FAST-TRACK CASE SETTLEMENT PROGRAM (NEW)

The IRS, on December 1, 2008, announced a program enabling tax-exempt organizations with issues under examination by the TE/GE Division to use a fast-track settlement (FTS) process to expedite resolution of their cases.[390.1] This program is intended to allow exempt organizations that have unagreed issues in at least one open period under examination to work with the Division and the Office of Appeals to resolve outstanding disputed issues while the case is still in the jurisdiction of the TE/GE Division. The Division and Appeals jointly administer this FTS process.

The procedures for using this FTS program are based on those the IRS developed to implement the Large and Mid-Size Business Division FTS dispute resolution program[390.2] and the Small Business/Self-Employed Taxpayer Division FTS dispute resolution program.[390.3] FTS is available for exemption, public charity/private foundation status, and certain other issues where the exempt organization has a written statement of its position and there is a "limited

---

Regional Commissioner positions were abolished as part of the reorganization. The IRS thereafter designated the Director, Examinations as that official (Delegation Order 193 (rev. 6); Internal Revenue Manual § 4.76.7.4). A federal district court magistrate judge ruled, on November 18, 2008, in a summons enforcement proceeding that, based on the constitutional law reasons for the church audit rules, the Director, Examinations is too low in rank to qualify and thus that a church tax inquiry and examination were improperly commenced (United States v. Living Word Christian Center, 102 A.F.T.R. 2d 2008-7220 (D. Minn. 2008)). The IRS filed its objections to this finding on December 3, 2008; the church filed its response on December 15, 2008.

The district court, on January 30, 2009, issued its opinion, which essentially adhered to the magistrate's opinion (2009-1 U.S.T.C. ¶ 50,199). The IRS, on July 31, 2009, proposed regulations that would denominate the Director, Exempt Organizations, as the appropriate Treasury official (REG-112756-09). A church sought a writ of mandamus that a church tax inquiry may not continue, for the reason articulated in the Living Word Christian Center opinion, but the complaint was dismissed on the ground that the remedy sought is available only in the context of a summons enforcement proceeding (Southern Faith Ministries, Inc. v. Geithner, WL 5125371 (D.D.C. 2009)).

* 390.1. Ann. 2008-105, 2008-48 I.R.B. 1219.
* 390.2. Rev. Proc. 2003-40, 2003-1 C.B. 1044.
* 390.3. Ann. 2006-61, 2006-2 C.B. 390.

number" of factual and/or law issues. FTS is not available for a list of matters, including issues designated for litigation, correspondence examination cases, frivolous issues, and cases involving civil or criminal fraud.

An organization that is interested in participating in this FTS process, or that has questions about the program and its suitability for a particular case, may contact the TE/GE group manager of the agent conducting the audit for the period(s) under examination. The organization, examining agent, or group manager may initiate an application[390.4] to the FTS process. A notice of proposed adjustment[390.5] or a revenue agent report will be prepared by the examining agent. If a case is not accepted for inclusion in the program, the IRS will discuss other dispute resolution opportunities with the organization.

FTS employs various alternative dispute resolution techniques to promote agreement. An FTS Appeals official will serve as a neutral party. This official thus will not perform in a traditional Appeals role but rather will use dispute resolution techniques to facilitate settlement. An FTS session report will be developed to assist in planning, and reporting on developments during, the FTS session. This report will include a description of the issues, the amounts in dispute, conference dates, and a plan of action for the session. If the parties resolve any of the issues at the session, the parties and the Appeals official will sign the session report acknowledging acceptance of the terms of settlement for purposes of preparing computations. The TE/GE FTS process is confidential.

FTS may be initiated at any time after an issue has been fully developed but before issuance of a 30-day letter (or its equivalent). This is a pilot program, available for two years. Thereafter, the Division and Appeals will evaluate the program, consider making adjustments, and decide whether to make it permanent.

§ 26.7 IRS DISCLOSURE TO STATE OFFICIALS

*p. 921, n. 393. Insert before period:

; Rev. Proc. 2009-9, 2009-1 C.B. 256 §§ 8.03, 8.04.

---

* 390.4. Form 14017.
* 390.5. Form 5701.

CHAPTER TWENTY-SEVEN

Operational Requirements

p. 924, n. 1, *first line*. Delete second citation.

§ 27.1 CHANGES IN OPERATIONS OR FORM

(a) Changes in Operations

*p. 924, n. 4. Delete text and substitute:

Rev. Proc. 2009-9, 2009-1 C.B. 256 § 12.

§ 27.2 ANNUAL REPORTING RULES

(a) Contents of Annual Information Return

(i) Form 990.

p. 927, n. 32. Delete *2005* and insert *2008*.

p. 927, *last paragraph*. Delete text (and footnotes) following first period and footnote 32 and substitute:

The annual information return filed by most tax-exempt organizations has been redesigned and is summarized below.[33]

pp. 928, 929, *and first four paragraphs on p. 930*. Delete (including footnotes).

p. 930, *fifth paragraph, first line*. Delete *(iv)* and insert *(ii)*.

p. 931, *first line*. Delete *(v)* and insert *(iii)*.

p. 932, *second paragraph, first line*. Delete *(vi)* and insert *(iv)*.

---

33. See § 27.2A.

p. 932, *fifth paragraph, first line.* **Delete** *(vii)* **and insert** *(v).*

p. 934, *second complete paragraph, first line.* **Delete** *(viii)* **and insert** *(vi).*

p. 934, *last paragraph, first line.* **Delete** *(ix)* **and insert** *(vii).*

(vii) Penalties.

p. 934, *first paragraph.* **Delete text (but not footnote) and insert:**

The IRS frequently denies recognition of tax-exempt status to or revokes the exempt status of an organization for failure to file annual information returns.

(ix) Miscellaneous.

∗p. 935, n. 129. Insert as third paragraph:

The Treasury Inspector General for Tax Administration (TIGTA) reviewed the efforts of the TE/GE Division to grapple with the problem of noncompliance by tax-exempt organizations with the annual information return filing requirements. The essence of the TIGTA's conclusions, embodied in a report that became public on April 14, 2009 (2009-10-056), is that the Exempt Organizations function, while engaged in "activities to secure delinquent returns," needs to do more to "fully identify and address non-filers." The term *non-filer* refers to tax-exempt organizations that are not required to file annual information returns (see § 27.2(b)) and those that are required to file but do not, plus exempt organizations that no longer exist.

(b) Exceptions to Reporting Requirements

(ii) Small Organizations.

p. 936, *last paragraph.* **Insert as last sentence:**

The IRS announced that, as of the 2010 tax year, this small organizations filing threshold will be increased to $50,000.[144.1]

p. 939. Insert following first complete paragraph, before heading:

§ 27.2A REDESIGNED ANNUAL INFORMATION RETURN (NEW)

The IRS, on June 14, 2007, released for public comment a discussion draft of a substantially revamped Form 990 (the annual information return filed with the IRS by most tax-exempt organizations).[172.1] The agency characterized this as a "significant redesign" of the annual return, which has not been substantially

---

144.1. See § 27.2A(b)(xxiv).
172.1. IR-2007-117.

revised since 1979.[172.2] The IRS, on December 20, 2007, released the final version of the annual information return for the 2008 tax year (returns to be filed in 2009).[172.3]

(a) IRS Guiding Principles

The IRS said that its retooling of this annual information return was based on these guiding principles:

- Enhancing transparency by providing the IRS and the public with a realistic picture of the filing organization and its operations, along with the basis for comparing the organization to similar organizations.

- Promoting compliance, by designing a return that accurately reflects the organization's operations and use of assets, so the IRS may efficiently assess the risk of its noncompliance.

- Minimizing the burden on filing organizations, by asking questions in a manner that makes it relatively easy to prepare the return and not impose unwarranted recordkeeping or information-gathering burdens to obtain and substantiate the reported information.

(b) Summary of Redesigned Annual Information Return

The redesigned Form 990 includes an 11-page "core form." There is a one-page summary of the organization (Part I), followed by ten additional parts (II–XI). Part II is the signature block. This core return is accompanied by 16 schedules.

(i) Part I (Summary). The summary requests a brief description of the organization's mission or most significant activities. It asks for the number of voting

---

172.2. The then-Acting Commissioner of Internal Revenue, on the occasion of the unveiling of the draft Form 990, said: "The tax-exempt sector has changed markedly since the Form 990 was last overhauled more than a quarter of a century ago. We need a Form 990 that reflects the way this growing sector operates in the 21st century. The new 990 aims to give both the IRS and the public an improved window into the way tax-exempt organizations go about their vital mission." The Director of the IRS's Exempt Organizations Division added: "Most organizations should not experience a change in burden. [Unfortunately, that statement is not accurate.] However, those with complicated compensation arrangements, related entity structures and activities that raise compliance concerns may have to spend more time providing meaningful information to the public."

172.3. IR-2007-204. On this occasion, the Commissioner, TE/GE, said: "When we released the redesigned draft form this past June, we said we needed a Form 990 that reflects the way this growing sector operates in the 21st century. The public comments we received in response to our draft form helped us develop a final form consistent with our guiding principles of transparency, compliance, and burden minimization."

members of the organization's governing body, the number of these board members who are independent, the number of employees, and the number of volunteers. Other questions include the amount of contributions and grants, program service revenue, investment income, other revenue, total gross unrelated business income total revenue and expenses, grants and similar amounts paid, compensation, professional fundraising expenses, other expenses,[172.4] and total assets and liabilities.

(ii) Part III. Part III of the redesigned Form 990 concerns the filing organization's program service accomplishments. It is required to describe its mission, new significant program services, any significant changes in the way it conducts a program, a cessation of any activity, and the exempt purpose achievements for each of its three largest program services by expenses. Charitable and social welfare organizations are required to report the amount of grants and allocations to others, total expenses, and any revenue for each program service reported.

(iii) Part IV. Part IV of the redesigned Form 990 is a checklist of required schedules. This schedule has 37 lines, with some lines containing up to four subparts.

(iv) Part V. Part V of the Form 990 pertains to a variety of activities and IRS filings. As to the former, there are questions about unrelated business income,[172.5] involvement in a prohibited tax shelter transaction,[172.6] use of supporting organizations,[172.7] use of donor-advised funds,[172.8] and payments with respect to personal benefit contracts.[172.9] As to the latter, there are questions about the filing of Forms 990-T, 1096, 1098-C, 8282, 8886-T, W-2G, and W-3.

(v) Part VI. Part VI of the Form 990 concerns governance, management, policies, and disclosure. As to the governing body and management (Section A), questions include the number of the voting members of the governing body and the number of board members who are "independent." Inquiry is made as to whether the organization has conflict-of-interest, whistleblower, and document retention and destruction policies, as well as policies governing the activities of chapters, affiliates, and "branches" (Section B). Additional questions pertain to various disclosures (Section C).[172.10]

172.4. See § 24.14.
172.5. See Chapter 24.
172.6. See § 27.15.
172.7. See § 12.3(c).
172.8. See § 11.8.
172.9. See § 27.12(c).
172.10. This Part VI of the Form 990 is an effort on the part of the IRS to substantially modify tax-exempt organizations' behavior in the governing context by encouraging the adoption and implementation of various practices and policies, none of which, for the most part, are required by law (Chapter 5; this Part VI is summarized in § 5.6(l)).

(vi) Part VII. Part VII of the Form 990 focuses on compensation of insiders and independent contractors. These persons currently in their positions must be listed (irrespective of compensation), along with a list of the organization's five highest compensated employees (other than insiders) who received compensation of more than $100,000 from the organization and any related organizations during the year; the organization's former officers, key employees, or highest compensated employees who received more than $100,000 of compensation from the organization and any related organizations during the year; and the organization's former directors or trustees who received (in that capacity) more than $10,000 of compensation from the organization and any related organizations during the year.

(vii) Parts VIII–XI. Part VIII of the Form 990 is a revenue statement, Part IX is a statement of expenses (including functional reporting), Part X is a balance sheet, and Part XI concerns financial statements.

(viii) Schedule A. Schedule A of the Form 990 is used by charitable organizations to report their public charity status.[172.11] Specific questions about supporting organizations include identification of the organization's type, a certification as to lack of control by disqualified persons, contributions from disqualified persons, and information about supported organizations.

There are separate public support schedules for the basic types of publicly supported charitable organizations. The public support computation period has been elongated to five years, which makes it consistent with the advance ruling period public support test. An organization can claim public charity status on the basis of the facts-and-circumstances test on this schedule.

(ix) Schedule B. Schedule B is the schedule used to report charitable contributions and grants. It is the same as the preexisting Schedule B.

(x) Schedule C. Schedule C comprises questions concerning political campaign and lobbying activities, principally by charitable organizations. Filing organizations are required to describe their direct and indirect political campaign activities, including the amounts of political expenditures and volunteer hours. There are separate parts for lobbying charitable organizations that are under the substantial part test and the expenditure test. Additional parts must be prepared by certain other types of tax-exempt entities.

(xi) Schedule D. Schedule D is used to report supplemental financial information, such as for investments, liabilities, conservation easements, donor-advised funds, art collections, trust accounts, and endowment funds.

172.11. See § 12.3.

(xii) Schedule E.   Schedule E is filed by organizations that constitute tax-exempt private schools.[172.12] Most of this schedule relates to the requirement that the organization cannot, to be tax-exempt, maintain a racially discriminatory policy. A question inquires as to whether the organization receives any financial aid or other assistance from a governmental agency.

(xiii) Schedule F.   The essence of Schedule F is the reporting of activities outside of the United States.[172.13] These activities, such as program services, grantmaking, and fundraising, are reported on a per region basis. Grantmakers are required to describe their procedures for monitoring the use of grant funds. Information must be supplied if a grantee or other recipient of assistance is related to any person with an interest in the grantmaking organization. Additional details are required in instances of grants or other assistance to organizations or individuals.

(xiv) Schedule G.   Schedule G largely concerns fundraising activities. The filing organization indicates the type or types of fundraising in which it is engaged and provides information about any fundraising contracts (including those with insiders). The organization is required to list the jurisdictions in which it is authorized to solicit funds. A part of this schedule focuses on fundraising events;[172.14] another part solicits details about gaming activities.[172.15]

(xv) Schedule H.   Schedule H is filed by tax-exempt hospitals.[172.16] The first part of this schedule (Part I) is a "community benefit report." The filing hospital indicates whether it provides free or discounted care to low-income individuals or to those who are "medically indigent." The hospital reports on its charity care (such care at cost, unreimbursed Medicaid services, and other unreimbursed costs in connection with government programs) and other community benefits (such as health improvement services, health professions education, subsidized health services, and research). The organization is asked whether it prepares an annual community benefit report and to describe its charity care policy.

The second part of this schedule (Part II) inquires as to the hospital's "community building" activities. These activities include physical improvements and housing, economic development, community support, environmental improvements, leadership development and training for community members, coalition-building, community health improvement advocacy, and workforce development.

Another part (Part III) pertains to bad debt, Medicare, and collection practices. A fourth part (Part IV) asks questions about the use of management

---

172.12. See § 12.3(a), text accompanied by note 134.
172.13. See § 27.16.
172.14. See § 24.5(h); *Fundraising* § 5.25(c).
172.15. See § 24.7(h).
172.16. See § 7.6(a).

companies and involvement in joint ventures. A fifth part (Part V) seeks information about the hospital's facilities. The schedule (Part VI) requests a description of how the organization assesses the healthcare needs of the communities it serves and how the organization informs patients about their eligibility for assistance under federal, state, or local government programs or under its charity care policy.

Parts I, II, III, IV, and VI of Schedule H are optional for 2008.

(xvi) Schedule I. Schedule I is used to solicit information about the organization's domestic grant and other assistance programs. For example, the organization is asked whether it maintains records to substantiate the amount of its assistance, and about the organization's selection criteria and grantees' eligibility. Information is required for grants of more than $5,000 to organizations and all grants to individuals.

(xvii) Schedule J. Schedule J is used to solicit supplemental information about compensation.[172.17] The organization must indicate (in Part I) if it provides to its insiders payments or items in forms such as first-class or charter travel, a discretionary spending account, a housing allowance, or health or social club dues; it is asked whether it follows a written policy in connection with such payments (or reimbursements) or items. The organization is asked how it determines certain executive compensation and, in the case of charitable and social welfare organizations, whether it provided any form of non-fixed payments.[172.18] The tax-exempt organization reports information concerning compensation paid to trustees, directors, officers, key employees, and highly compensated employees (Part II). There is a breakdown as to base compensation, bonus and incentive compensation, deferred compensation and nontaxable benefits.

(xviii) Schedule K. Schedule K is used to solicit information about tax-exempt bond issues (Part I) and the use of the proceeds (Part II). There are questions about the private use rules (Part III) and arbitrage (Part IV). Parts II, III, and IV of this schedule are optional for 2008.

(xix) Schedule L. Schedule L concerns excess benefit transactions,[172.19] and loans to and from interested persons.[172.20] Information sought includes the name of the debtor/creditor, original principal amount, balance due, the purpose of the loan, and whether there is a written agreement. Questions are also asked about grants or other forms of assistance benefiting, and business transactions involving, interested persons.

172.17. See, e.g., § 20.4.
172.18. See § 21.4(b).
172.19. See Chapter 21.
172.20. See, e.g., § 20.5(b).

(xx) Schedule M. The focus of Schedule M is on noncash contributions. Thus, information is sought about gifts of art (including fractional interests), books, clothing and household goods, automobiles, airplanes, boats, intellectual property, securities, qualified conservation property, real estate, collectibles, food inventory, drugs and medical supplies, taxidermy, historical artifacts, scientific specimens, and archeological artifacts.

This schedule inquires as to the number of Forms 8283 received by the organization for contributions for which the organization completed the donee acknowledgment portion; whether the organization received any property that it must hold for at least three years from the date of its contribution, which is not required to be used for exempt purposes during the entire holding period; whether the organization has a gift acceptance policy that requires the review of non-standard contributions; and whether the organization used third parties or related organizations to solicit, process, or sell non-cash distributions.

(xxi) Schedule N. Schedule N pertains to liquidations, terminations, dissolutions, and significant dispositions of assets. Questions include a description of the assets involved, their value, the method of determining the value, the date of the distribution, and the name and address of the recipient. Other questions concern the involvement of an insider with the successor or transferee organization, notification of one or more state officials, and other compliance with state laws. Additional information is sought concerning transfers of more than 25 percent of the organization's assets.

(xxii) Schedule O. Schedule O is used by filing organizations to provide additional information for responses to specific questions in the Form 990 and/or its schedules, and to provide additional information.

(xxiii) Schedule R. Schedule R has as one of its purposes the identification of disregarded entities and related tax-exempt organizations. Related organizations taxable as a partnership and as a corporation or trust are also required to be identified. There is a series of questions about transactions with related organizations and unrelated organizations taxable as a partnership.

(xxiv) Transition Rules. The IRS also announced a graduated three-year transition period for annual information return filings. For the 2008 tax year (returns filed in 2009), organizations with gross receipts of more than $1 million or total assets in excess of $2.5 million are required to file the Form 990. For the 2009 tax year (returns filed in 2010), organizations with gross receipts over $500,000 or total assets over $1.25 million will be required to file the Form 990. Exempt organizations below these thresholds are allowed to file the Form 990-EZ (with the option to file the new Form 990). (The Form 990-EZ for 2008 was also released on December 20, 2007.)

The filing threshold will be permanently set, beginning with the 2010 tax year, at $200,000 in gross receipts and $500,000 in total assets. Starting with the 2010 year, the filing threshold for organizations required to file Form 990-N (the e-postcard) will be increased to $50,000 (from $25,000).

(c) Implementing Regulations (New)

The IRS, on September 8, 2008, issued final, temporary, and proposed regulations to implement the redesigned Form 990.[172.21] These regulations eliminate the advance ruling process for new charitable entities that are seeking classification as publicly supported charities[172.22] and introduce a new public support computation period.[172.23]

(i) Compensation Reporting.   The preexisting regulations required that tax-exempt organizations report on the Form 990 the names and addresses of all officers, directors, trustees, and persons having responsibilities or powers similar to those of officers, directors, or trustees of the organization.[172.24] The redesigned Form 990 expanded the definition of *key employee* to cover not only persons having these similar responsibilities but also persons who manage a discrete segment or activity of the organization that represents a substantial portion of its activities, assets, income, or expenses. The new Form 990 requires reporting only for those key employees whose compensation exceeds $150,000. The temporary regulations add key employees to the list of persons who may be required to be reported on Form 990, as prescribed by publication, form, or instructions.[172.25]

The preexisting regulations also required exempt organizations that make payments of more than $30,000 annually to employees and independent contractors to report these persons' names and addresses on Form 990.[172.26] The regulations required a schedule showing the compensation or other payments made to these persons.[172.27] The redesigned Form 990 requires an organization to report, for each person listed (other than a key employee or former director or trustee of the organization), compensation and other payments totaling more than $100,000 annually paid by the organization and its related organizations to the person. For key employees, the new Form 990 requires an organization to report compensation and other payments totaling more than $150,000 annually paid by the organization and its related organizations to the person. For former directors and trustees, the new Form 990 requires an organization to

---

172.21. T.D. 9423, REG-142333-07. Also IR-2008-102.
172.22. See § 12.3(b).
172.23. See §§ 12.3(b)(i), text accompanied by notes 155–155.2; 12.3(b)(iv), text accompanied by notes 180–180.2.
172.24. Reg. § 1.6033-2(a)(2)(ii)(g).
172.25. Reg. § 6033-2T(a)(2)(ii)(g).
172.26. Reg. § 1.6033-2(a)(2)(ii)(g).
172.27. Reg. § 1.6033-2(a)(2)(ii)(h).

report compensation and other payments totaling more than $10,000 annually paid by the organization and its related organizations to the person solely on account of the person's past services as a director or trustee of the organization. The temporary regulations provide the IRS with the discretion to revise these threshold amounts for reporting by form and instructions.[172.28]

Moreover, the preexisting rule, which generally requires the reporting of compensation paid by an organization during its annual accounting period (or during the calendar year ending within the period), did not impose a requirement that the compensation reported on Form 990 be consistent with what is reported on Form W-2 or 1099.[172.29] The preexisting rule permitted, but did not require, a fiscal year organization to report paid compensation on a calendar-year basis. The redesigned Form 990, in Part VII and Schedule J, requires that compensation reported as paid to officers and other employees be consistent with Form W-2 and that compensation reported as paid to directors, individual trustees, and independent contractors be consistent with Form 1099.

The temporary regulations require an exempt organization to report compensation it has paid during a calendar year ending with or within the organization's annual accounting period, or during such other period as specified by form or instructions.[172.30] A fiscal-year organization will continue to be required to use fiscal-year accounting when reporting aggregate compensation as an expense item (Form 990, Part IX). An organization will not be required to reconcile compensation for individuals reported in Part VII with compensation for these individuals included in the Part IX statement of expenses.

(ii) Asset Disposition Reporting.   Form 990, Schedule N, requires information about organizations that liquidate, terminate, or dissolve, or sell, exchange, dispose of, or otherwise transfer more than 25 percent of the organization's assets. Two statutes authorize the collection of this information.[172.31] While the second of these laws and its companion penalty provision[172.32] contemplate a separate return, this information has been collected on Form 990 since 1981.

To eliminate the potential for inconsistency and confusion, the regulations accompanying this second law have been amended to be consistent with the rule under the first of these laws, as well as Schedule N. Generally, the preexisting regulations excused from the information-reporting requirement of the second law organizations other than former charitable organizations.[172.33] The IRS now believes that this exception is overly broad; therefore, the temporary regulations amend the preexisting regulations to accord discretion to the IRS to narrow the exception and require reporting from other exempt organizations

---

172.28.   Reg. § 1.6033-2T(a)(2)(ii)(g).
172.29.   Reg. § 1.6033-2(a)(2)(ii)(h).
172.30.   Reg. § 1.6033-2T(a)(2)(ii)(h).
172.31.   IRC §§ 6033, 6043(b).
172.32.   IRC § 6652(c).
172.33.   Reg. § 6043-3(b)(8).

by form or instructions.[172.34] Also, the temporary regulations remove the definition of *substantial contraction* from the preexisting regulations,[172.35] leaving this term to be defined by form or instructions.[172.36]

(d) Instructions (New)

The IRS, on April 7, 2008, issued draft instructions to accompany the redesigned Form 990. The final version of these instructions (from the standpoint of the IRS) was released on August 19, 2008.[172.37] The actual final version of these regulations (following IRS Forms and Publications unit approval) were issued in late 2008; there were no significant changes in content.

The instructions contain summaries of the law, a glossary, and a *sequencing list*, the latter to assist organizations in completing the return and its schedules.[172.38] As the IRS noted in the draft of these instructions, "certain later parts of the form must first be completed in order to complete earlier parts." Following are the highlights of the draft and final Form 990 instructions.

(i) Draft Instructions for Part VI (Governance). The draft instructions that underlie Part VI of the new Form 990 are quite remarkable in their contents (as is Part VI itself). These instructions open with the following extraordinary observation: "Even though certain governance, management, and disclosure policies and procedures may not be required under the Internal Revenue Code, the IRS considers such policies and procedures to generally improve tax [law] compliance."

A concept introduced into the federal tax law by the new Form 990 is that of the independent member of a tax-exempt organization's governing board. Pursuant to the draft instructions, a voting member of a board is considered *independent* only if the following four circumstances applied at all times during the organization's tax year:

1. The member was not compensated as an employee of the organization or a related organization (see Schedule R and its draft instructions), except for a religious entity exception.

2. The member did not receive total compensation or other payments exceeding $10,000 for the year from the organization or a related organization as an independent contractor, other than reimbursement of expenses or reasonable compensation for services provided in the capacity of a member of the governing body.

172.34. Reg. § 1.6043-3T(b)(8).
172.35. Reg. § 1.6043-3(d)(1).
172.36. Reg. § 1.6043-3T(d).
172.37. IR-2008-96.
172.38. See § 27.2A(d)(x).

3. The member did not otherwise receive, directly or indirectly, material financial benefits from the organization or a related organization (see the Schedule L draft instructions).

4. The member did not have a family member that received compensation or other material financial benefits from the organization or a related organization.

One of the questions in this part (line 3) concerns use of a management company or other person to perform management duties customarily performed by or under the direct supervision of trustees, directors, officers, or key employees. The draft instructions point out that these management duties include hiring, firing, and supervising personnel; planning or executing budgets or financial operations; or supervising exempt operations or unrelated businesses of the organization.

Another question in this part (line 4) concerns significant changes to organizing or enabling documents of the filing organization. The draft instructions state that examples of these changes include changes:

- In the number, composition, qualifications, authority, or duties of the governing body's voting members
- In the number, composition, qualifications, authority, or duties of the organization's officers or key employees
- In the distribution of assets on dissolution
- In the provisions to amend the organizing or enabling document or bylaws
- In the organization's exempt purposes or mission
- In the policies or procedures regarding compensation of trustees, directors, officers, or key employees
- In the policies or procedures concerning conflicts of interest, whistle-blowing, or document retention and destruction
- In the composition or procedures of an audit committee

It may be noted that the last three items are rarely in an organization's governing or enabling documents.

A question (line 8) concerns contemporaneous documentation of meetings and actions by governing bodies and committees. The draft instructions provide that *documentation* includes approved minutes, strings of emails, or similar writings that explain the action taken, when it was taken, and who made the decision. For this purpose, the draft instructions state that *contemporaneous* means by the later of (1) the next meeting of the governing body or committee or (2) 60 days after the date of the meeting or written action.

In a discussion of conflict-of-interest policies, the draft instructions state that a *conflict of interest* arises "when a person in a position of authority over an organization, such as an officer, director, or manager, may benefit financially from a decision he or she could make in such capacity, including indirect benefits such as to family members or businesses with which the person is closely associated." A conflict of interest "does not include questions involving a person's competing or respective duties to the organization and to another organization, such as by serving on the boards of both organizations, that do not involve a material financial interest of, or benefit to, such person."

An organization can answer "yes" to line 16b of this part if the organization has (1) adopted a written policy or procedure that requires the organization to negotiate in its transactions and arrangements with other members of a partnership such terms and safeguards that are adequate to ensure that the organization's tax exemption is protected, and (2) taken steps to safeguard the organization's exempt status with respect to the venture or arrangement. The draft instructions provide examples of these *safeguards*: control over the venture or arrangement sufficient to ensure that the venture furthers the exempt purposes of the organization; requirements that the venture or arrangement give priority to exempt purposes over maximization of profits for the other participants; a policy that it not engage in activities that would jeopardize the organization's exemption; and a policy that all contracts entered into with the organization be on terms that are arm's length or more favorable to the organization.

(ii) Draft Instructions for Schedule G (Fundraising and Gaming). The greatest import of the draft instructions that accompany Schedule G is in the definitions. For example, the term *fundraising activities* means "activities undertaken to induce potential donors to contribute money, securities, services, materials, facilities, other assets, or time." According to this sweeping definition, if a representative of a tax-exempt organization asks an individual to serve on its governing board or to otherwise act as a volunteer for the organization, the organization has engaged in fundraising. This definition of the term goes far beyond state law concepts that have been applied for decades.

This definition of *fundraising activities* is broad; conventionally, the solicitation of *services* or *time* is not considered to be *fundraising*. The fundraising community, long ago, differentiated among contributions of "time, treasure, and talent." Fundraising pertains to the solicitation of money and/or other property; it does not relate to solicitations of services or time. If a charitable organization's president asks an individual to serve on the charity's board of trustees, the president is not engaged in fundraising. If a charitable organization's executive director asks an individual to volunteer to assist with a particular project (even a fundraising event), the executive director is likewise not engaged in fundraising. The IRS has overlooked the fact that the concept of and the word *fundraising* not only contains the word *fund* but is predicated on it.

Fundraising activities, according to the draft instructions, include publicizing and conducting fundraising campaigns; maintaining donor mailing lists; conducting fundraising events; preparing and distributing fundraising manuals, instructions, and other materials; and conducting other activities involved with the solicitation of contributions and grants from individuals, private foundations, governments, and others.

The phrase *professional fundraising services* includes services "performed (other than by an officer, director, or employee in his or her capacity as an officer, director, or employee) for the organization requiring the exercise of professional judgment or discretion consisting of planning, management, the preparation of materials, e.g., direct mail solicitation packages, or the provision of advice and consulting regarding solicitation of contributions; or the direct solicitation of contributions."

(iii) Draft Instructions for Schedule M (Non-Cash Contributions).   One of the more complex schedules that accompanies the new Form 990 is Schedule M, by means of which organizations report on contributions to them of property other than cash. The draft instructions make it clear that (1) all tax-exempt organizations, not just charitable entities, must file this schedule, if they received non-cash gifts; (2) a contribution is a non-cash contribution irrespective of whether it is deductible; and (3) gifts of donated services are not non-cash gifts for purposes of the schedule.

The draft instructions for Schedule M include definitions for various terms, such as *works of art, historical treasure, household goods, intellectual property, collectibles, archeological artifact, ethnological artifact,* and *taxidermy*. The instructions also define *nonstandard contribution*, a term to apply when answering the question about a gift acceptance policy. The scheme involving the contribution of successor member interests, by means of limited liability companies, to charitable organizations (see the January 2008 issue) is identified as an example of a nonstandard contribution.

(iv) Draft Instructions for Schedule A (Public Charities).   The new Schedule A introduced, as the draft instructions explain, separate schedules for computation of the public support tests. Donative-type publicly supported charities prepare Part II; service-provider publicly supported charities prepare Part III. The public support measuring period has been lengthened to five years.

The IRS has ceased issuing advance rulings. An organization seeking public charity status as a publicly supported entity will receive a determination letter (if it qualifies). The organization will have five years to establish satisfaction of the public support requirement (if it can). At the end of the five-year period, the organization will not have to file Form 8734. Beginning with its sixth tax year, the organization will have to establish on Schedule A that it continues to be a public charity (if it can).

(v) Draft Instructions for Schedule F (Foreign Activities). The draft instructions require organizations operating or funding outside the United States to report activities on a regional basis, with the regions generally patterned on the regional breakdown used by the World Bank. The draft instructions do not provide a list of the countries within each region; this topic will be addressed in the final regulations.

(vi) Draft Instructions for Schedule L (Transactions with Interested Persons). The draft instructions focus on Part IV of Schedule L. There, reporting is based on whether the organization made payments in connection with an interested person, transaction, or arrangement during the year. A "large board" exception is provided for organizations with large boards that rely on an executive committee for ongoing governance decisions.

(vii) Draft Instructions for Schedule N (Significant Dispositions). Schedule N is used to report certain major transactions or events. The new Form 990 expands this reporting to include a significant disposition of assets for which adequate consideration is received. The draft instructions provide that a *significant disposition* includes a sale or exchange of more than 25 percent of the organization's net assets or a substantial contraction of net assets.

(viii) Final Instructions. The final instructions issued by the IRS to accompany the redesigned Form 990 include many changes in content and format that are intended to provide greater clarity. They provide additional examples to illustrate key points, reduce information-gathering and reporting burdens in certain areas, and establish or revise definitions or standards in certain areas. Here are the significant changes:

- Provision of a definition of *key employee* for purposes of reporting executive compensation in Part VII and Schedule J, identifying transactions with interested persons in Schedule L, answering questions about governance in Part VI, and for other purposes

- Listing of countries included in nine geographic regions to be used for reporting foreign activities on Schedule F

- Specification of reporting requirements for which the filing organization may rely on an express reasonable efforts process to obtain information required from interested persons or third parties, in Part VI, Section A of Part VII, and Parts III and IV of Schedule L

- Revision of definition of *independent voting member* of a governing body, for purposes of Part VI, line 1b

- Making of several changes to Schedule H
- Exemption concerning reporting of certain refunding bonds on Schedule K
- Clarification as to compensation reporting in Part VII and Schedule J, Part II
- Narrowing of the scope of business relationship reporting in Part VI.
- Making of changes to Schedule L
- Clarification of the definition of *officer* for purposes of reporting executive compensation in Part VII and Schedule J, identification of transactions with interested persons in Schedule L, reporting as to governance in Part VI, and for other purposes
- Expansion of required narrative reporting in Schedule O to include several items

(ix) Sequencing List.   The instructions include a *sequencing list*, to assist an organization in completing the form and its schedules. According to this list, here is the way to approach preparation of the new Form 990:

1. Complete lines A–F and H(a)–M in the heading of the return.
2. Determine the organization's related organizations (see Schedule R instructions) for which reporting will be required.
3. Determine the organization's officers, directors, trustees, key employees, and five highest compensated employees required to be listed in Form 990, Part VII, Section A.
4. Complete Parts VIII, IX, and X (revenue and expense statements, and balance sheet).
5. Complete line G in the heading (gross receipts).
6. Complete Parts III, V, VII, and XI.
7. Complete Schedule L (concerning transactions with interested persons) if required.
8. Complete Part VI.
9. Complete Parts I.
10. Complete Part IV.
11. Complete remaining applicable schedules (for which "yes" boxes were checked in Part IV). Schedule O is to be used to provide required supplemental information and other narrative.
12. Complete Part II (signature block).

§ 27.3 SMALL ORGANIZATIONS NOTIFICATION REQUIREMENT

*p. 939, *second complete paragraph, third line.* Insert following *must*:

, to remain exempt,[173.1]

*p. 939, n. 174. Insert before first period:

; Reg. § 1.6033-6

*p. 939, n. 174. Insert following first period:

This notification requirement, applicable with respect to tax years beginning after December 31, 2007, entails the submission of Form 990-N (otherwise known as the *ePostcard*). This notice is not a *return* and it is not *filed* but rather it is *submitted*; a significance of these distinctions is that the submission of this electronic notification does not start the running of the statute of limitations for assessment of tax. The voluntary filing of an annual information return (presumably, a Form 990-EZ (see § 27.2(a)(iv)) that is completely prepared can be done without filing electronically and that filing triggers the running of the statute of limitations.

The IRS, on February 25, 2008, announced the launch of a "simple electronic filing system" that small tax-exempt organizations may use to comply with the law requiring them to annually file the ePostcard (IR-2008-25).

The IRS, during the second half of 2007, mailed educational letters to over 650,000 small tax-exempt organizations about these rules (IR-2007-129). The IRS is expecting a "substantial" number of by-operation-of-law revocations of tax exemption in 2010 because "many" organizations that were required to submit electronic notification for the 2007 annual period have yet to do so (based on the discrepancy between the number of organizations notified of this obligation and the number of submitters) (PMTA 2009-155).

*p. 939. Insert as third and fourth complete paragraphs, before heading:

This filing threshold of $25,000 will be increased to $50,000 beginning with the 2010 tax year.[175.1]

This notice is not a *return*; it is not *filed* but rather is *submitted*. The significance of these distinctions is that the submission of this electronic notification does not trigger the running of the statute of limitations for assessment of tax. Also, inasmuch as the requirement that the notice be submitted *electronically* is statutory, the IRS lacks the authority to allow submissions of the notice in hardcopy form. The voluntary filing of an annual information return,[175.2] by contrast, starts the running of the limitations period and can be filed in paper form. If this is done, however, the return must be prepared in full. If a small

---

* 173.1. See § 27.4.
  175.1. See § 27.2(b)(ii).
* 175.2. Presumably, a Form 990-EZ. See § 27.2(a)(iv).

organization is a subordinate entity as part of a group exemption[175.3] and its information is included in the central organization's group return, the small organization need not submit this notice.[175.4]

§ 27.4   FILING REQUIREMENTS AND TAX-EXEMPT STATUS

*p. 940. Insert as first complete paragraph:

The IRS is required to publish and maintain a list of organizations the tax-exempt status of which has been revoked by operation of this law.[180.1] This publication will be on the IRS Web site, rather than in the Internal Revenue Bulletin (IRB), although there will be initial notices of this changeover in practice in the IRB, along with advisories as to when this electronic list of revoked organizations is updated.[180.2]

*p. 940, n. 182. Insert as first sentence:

A central organization, with a group exemption, may not reinstate the revoked tax-exempt status of a subordinate organization, where the revocation is by operation of this law, by listing the subordinate entity on the central organization's annual group ruling information filing with the IRS (see § 25.6) (PMTA 2009-156).

*p. 940. Insert as third complete paragraph, before heading:

The IRS is in the process of developing a voluntary compliance program to assist tax-exempt organizations that are not presently filing annual returns, in order to preclude inadvertent loss of exemption because of this three-year rule.

§ 27.5   REPORTING BY POLITICAL ORGANIZATIONS

(a)   General Rules

p. 941, *fourth paragraph*. Insert as second sentence:

The IRS issued guidance providing the elements of a safe harbor for establishing that failure by a political organization to report certain contributor information satisfies this waiver regime.[189.1]

---

* 175.3. See § 25.6.
* 175.4. The filing of this notice is a requirement that is applicable to organizations that are tax-exempt by reason of description in a subsection of IRC § 501(c). Thus, small political organizations (see Chapter 17) are not required to file this notice; they may, however, having other reporting requirements (see § 27.5).
* 180.1. *Id.*
* 180.2. PMTA 2009-155.
* 189.1. Rev. Proc. 2007-27, 2007-1 C.B. 887.

§ 27.7 UNRELATED BUSINESS INCOME TAX RETURNS

p. 944, *third paragraph*. Insert as last sentences:

The IRS issued interim guidance in connection with these disclosure rules,[204.1] which will remain in effect until tax regulations are promulgated.[204.2] The three-year limitation on making annual information returns available[204.3] also applies with respect to the unrelated business income tax return filed by charitable organizations; the IRS is required to make this Form 990-T publicly available, subject to the usual redaction procedures.[204.4] The IRS thereafter provided additional interim guidance concerning these rules by stating that schedules, attachments, and other supporting documents filed with a Form 990-T that do not relate to the imposition of unrelated business income tax are not required to be made available for public inspection and copying.[204.5] The IRS subsequently published the procedures that are to be used to request a charitable organization's Form 990-T for purposes of the inspection and photocopying rules.[204.6]

p. 944, n. 202. Delete text and substitute:

See §§ 27.8, 27.9.

p. 945, n. 215. Insert before existing material:

A six-month extension of time to file Form 990-T may be requested by filing Form 8868.

§ 27.8 IRS DOCUMENT DISCLOSURE RULES

(a) Federal Tax Law Disclosure Requirements

(ii) Exempt Organizations Documents.

---

* 204.1. Notice 2007-45, 2007-1 C.B. 1320.
  204.2. All charitable organizations that file Form 990-T are required to make the return public, even if the organization is not otherwise subject to the disclosure requirements, such as a church (see § 25.3(a), text accompanied by note 137; § 27.2(b)(i)). Also, state colleges and universities, and certain other entities, have tax exemption (exclusion) based on IRC § 115 (see § 19.19(b)); if that is the sole basis for exemption and the organization has reportable unrelated business income, the organization need not make its Forms 990-T public, whereas if the organization also has tax exemption based on IRC § 501(c)(3), the Forms 990-T must be made publicly available.
  204.3. See § 27.9(a).
  204.4. See § 27.8(a). Clarification as to these two rules came about as a result of enactment of the Tax Technical Corrections Act of 2007 (Pub. L. No. 110-172, 110th Cong., 1st Sess. (2007) § 3(g)).
* 204.5. Notice 2008-49, 2008-1 C.B. 979.
  204.6. Ann. 2008-21, 2008-13 I.R.B. 691. Form 4506-A is used for this purpose.

*p. 947, n. 231, *first line.* **Insert before first period***:*

> ; Rev. Proc. 2009-9, 2009-1 C.B. 256 § 8.01(1).

*p. 948, n. 252, *first paragraph.* **Insert following existing material:**

> Rev. Proc. 2009-9, 2009-1 C.B. 256 § 8.02. The IRS, on August 13, 2007, issued proposed regulations to amend the existing regulations to bring them into accord with this court opinion and the current IRS practice (REG-116215-07).

§ 27.9 DOCUMENT DISCLOSURE OBLIGATIONS OF EXEMPT ORGANIZATIONS

(a) General Rules

*p. 950, n. 269, *first line.* **Insert before first period:**

> ; Rev. Proc. 2009-9, 2009-1 C.B. 256 § 8.01(2).

§ 27.12 INSURANCE ACTIVITIES

(c) Applicable Insurance Contract Reporting Requirements

p. 962, n. 364. Insert following existing material:

> The IRS solicited public comment on two draft IRS forms designed to implement this information reporting requirement (Notice 2007-34, 2007-12 I.R.B. 750). Form 8921 will be used to report information to the IRS about structured transactions under which there have been reportable acquisitions of applicable insurance contracts made by an applicable exempt organization. Form 8922 will be used to report information to the IRS about the applicable insurance contracts that are part of a structured transaction required to be reported on a Form 8921.

§ 27.14 TAX-EXEMPT ENTITY LEASING RULES

p. 973. Insert following fourth paragraph, before heading:

(h) Interrelationship with Certain Tax Shelter Rules (New)

A law change in 2007[466.1] provided tax relief for certain investment partnerships, the investors in which include tax-exempt organizations. This law change, affecting university endowment funds, pension funds, and the like, enables these exempt institutions to sidestep law that attempts to curb the use

---

466.1. Tax Technical Corrections Act of 2007 (Pub. L. No. 110-172, 110th Cong., 1st Sess. (2007)) § 7(c), amending the American Jobs Protection Act of 2004 (Pub. L. No. 108-357, 108th Cong., 2nd Sess. (2004)) § 848.

of two tax shelters involving purchases by corporations of assets of government entities (usually cities or states), followed by lease of them back to the governments, generating tax benefits to the corporations.

The IRS barred the tax shelters—known as lease-in, lease-out (LILO) or sale-in, sale-out (SILO) arrangements—in 2002 and 2005, respectively. These partnerships involving exempt organizations did not, however, engage in LILO or SILO transactions; a moratorium on application of the anti-shelter law to these partnerships nonetheless would have expired at the close of 2007.

The federal tax law applies limitations on deductions allocable to property leased to government entities or other tax-exempt organizations.[466.2] This rule applies with respect to tax-exempt use property, generally defined in the tax-exempt entity leasing rules.[466.3] This legislation was enacted because the manner of application of these deduction limitations in the case of property owned by a partnership in which a tax-exempt entity is a partner was unclear.

The new rule provides that tax-exempt use property does not include any property that would be tax-exempt use property solely because of the fact that the property is in a partnership.[466.4] The provision[466.5] refers to the tax law rules as to circumstances where partnership is treated as a lease to which the tax-exempt entity leasing rules apply.[466.6] Thus, if a partnership is recharacterized as a lease and a provision of the tax-exempt entity leasing rules (other than the carve-out rule[466.7]) applies to cause the property characterized as leased to be treated as a tax-exempt use property, the deduction limitations (loss deferral) rules apply.

§ 27.15 TAX-EXEMPT ORGANIZATIONS AND TAX SHELTERS

(j) Excise Tax Penalties

p. 980. Insert as second and third paragraphs, before heading:

The IRS issued temporary and proposed regulations providing guidance relating to entity-level and manager-level excise taxes with respect to prohibited tax shelter transactions to which tax-exempt organizations are parties, to certain disclosure obligations with respect to these transactions, and to the requirement of a return and time for filing with respect to these taxes.[526.1] These regulations, in addition to addressing the definition of the term *tax-exempt entity*, coordinate the term *prohibited tax shelter transaction* with the

---

466.2. IRC § 470.
466.3. IRC § 168(h). See § 27.14(f).
466.4. IRC § 168(h)(6); new IRC § 470(c)(2)(B).
466.5. New IRC § 470(c)(2)(C).
466.6. IRC § 7701(e).
466.7. IRC § 168(h)(6).
526.1. REG-139268-06, REG-142039-06; T.D. 9334, T.D. 9335.

term *reportable transaction*[526.2] and define the term *subsequently listed transaction* as a transaction (other than a reportable transaction) to which an exempt entity becomes a party before the transaction becomes a listed transaction. The most significant element of these regulations is the threshold definition of *party* to a prohibited tax shelter transaction, which (1) means an exempt entity that facilitates a prohibited tax shelter transaction by reason of its exempt (or tax-indifferent or tax-favored) status and (2) includes an exempt entity that enters into a listed transaction and reflects on its tax return a reduction or elimination of its liability for federal employment, excise, or unrelated business income taxes that is derived directly or indirectly from tax consequences or tax strategy described in the published guidance that lists the transaction.[526.3] These proposed regulations also clarify the definition of the term *entity manager*, address the meaning of the phrase *knowing or having reason to know*, define *net income* and *proceeds*, provide rules regarding the manner and timing of the requisite disclosures, and specify the tax forms used to pay the taxes under this regime.

Thereafter, the IRS issued final regulations on the matter of reportable transactions, including a new category of arrangements that must be disclosed, known as *transactions of interest*.[526.4] The identification of a transaction (or a substantially similar one) as a transaction of interest alerts persons involved with these transactions to "certain responsibilities" that may arise from their involvement with the transaction.[526.5] The first transaction of interest announced by the IRS[526.6] concerns a transaction in which a taxpayer directly or indirectly acquires certain rights in real property or in an entity that directly or indirectly holds real property, transfers the rights more than one year after the acquisition to a charitable organization, and claims a charitable contribution deduction that is significantly higher than the amount that the taxpayer paid to acquire the rights.[526.7] Thereafter, the IRS launched an examination program pertaining to charitable contributions of certain *successor member interests*, by means of a prototype letter and information document request that was made public in late October 2007.[526.8]

Following that, the IRS announced another transaction of interest involving charitable remainder trusts, this one involving a coordinated disposition of trust assets by the grantor and the trust, in a manner that ostensibly manipulates the basis rules to avoid tax on the gain from the disposition of appreciated

---

526.2. IRC § 6011
526.3. Reflecting guidance that was issued previously (Notice 2007-18, 2007-9 I.R.B. 608), the proposed regulations provide that a tax-exempt entity does not become a party to a prohibited tax shelter transaction solely because it invests in an entity that in turn becomes involved in such a transaction.
526.4. T.D. 9350, T.D. 9351, T.D. 9352.
526.5. IRC §§ 6111, 6112; Reg. § 1.6011-4(b)(6).
526.6. IR-2007-143.
526.7. Notice 2007-72, 2007-36 I.R.B. 544.
526.8. See *IRS Audits* § 4.9(b).

assets that were contributed to the trust (and as to which the grantor claimed a charitable deduction for the contribution of the remainder interest).[526.9]

§ 27.17 RECORD-KEEPING REQUIREMENTS

*p. 983. Insert as third complete paragraph:

The IRS ruled that an organization will not jeopardize its tax-exempt status as a charitable entity, even if it distributes funds to nonexempt organizations, as long as it retains control and discretion over the use of the funds and maintains records establishing that the funds were used for charitable purposes.[548.1]

*p. 983, n. 549. Insert following existing material:

See § 26.6(a)(i), text accompanied by note 296.1.

---

* 526.9. Notice 2008-99, 2008-2 C.B. 979.
* 548.1. Rev. Rul. 68-489, 1968-2 C.B. 210.

PART SEVEN

Interorganizational Structures and Operational Forms

Tax-Exempt Organizations and Exempt Subsidiaries

§ 28.2   CHARITABLE ORGANIZATIONS AS SUBSIDIARIES

(e)   Subsidiaries of Foreign Charitable Organizations

*p. 995, n. 59. Insert following fifth period:

Because an organization did not "review and approve the disbursements" and did not "maintain control and discretion over the use of the funds," it was found by the IRS to be a conduit entity; the funds did not flow through to a foreign charity, however, but flowed through to individuals (scholarship recipients). Priv. Ltr. Rul. 200931059.

*p. 995, n. 59. Convert text following fifth period to second paragraph of note.

§ 28.6   REVENUE FROM TAX-EXEMPT SUBSIDIARY

*p. 1002, n. 123, *second line.* **Delete** *2007* **and insert** *2009.*

*p. 1002, n. 123. Insert following existing material:

The Tax Extenders Act of 2009 (H.R. 4213), which passed the House of Representatives on December 9, 2009, would extend this provision through 2010 (Act § 136); this measure is pending in the Senate.

Tax-Exempt Organizations and For-Profit Subsidiaries

§ 29.2   POTENTIAL OF ATTRIBUTION TO PARENT

p. 1010, *last paragraph*. Insert as last sentence:

Yet, the IRS, in 2008, in a rare ruling on the point, revoked a charitable organization's tax-exempt status on the grounds of attribution, where the organization controlled the affairs of its wholly owned subsidiary to the point that it was considered a mere instrumentality of the parent.[48.1]

§ 29.7   REVENUE FROM FOR-PROFIT SUBSIDIARY

(b)   Tax Treatment of Income from Subsidiary

p. 1018, n. 100. Insert following existing text:

Applying these rules, the IRS held (in a controversial private letter ruling) that a tax-exempt hospital that constructively owns several professional medical corporations received unrelated business income from them (Priv. Ltr. Rul. 200716034).

(d)   Temporary Rule

*p. 1020, *first paragraph, third line*. Delete *2008* and insert *2010*.

48.1. Priv. Ltr. Rul. 200842050. In this ruling, the IRS did not explain the factors that led to this conclusion. In any event, the test is not *control* (which is obviously always present when the subsidiary is wholly owned), but is *day-to-day management*.

*p. 1020, n. 112. Insert following existing material:

The Tax Extenders Act of 2009 (H.R. 4213), which passed the House of Representatives on December 9, 2009, would extend this provision through 2010 (Act § 136); this measure is pending in the Senate.

p. 1020, *first paragraph.* Insert as third sentence:

This temporary rule applies, however, only with respect to payments made pursuant to a binding written contract in effect on August 17, 2006, or a contract that is a renewal under substantially similar terms of a contract in effect on that date.[113.1]

*p. 1020, *third paragraph, first line.* Delete *is* and insert *was required.*

113.1. IRC § 512(b)(13)(E)(iii).

CHAPTER THIRTY

Tax-Exempt Organizations
and Joint Ventures

§ 30.1 PARTNERSHIPS AND JOINT VENTURE BASICS

(b) Joint Ventures

*p. 1028, *first complete paragraph*. **Insert as last sentence:**

By contrast, where an exempt organization participates in a joint venture with one or more other exempt organizations, in furtherance of exempt purposes, the exempt activities of the venture are attributed to the partners and their exemption is not jeopardized by reason of their involvement in the venture.[26.1]

§ 30.5 LOW-INCOME HOUSING VENTURES

p. 1051, *first complete paragraph, last line*. **Insert footnote following period:**

[123.1] In general, Myers, "The Low-Income Housing Tax Credit: A Proposal to Address IRS Concerns Regarding Non-Profit and For-Profit Partnerships," 60 *Tax Law.* (No. 2) 415 (Winter 2007).

§ 30.7 ALTERNATIVES TO PARTNERSHIPS

p. 1053, n. 137, *second paragraph, first line*. **Insert following first comma:**

Kirk, "Self-Dealing and the Lobster Pot of Joint Ventures," 49 *Exempt Org. Tax Rev.* (No. 2) 221 (Aug. 2005);

---

* 26.1. E.g., Priv. Ltr. Rul. 200902013 (where two tax-exempt hospitals operated a network of six freestanding family health care clinics in medically underserved areas of their community). In this instance, the joint venture was converted to a formal partnership (see § 30.1(a)).

CHAPTER THIRTY-ONE

Tax-Exempt Organizations: Other Operations and Restructuring

§ 31.3   MERGERS

*p. 1064, *carryover paragraph.* Insert as last sentence:

In another instance, two public charities (one the sole member of the other) merged, to simplify their governance structure and reduce administrative expenses.[63.1]

*p. 1065, n. 75, *first line.* Insert following fourth period:

The IRS, in May 2009, issued a fact sheet on mergers of tax-exempt organizations (Pub. 4779).

p. 1065, *carryover paragraph.* Insert as last sentence:

In still another instance, the IRS approved a consolidation of industry regulatory functions between two affiliated business leagues[75.1] and a nonprofit (nonexempt) corporate subsidiary of a publicly traded company; the effect of the transaction was said by the agency to produce benefits for the industry and the public that relies on the business leagues to ensure fairness in the industry.[75.2]

63.1. Priv. Ltr. Rul. 200843040.
75.1. That is, organizations described in IRC § 501(c)(6) (see Chapter 14).
75.2. Priv. Ltr. Rul. 200723029.

§ 31.6 SINGLE-MEMBER LIMITED LIABILITY COMPANIES

p. 1070. Insert following carryover paragraph:

- An exempt public charity operated an activity in a wholly owned for-profit subsidiary. The organization, having determined that this activity is an exempt function, merged the subsidiary corporation into a SMLLC, of which the charity is the member, and thereafter continued these operations as a charitable activity.[119.1]

*p. 1070. Insert following second complete paragraph, before heading:**

§ 31.6A LOW-PROFIT LIMITED LIABILITY COMPANIES (NEW)

State statutory law additions in recent years have brought a new type of entity: the *low-profit limited liability company* (L3C). Most L3C organizations are for-profit, taxable entities, with one or more taxable members. Thus, an L3C is not likely to qualify as a tax-exempt charitable organization (although it could if it had only charitable organizations as members). Nonetheless, an L3C has as its primary purpose the accomplishment of one or more charitable purposes. The production of income is a permitted secondary purpose of an L3C.

The principal federal tax law issue in this regard is whether an investment by a private foundation in an L3C qualifies as a program-related investment.[124.1] The requirements in this regard appear to be essentially identical to preexisting law concerning these investments. The IRS's evaluation of an L3C would not be affected by the classification of the entity as charitable or noncharitable under state law.

119.1. Priv. Ltr. Rul. 200723030.
* 124.1. See § 12.4(d). Also *Private Foundations* § 8.3.

*A P P E N D I X   A

Sources of the Law (Revised)

*pp. 1095–1101. Delete Appendix A and substitute:

The law as described in this book is derived from many sources. For those not familiar with these matters and/or wishing to understand precisely what the law regarding tax-exempt organizations is, the following explanation should be of assistance.

§ 1 FEDERAL LAW

The U.S. Constitution created three branches of government. Article I of the Constitution established the U.S. Congress as a bicameral legislature, consisting of the House of Representatives and the Senate. Article II of the Constitution established the Presidency. Article III of the Constitution established the federal court system.

(a) Congress

Congress created the legal structure underlying the federal law for non-profit organizations. Most of this law is manifested in the tax law and thus appears in the Internal Revenue Code. Other laws written by Congress that can affect tax-exempt organizations include the antitrust, consumer protection, corporate responsibility, education, employee benefits, health care, political campaign financing, labor, postal, and securities laws.

Statutory Law in General. Tax laws for the United States must originate in the House of Representatives (U.S. Constitution, Article I § 7). The nation's tax laws are formally initially written by the members and staff of the House Committee on Ways and Means and the Senate Committee on Finance. A considerable portion of this work is performed by the staff of the Joint Committee on Taxation, which consists of members of the House and Senate. Frequently, these laws are generated by work done at the House subcommittee level, usually the Subcommittee on Oversight or the Subcommittee on Select Revenue Measures. Most tax legislation is the subject of hearings before the House Ways and Means Committee and the Senate Finance Committee. Nearly all of this legislation is finalized by a House-Senate conference committee, consisting of senior members of the House Ways and Means Committee and the Senate Finance Committee.

A Congress sits for two years, which is termed a *session*. Each Congress is sequentially numbered. For example, the 111th Congress is meeting during the calendar years 2009–2010. A legislative development that took place in 2010 is referenced as occurring during the 111th Congress, 2nd Session ("111th Cong., 2nd Session (2010)").

A bill introduced in the House of Representatives or Senate during a particular Congress is given a sequential number in each house. For example, the 3,000th bill introduced in the House of Representatives in 2010 is cited as "H.R. 3000, 111th Cong., 2nd Sess. (2010)" (see, e.g., § 19.22, second item); the 2,000th bill introduced in the Senate in 2010 is cited as "S. 2000, 111th Cong., 2nd Sess. (2010)" (see, e.g., § 19.22, first item).

A tax bill, having passed the House and Senate, and usually blended by a conference committee, is sent to the President for signature. Once signed, the measure becomes law, causing enactment of one or more new and/or amended Code sections. As is the case with any act that has passed Congress, it is assigned a public law (Pub. L.) number. Thereafter, it is given a United States statutes designation (citation) and becomes part of the United States Code (USC).

Legislative History. A considerable amount of the federal tax law for nonprofit organizations is found in the legislative history of these statutory laws. Most of this history is in congressional committee reports. Reports from committees in the House of Representatives are cited as "H. Rep." (see, e.g., Chapter 1, note 41); reports from committees in the Senate are cited as "S. Rep." (see, e.g., Chapter 1, n. 112); conference committee reports are cited as "H. Rep." The IRS wrote that committee reports are "useful tools in determining Congressional intent behind certain tax laws, and helping examiners apply the law properly."[1]

Transcripts of the debate on legislation, formal statements, and other items are printed in the Congressional Record (*"Cong. Rec."*). The Congressional Record is published every day one of the houses of Congress is in session and is cited as "____ *Cong. Rec.* ____ (daily ed., [date of issue])." The first number is the annual volume number; the second number is the page in the daily edition

---

1. Internal Revenue Manual (IRM) 4.75.13.6.2 § 3.

on which the item begins. Periodically, the daily editions of the Congressional Record are republished as a hardbound book and are cited as "____ *Cong. Rec.* ____ ([year])." As before, the first number is the annual volume number and the second is the beginning page number. The bound version of the Congressional Record then becomes the publication that contains the permanent citation for the item.

Internal Revenue Code. The Internal Revenue Code, the current version of which is the Internal Revenue Code of 1986, as amended, is the primary source of the federal tax law.[2] This Code is officially codified in Title 26 of the USC and referenced throughout this book as the "IRC" (see Chapter 1, note 2)). (The United States Code consists of 50 titles. The IRC imposes income, estate, gift, generation-skipping, excise, and employment taxes, and includes penalties and other provisions concerning the administration of federal taxation.

The IRC includes subtitles (of which there are 11), chapters, subchapters, parts, and sections. Code sections are divided into subsections, paragraphs, subparagraphs, and clauses.[3] The most relevant of the subtitles are the following:

Subtitle	**Contents**	**IRC Sections**
A	Income Taxes	1–1563
B	Estate and Gift Taxes	2001–2704
C	Employment Taxes	3101–3510
D	Excise Taxes	4041–5000
F	Procedure and Administration	6001–7873
G	Joint Committee on Taxation	8001–8023

Sections of the IRC are usually arranged in numerical order. When the IRS cites an IRC section, it does not usually reference the title, subtitle, chapter, subchapter, or part. It references a Code section as "IRC §" (as does this book). As noted, IRC sections are divided into subsections, paragraphs, subparagraphs, and clauses. For example, IRC § 170(b)(1)(A)(vi) is structured as follows:

1. IRC § 170—Code section, Arabic number

2. Subsection (b)—lowercase letter in parentheses

3. Paragraph (1)—Arabic number in parentheses

4. Subparagraph (A)—uppercase letter in parentheses

5. Clause (vi)—lowercase Roman numeral in parentheses

---

2. The IRS, in a peculiar understatement, advises its examiners that "[i]t is often necessary to cite Internal Revenue Code sections in reports and to taxpayers in support of a position on an issue" (IRM 4.75.13.6.1.2 § 1).
3. According to the IRS, this structure results in "ease of use" of the IRC (IRM 4.75.13.6.1 § 2).

Inasmuch as IRC sections are usually arranged in numerical order, this practice sometimes leads to the need to show a Code section number followed by a capital letter that is not in parentheses. An example of this is IRC § 409A. This came about because Congress created an IRC § that needed to immediately follow IRC § 409 and IRC § 410 already existed.[4]

The IRC is generally binding on the courts. As the IRS has written, the courts "give great importance to the literal language of the Code, but the language does not solve every tax controversy."[5] Thus, courts also consider the legislative history underlying a Code section, its relationship to other Code sections, tax regulations, and various IRS pronouncements.

(b) Executive Branch

A function of the Executive Branch in the United States is to administer and enforce the laws enacted by Congress. This "executive" function is performed by departments and agencies, and "independent" regulatory commissions (such as the Federal Trade Commission or the Securities and Exchange Commission). The federal tax laws are administered and enforced overall by the Department of the Treasury.

Tax Regulations. The Code of Federal Regulations ("CFR") is a codification of the general and permanent rules published in the Federal Register by the executive departments and agencies of the federal government (see, e.g., Chapter 6, note 99). The CFR is divided into 50 titles representing broad areas subject to federal regulation. Each title is divided into chapters that usually bear the name of the issuing agency. Each chapter is subdivided into parts covering specific regulatory areas. Title 26 of the CFR consists of the federal tax regulations.

One of the ways in which the Department of the Treasury executes its functions is by the promulgation of regulations ("Reg."), which are designed to interpret and amplify the related statute (see, e.g., Chapter 1, note 67). Treasury regulations are the official interpretations of the Department of the IRC; they follow the numbering sequence of IRC sections. Generally, tax regulations are subject to a public notice and comment process (see below).

Tax regulations are written by the Legislative and Regulations Division or Tax Exempt and Government Entities Office of Associate Chief Counsel (Technical), IRS; the Department of the Treasury must approve regulations for them to take effect. There are three classes of tax regulations:

- *Proposed regulations.* Proposed regulations provide guidance concerning the Treasury Department's interpretation of an IRC section but do not have authoritative weight (because they are in proposed form); thus they

---

4. IRC § 409A is a part of the federal tax law of employee benefits and can be applicable with respect to tax-exempt organizations.
5. IRM 4.75.13.6.1.

are not binding on taxpayers and IRS examiners. The public is accorded an opportunity to comment on a proposed regulation; a public hearing on the proposal may be held if sufficient written requests are received. Proposed regulations become effective when adopted by a Treasury Decision and become final regulations.

- *Temporary regulations.* Temporary regulations are often issued soon after a major statutory law change to provide guidance to the public and IRS employees with respect to procedural and computational matters. Temporary regulations are authoritative and have the same weight as final regulations. Public hearings are not held on temporary regulations.

- *Final regulations.* Final regulations are issued after public comments on the regulations in proposed form are evaluated. They supersede any temporary regulations on the point. A final regulation is effective as of the day it is published in the Federal Register as a Treasury Decision, unless otherwise stated.

Tax regulations (like other rules made by other government departments, agencies, and commissions) generally have the force of law, unless they are overly broad in relation to the accompanying statute or are unconstitutional, in which case they can be rendered void by a court. These regulations are not binding on courts; they are, however, binding on the IRS. If temporary and proposed regulations have been issued in connection with the same Code provision, and the texts of both are similar, examiners' positions should be based on the temporary regulations. If neither temporary nor final regulations have been issued, IRS examiners may use a proposed regulation to support a position; they should, however, indicate that the proposed regulation lacks authoritative weight but is the best (at least from the standpoint of the IRS) interpretation of the statutory law involved that is available. Regulations may apply only to a particular time period. Regulations do not always reflect changes in the law.

There are two types of final tax regulations: legislative and interpretative. The standard of review by a court applicable to a final regulation differs as between these types of regulations. A *legislative regulation* is a final regulation issued under a specific grant of congressional authority to prescribe a method of executing a statutory provision. In this instance, a Code provision will state: "The Secretary shall provide such regulations. . . ."[6] In contrast, an *interpretative regulation* is promulgated pursuant to the Treasury's general authority to prescribe regulations.[7] Courts accord a higher degree of deference to a legislative regulation than to an interpretative one.

The deference accorded a legislative regulation is so high that the regulation has controlling weight unless it is arbitrary, capricious, or manifestly contrary

---

6. E.g., Snap Drape, Inc. v. Comm'r, 98 F.3d 194 (5th Cir. 1996).
7. IRC § 7805(a).

to the underlying statute.[8] This standard of deference is sometimes referred to as the *Chevron deference*.[9] Thus, when reviewing a legislative regulation, a court "may not substitute its own construction of a statutory provision for a reasonable interpretation made by the administrator of an agency."[10]

The Administrative Procedure Act[11] (APA) requires federal government agencies to adhere to notice and comment procedures in the case of rules or regulations that are intended to have the force of law, but not in instances of "interpretative rules, general statements of policy, or rules of agency organization, procedure or practice."[12] This is a different dichotomy than the court-fashioned law referenced above.[13] Consequently, it would appear that all tax regulations, whether legislative or interpretative (as defined above), are substantive regulations to which the APA's notice and comment requirements apply.[14] Generally, as noted, the Department of the Treasury follows a notice and comment procedure with respect to its regulations. It has been suggested that the Department does this at its discretion, maintaining the position that tax regulations are merely "interpretative" for APA purposes and thus not subject to the APA notice and comment requirements.[15]

A tax regulation may be made retroactive; this type of regulation can be reviewed by a court for abuse of discretion. The IRS "does not have carte blanche" authority to issue retroactive regulations.[16] The efficacy of a retroactive regulation is tested against these factors: whether or to what extent the taxpayer justifiably relied on settled law or policy and whether or to what extent the putatively retroactive regulation alters that law or policy; the extent to which the prior law or policy has been implicitly approved by Congress, as

---

8. E.g., Chevron, U.S.A., Inc. v. Natural Resources Defense Council, Inc., 467 U.S. 837 (1984); Fransen v. United States, 191 F.3d 599 (5th Cir. 1999).
9. E.g., Belt v. EmCare, Inc., 444 F.3d 403, 416, note 35 (5th Cir. 2006); Klamath Strategic Investment Fund, LLC v. United States, 2007-1 U.S.T.C. ¶ 50,410 (E.D. Tex. 2007). In Klamath, the regulation at issue was held to be an interpretative regulation.
10. Chevron, U.S.A., Inc. v. Natural Resources Defense Council, Inc., 467 U.S. 837, 843-844 (1984). E.g., Littriello v. United States, 484 F.3d 372 (6th Cir. 2007) (holding that the check-the-box entity classification regulations [*Tax-Exempt Organizations* § 4.1(b)] are valid, using the *Chevron deference* standard).
11. 5 U.S.C. § 551.
12. *Id.* § 553(b).
13. The U.S. Tax Court wrote that, "[i]n the case of regulations, tax law has used a different basis to distinguish between legislative and interpretive rules" (Swallows Holding v. Commissioner, 126 T.C. 96, 176 (2006)).
14. E.g., Hickman, "Coloring Outside the Lines: Examining Treasury's (Lack of) Compliance with Administrative Procedure Act Rulemaking Requirements," 82 *Notre Dame L. Rev.* 1727 (2007); Cummings, Jr., "Treasury Violates the APA?," 117 *Tax Notes* 263 (Oct. 15, 2007).
15. Berg, "Judicial Deference to Tax Regulations: A Reconsideration in Light of *National Cable, Swallows Holding,* and Other Developments," 61 *Tax Law.* (No. 2) 481, 487, note 23 (Winter 2008).
16. Snap Drape, Inc. v. Comm'r, 98 F.3d 194, 202 (5th Cir. 1996).

by legislative reenactment of the pertinent Code provision(s); whether retroactivity would advance or frustrate the interest in equality of treatment among similarly situated taxpayers; and whether according retroactive effect would produce an inordinately harsh result.[17]

Revenue Rulings and Procedures. Within the Department of the Treasury is the Internal Revenue Service (IRS). The IRS is, among its many roles, a tax-collecting agency. The IRS, while headquartered in Washington, D.C. (its National Office), has regional and field offices throughout the country.

The IRS's jurisdiction over tax-exempt organizations is principally lodged within the office of the Director, Exempt Organizations, who is responsible for planning, managing, directing, and executing nationwide activities for exempt organizations. The Director reports to the Commissioner, Tax Exempt Entities/ Government Entities Division. The Director supervises the activities of the offices of Customer Education and Outreach, Rulings and Agreements, and Examinations.

The IRS (from its National Office) prepares and disseminates guidance in interpreting tax statutes and tax regulations. This guidance has the force of law, unless it is overly broad in relation to the statute and/or Treasury regulation involved, or is unconstitutional. The Internal Revenue Bulletin ("I.R.B."), published weekly, is the publication used by the IRS to announce official IRS rulings and procedures, and for publishing Treasury Decisions, Executive Orders, Tax Conventions, legislation, court decisions, and other items of general interest. Every six months, the I.R.B.s are republished as hardbound books, with the resulting publication termed the Cumulative Bulletin ("C.B.").

The C.B. is a consolidation of items of a permanent nature first published in the I.R.B.; it consists of four parts:

1. *Part I*—This part is divided into two subparts based on provisions of the IRC. Arrangement is sequential according to IRC and regulation sections. The Code section is shown at the top of each page.

2. *Part II*—This part is divided into two subparts, one concerning tax conventions and the other pertaining to legislation and related congressional committee reports.

3. *Part III*—This part concerns various administrative, procedural, and miscellaneous matters.

4. *Part IV*—The preambles and text of proposed regulations that were published in the Federal Register during the six-month period involved are printed in this part. Also included in this portion of the C.B. is a list of individuals disbarred or suspended from practice before the IRS.

---

17. E.g., Anderson, Clayton & Co. v. United States, 562 F.2d 972 (5th Cir. 1977); Klamath Strategic Investment Fund, LLC v. United States, 2007-1 U.S.T.C. ¶ 50,410 (E.D. Tex. 2007).

The IRS publishes in the I.R.B. all substantive rulings necessary to promote uniform application of the federal tax laws, including rulings that supersede, revoke, modify, or amend rulings previously published in the I.R.B. All published rulings apply retroactively, unless otherwise indicated. Procedures pertaining solely to matters of internal IRS management are not published in the I.R.B. Nonetheless, statements of internal practices and procedures that affect the rights and duties of taxpayers are so published.

IRS public determinations on a point of law usually are in the form of "revenue rulings" ("Rev. Rul.") (see, e.g., Chapter 3, note 29); those that are rules of procedure are termed "revenue procedures" ("Rev. Proc.") (see, e.g., Chapter 4, note 2). A Rev. Rul. represents the conclusion(s) of the IRS on application of the law to the facts stated in the ruling. Some Rev. Ruls. are based on positions taken by the IRS in private letter rulings or technical advice memoranda. A Rev. Proc. is issued to assist taxpayers in complying with procedural issues. The purpose of these rulings and procedures is to promote uniform application of the tax laws. IRS employees must follow them; taxpayers may rely on them or appeal their position to the courts. Revenue rulings and revenue procedures are almost never accorded a public notice and comment process.

Rev. Ruls. and Rev. Procs. that have an effect on previous rulings use the following terms to describe the effect:

- *Amplified* describes a situation where a change is not being made in a prior published position of the IRS but the prior position is being extended (amplified) to apply to a variation of the original fact situation.

- *Clarified* is used in instances where the language in a prior ruling is being made clearer because the original language has or may cause confusion.

- *Distinguished* describes a situation where a ruling makes reference to a previously published ruling and points out one or more essential differences between them.

- *Modified* is used where the substance of a previously published position is being changed.

- *Obsoleted* describes a previously published ruling that is not considered determinative with respect to future transactions. The term is most commonly used in a ruling that lists previously published rulings that are obsolete because of changes in the statutory law or regulations. A ruling may also be rendered obsolete because the substance of it has been included in subsequently adopted regulations.

- *Revoked* describes situations where the position of the IRS in a previously published ruling is not correct and the correct position is being stated in a new ruing.

- *Superseded* describes a situation where the new ruling does nothing more than restate the substance and situation of a previously published ruling or rulings. The term is used by the IRS when it is desirable to republish in a single ruling a series of situations and the like that were previously published over a period of time in separate rulings. If the new ruling does more than restate the substance of a prior ruling, a combination of terms is used. For example, *modified and superseded* describes a situation where the substance of a previously published ruling is being changed in part and is being continued without change in part, and the IRS desires to restate the valid portion of the previously published ruling in a new ruling that is self-contained. In this case, the previously published ruling is first modified and then, as modified, is superseded.

- *Supplemented* is used in situations in which a list is published in a ruling and that list is expanded by adding items in subsequent rulings. After the original ruling has been supplemented several times, a new ruling may be published that includes the list in the original ruling and the additions, and supersedes all prior rulings in the series.

- *Suspended* is used in rare situations to show that a previously published ruling will not be applied pending some future action, such as the issuance of new or amended regulations, the outcome of cases in litigation, or the outcome of an IRS study.

The IRS considers itself bound by its revenue rulings and revenue procedures. These determinations are the "law," particularly in the sense that the IRS regards them as precedential, although they are not binding on the courts. Rulings do not have the force and effect of regulations. In applying rulings, the effects of subsequent legislation, regulations, court decisions, and other rulings and procedures need to be considered.

Thus, as in the case of the IRS, not all agency determinations are in the form of regulations. Agencies charged with applying a statute "necessarily make all sorts of interpretive choices and . . . not all of those choices bind judges to follow them."[18] Even where not binding, these agency choices "certainly may influence courts facing questions the agencies have already answered," and, in this type of instance, the "fair measure of deference to an agency administering its own statute has been understood to vary with circumstances."[19] The weight given to an agency's interpretation in this context depends on the "degree of the agency's care, its consistency, formality, and relative expertness, and to the persuasiveness of the agency's position."[20] (This is known as *Skidmore defer-ence*.) It has been held that a revenue ruling is entitled to *Skidmore* (not *Chevron*) deference.[21] The same is the case with respect to a revenue procedure.[22]

---

18. United States v. Mead Corp., 533 U.S. 218, 227 (2001).
19. *Id.*
20. *Id.*, citing Skidmore v. Swift & Co., 323 U.S. 134 (1944).
21. Omohundro v. United States, 300 F.3d 1065 (9th Cir. 2002).
22. Tualatin Valley Builders Supply v. United States, 2008-1 U.S.T.C. ¶ 50,280 (9th Cir. 2008).

Other IRS Pronouncements. The IRS also issues forms of "public" law in the name of "notices" and "announcements," as well as "Delegation Orders." A notice or Delegation Order is initially published in the I.R.B. and then republished in the C.B. An announcement, however, although published in the I.R.B., is not republished in the C.B.

Announcements are public pronouncements on matters of general interest, such as the effective dates of temporary regulations, and clarification of rulings and form instructions. They are issued when guidance of a substantive or procedural nature is needed quickly. Announcements can be relied on to the same extent as revenue rulings and revenue procedures, when they include specific language to that effect. Announcements are identified by a two-digit number, representing the year involved, and a sequence number (e.g., Ann. 2008-25). Notices are public announcements that are identified in the same manner as announcements (e.g., Notice 2008-50).

Commissioner Delegation Orders formally delegate, by the Commissioner of Internal Revenue, authority to perform certain tasks or make certain decisions to specified employees of the IRS. Agreements entered into by IRS personnel pursuant to these orders are binding on taxpayers and the agency. Delegation Orders are identified by a number, sometimes followed by a revision date (e.g., Del. Order 250).

The IRS issues plain-language publications to explain aspects of the federal tax law. They typically highlight changes in the law, provide examples of IRS positions, and include worksheets. These publications, which do not necessarily cover all positions for a given issue, are not binding on the IRS. While a good source of general information, IRS examiners are not supposed to cite to these publications in support of a position.

Private Determinations. By contrast to these forms of "public" law, the IRS (again from its National Office) also issues "private" or nonprecedential determinations. These documents principally are private letter rulings and technical advice memoranda. As a matter of law, these determinations may not be cited as legal authority.[23] Nonetheless, these pronouncements can be valuable in understanding IRS thinking on a point of law and, in practice (the statutory prohibition notwithstanding), these documents are cited as IRS positions on issues, such as in court opinions,[24] articles, and books.

The IRS issues private letter rulings in response to written questions (termed *ruling requests*) submitted to the IRS by individuals and organizations. An IRS district office may refer a case to the IRS National Office for advice (termed *technical advice*); the resulting advice is provided to the IRS district office in the form of a technical advice memorandum. In the course of preparing a revenue ruling, private letter ruling, or technical advice memorandum, the IRS

---

23. IRC § 6110(k)(3).
24. E.g., Glass v. Comm'r, 471 F.3d 698 (6th Cir. 2006); Woods Investment Co. v. Comm'r, 85 T.C. 274, 281, n. 15 (1985).

National Office may seek legal advice from its Office of Chief Counsel; the resulting advice was provided, until recently, in the form of general counsel memorandum. These documents are eventually made public, albeit in redacted form. The chief counsel advice memorandum has replaced the general counsel memorandum.

Private letter rulings and technical advice memoranda are identified by seven- or nine-digit numbers, as in "Priv. Ltr. Rul. 201026007" (see, e.g., Chapter 3, note 115; Chapter 4, note 138). The first two (or four) numbers are for the year involved (here, 2010), the next two numbers reflect the week of the calendar year involved (here, the twenty-sixth week of 2010), and the remaining three numbers identify the document as issued sequentially during the particular week (here, this private letter ruling was the seventh one issued during the week involved).

The agency has, pursuant to court order,[25] also commenced issuance of rulings denying or revoking tax-exempt status. These exemption denial and revocation letters initially were identified by eight numbers, followed by an *E* (see, e.g., Chapter 4, note 11). This practice was discontinued by the IRS, however; these letters are now being issued as private letter rulings.

(c) Judiciary

The federal court system has three levels; trial courts (including those that initially hear cases where a formal trial is not involved), courts of appeal ("appellate" courts), and the U.S. Supreme Court. The trial courts include the various federal district courts (at least one in each state, the District of Columbia, and the U.S. territories), the U.S. Tax Court,[26] and the U.S. Court of Federal Claims.[27] There are 13 federal appellate courts (the U.S. Court of Appeals for the First through the Eleventh Circuits, the U.S. Court of Appeals for the District of Columbia, and the U.S. Court of Appeals for the Federal Circuit).

Cases involving tax-exempt organization issues at the federal level can originate in any federal district court, the U.S. Tax Court, and the U.S. Court of Federal Claims. Under a special declaratory judgment procedure available only to charitable organizations and farmers' cooperatives,[28] cases can originate only with the U.S. District Court for the District of Columbia, the U.S. Tax Court, and the U.S. Court of Federal Claims. Cases involving tax-exempt organizations are considered by the U.S. Courts of Appeals and the U.S. Supreme Court.

---

25. Tax Analysts v. Internal Revenue Service, 350 F.3d 100 (D.C. Cir. 2003) (see *The Law of Tax-Exempt Organizations* § 28.8(a)(ii), text accompanied by notes 245–252).
26. The Tax Court was created in 1942; its predecessor was the Board of Tax Appeals. Some B.T.A. decisions still retain precedential value.
27. This court was created (renamed) in 1982; its predecessor was the U.S. Claims Court.
28. IRC § 7428.

Most opinions emanating from a U.S. district court are published by the West Publishing Company in the "Federal Supplement" series ("F. Supp." or "F. Supp. 2d"). Thus, a citation to one of these opinions appears as "___ F. Supp. ___" or "___ Supp. 2d ___," followed by an identification of the court and the year of the opinion. The first number is the annual volume number, the other number is the page in the book on which the opinion begins (see, e.g., Chapter 1, note 78). Some district court opinions appear sooner in Commerce Clearinghouse or Prentice Hall publications (see, e.g., Chapter 3, note 2); occasionally, these publications will contain opinions that are never published in the Federal Supplement series.

Most opinions emanating from a U.S. court of appeals are published by the West Publishing Company in the "Federal Reporter" series (usually "F.2d" or "F.3d"). Thus, a citation to one of these opinions appears as "___ F.2d ___" or "___ F.3d ___," followed by an identification of the court and the year of the opinion. The first number is the annual volume number; the other number is the page in the book on which the opinion begins (see, e.g., Chapter 1, note 75). Appellate court opinions appear sooner in Commerce Clearinghouse or Prentice Hall publications (see, e.g., Chapter 3, note 158); occasionally these publications contain opinions that are never published in the Federal Second or Federal Third series. Opinions from the U.S. Court of Federal Claims are also published in the Federal Second or Federal Third.

Opinions from the U.S. Tax Court are published by the U.S. government (Government Printing Office) and are usually in the form of "regular opinions" and cited as "___ T.C. ___," followed by the year of the opinion (see, e.g., Chapter 3, note 2). Some Tax Court opinions that are of lesser precedential value (because they primarily involve determinations of fact and application of well-established rules of law) are published by the federal government as "memorandum decisions" and are cited as "___ T.C.M. ___" followed by the year of the opinion (see, e.g., Chapter 3, n. 129). As always, the first number of these citations is the annual volume number; the second number is the page in the book on which the opinion begins. Commercial publishers publish regular opinions and memorandum decisions.

U.S. district court and Tax Court opinions may be appealed to the appropriate U.S. court of appeals. For example, cases in the states of Maryland, North Carolina, South Carolina, Virginia, and West Virginia are appealable (from either court) to the U.S. Court of Appeals for the Fourth Circuit. Cases from any federal appellate or district court, the U.S. Tax Court, and the U.S. Court of Federal Claims may be appealed to the U.S. Supreme Court.

District courts must follow the decisions of the court of appeals for the circuit in which they are located. If the court of appeals that is potentially involved in a case has not rendered a decision on a particular issue, the district court may reach its own decision or follow the decision of another circuit court that has rendered a decision on the issue. A circuit court is not bound by a decision of another circuit court.

The U.S. Supreme Court usually has discretion as to whether to accept a case.[29] This decision is manifested as a *writ of certiorari*. When the Supreme Court agrees to hear a case, it grants the writ (*"cert. gr."*); otherwise, it denies the writ (*"cert. den."*) (see, e.g., Chapter 3, note 6).

In this book, citations to Supreme Court opinions are to the "United States Reports" series, published by the U.S. government, when available ("___U.S. ___," followed by the year of the opinion) (see, e.g., Chapter 1, note 27). When the United States Reports series citation is not available, the "Supreme Court Reporter" series, published by the West Publishing Company, reference is used ("___ S. Ct. ___," followed by the year of the opinion) (see. e.g., Chapter 10, note 55). As always, the first number of these citations is the annual volume number; the second number is the page in the book or which the opinion begins. There is a third way to cite Supreme Court cases, which is by means of the "United States Supreme Court Reports—Lawyers Edition" series, published by The Lawyers Co-Operative Publishing Company and the Bancroft-Whitney Company, but that form of citation is not used in this book. Supreme Court opinions appear earlier in the Commerce Clearinghouse or Prentice Hall publications.

In most instances, court opinions are available on Westlaw and LEXIS in advance of formal publication.

Decisions made at various levels of the court system are considered to be interpretations of the tax laws and may be used by examiners and taxpayers to support a position. Some court opinions lend more weight to a position than others. An opinion emanating from a case decided by the U.S. Supreme Court becomes the "law of the land" and takes precedence over decisions of lower courts. The IRS must follow Supreme Court decisions. In that sense, Supreme Court decisions have the same weight as the IRC. Decisions made by lower courts are binding on the IRS only for the particular taxpayer and the years litigated. Adverse decisions of lower courts do not require the IRS to alter its position for other taxpayers.

Action on Decisions. It is the policy of the IRS to announce at an early date whether it will follow the holding(s) in certain court cases; such an announcement is an Action on Decision ("AOD"). An AOD is issued at the discretion of the IRS only on unappealed issues that have been decided adverse to the position of the government. Generally, an AOD is issued when guidance would be helpful to IRS personnel working with the same or similar issues. Unlike a tax regulation or a revenue ruling, an AOD is not an affirmative statement of the IRS's position. It is not intended to serve as guidance to the public and is not to be cited as precedent.

---

29. The IRS observed that "[o]nly a limited number of tax cases are heard" by the Court (IRM 4.75.13.6.8.6 § 1).

An AOD may be relied on within the IRS only as to the conclusion, applying the law to the facts in the particular case at the time the AOD was issued. IRS examiners are to exercise caution when extending the recommendation of an AOD to another case, where the facts may be different. An AOD may be superseded by legislation, regulations, rulings, court opinions, or a subsequent AOD.

An AOD may state that the IRS acquiesces in the holding of a court in a case and that the IRS will follow it in disposing of cases with the same facts; this *acquiescence* indicates neither approval nor disapproval of the reasons relied on by the court for its conclusions. An *acquiescence in result only* indicates IRS disagreement or concern with some or all of those reasons. *Nonacquiescence* signifies that, although no further review was sought, the IRS does not agree with the holding of the court and generally will not follow it in disposing of cases involving other taxpayers. With respect to an opinion of a circuit court of appeals, a nonacquiescence indicates that the IRS will not follow the holding on a nationwide basis; the IRS will, however, recognize the precedential impact of the opinion on cases arising within the venue of the deciding circuit court.

AODs are published in the I.R.B. and thereafter in the appropriate C.B. An examiner is required to include in the citation to a court opinion any acquiescence ("acq."), acquiescence in result only ("acq. in result"), or nonacquiescence ("nonacq.").

§ 2 STATE LAW

(a) Legislative Branches

Statutory laws in the various states are created by their legislatures. There are no specific references to state statutory laws in this book (although most, if not all, of the states have such forms of law relating, directly or indirectly, to tax-exempt organizations).

(b) Executive Branches

The rules and regulations published at the state level emanate from state departments, agencies, and the like. For tax-exempt organizations, these departments are usually the office of the state's attorney general and the state's department of state. There are no specific references to state rules and regulations in this book.

(c) Judiciary

Each of the states has a judiciary system, usually a three-tiered one modeled after the federal system. Cases involving nonprofit organizations are heard in all of these courts. There are no references to state court opinions in this book (although most, if not all, of the states have court opinions relating, directly or indirectly, to tax-exempt organizations).

State court opinions are published by the governments of each state and the principal ones by the West Publishing Company. The latter sets of opinions are published in "Reporters" relating to court developments in various regions throughout the country. For example, the *Atlantic Reporter* contains court opinions issued by the principal courts in the states of Connecticut, Delaware, Maine, Maryland, New Hampshire, New Jersey, Pennsylvania, Rhode Island, and Vermont, and the District of Columbia, while the *Pacific Reporter* contains court opinions issued by the principal courts of Arizona, California, Colorado, Idaho, Kansas, Montana, Nevada, New Mexico, Oklahoma, Oregon, Utah, Washington, and Wyoming.

§ 3 PUBLICATIONS

Articles, of course, are not forms of the "law." They can be cited, however, particularly by courts, in the development of the law. Also, as research tools, they contain useful summaries of the applicable law. In addition to the many law school "law review" publications, the following periodicals (not an inclusive list) contain material that is of help in following developments concerning tax-exempt organizations:

Advancing Philanthropy (Association of Fundraising Professionals)
Bruce R. Hopkins' Nonprofit Counsel (John Wiley & Sons, Inc.)
The Chronicle of Philanthropy
Daily Tax Report (Bureau of National Affairs, Inc.)
Exempt Organization Tax Review (Tax Analysts)
Foundation News (Council on Foundations)
Giving USA (Center on Philanthropy, Indiana University)
The Journal of Taxation (Warren, Gorham & Lamont)
The Journal of Taxation of Exempt Organizations (Faulkner & Gray)
The Philanthropy Monthly (Non-Profit Reports, Inc.)
Tax Law Review (Rosenfeld Launer Publications)
The Tax Lawyer (American Bar Association)
Tax Notes (Tax Analysts)
Taxes (Commerce Clearinghouse, Inc.)

Federal Election Campaign Laws and Tax-Exempt Organizations (New)

*p. 1171. Insert following existing material:

The federal election campaign law,[1] which has considerable applicability to tax-exempt organizations, is embodied in the Federal Election Campaign Act of 1971, as amended,[2] and augmented by rules promulgated by the Federal Election Commission[3] and court opinions, including several from the U.S. Supreme Court. This body of statutory law was substantially amended by enactment of the Bipartisan Campaign Reform Act of 2002.[4]

---

1. 2 U.S.C. Chapter 14.
2. 2 U.S.C. § 431 *et seq.* Also 2 U.S.C. § 431(19). Hereinafter "FECA."
3. See § 3.
4. Pub. L. No. 107-155, 107th Cong., 2nd Sess. (2002); 116 Stat. 81. Hereinafter "BCRA."

§ 1 FEDERAL ELECTION LAW INTRODUCTION

Participation in the electoral process—whether by individuals, for-profit corporations, tax-exempt organizations, or other entities—entails forms of political speech, thus implicating the free speech principles of the First Amendment.[5] Ample tension between free speech principles and regulation of political campaign activity has existed since the outset of this type of statutory law. Particularly contentious have been limitations on contributions and expenditures for political purposes.

The BCRA is the most recent federal enactment designed to "purge national politics of what was conceived to be the pernicious influence of 'big money' campaign contributions."[6] The first of these enactments, in 1907, completely banned corporate contributions of money in connection with a federal election. This law was extended in 1925, 1942, 1947, 1971 (FECA), and 1974.[7]

The Supreme Court in 1976 characterized this body of law as an "intricate statutory scheme."[8] These rules were made more complex in 2002, with enactment of the BCRA. The Court wrote that "BCRA's central provisions are designed to address Congress' concerns about the increasing use of soft money and issue advertising to influence federal elections."[9]

The Supreme Court upheld nearly all of the 2002 enactment, in response to free speech and other challenges, as being constitutional on its face.[10] Yet, this decision was initially misunderstood in some quarters, in that this action by the Court did not immunize this body of law from lawsuits asserting unconstitutionality of it when applied to a specific set of facts—known as *as-applied* challenges.[11]

---

5. See § 2.
6. United States v. Automobile Workers, 352 U.S. 567, 572 (1957).
7. The history of the federal campaign legislation is traced in McConnell v. Federal Election Comm'n, 540 U.S. 93, 115–132 (2003). The Court as constituted in 2003 seemed quite enamored with this law (see, e.g., text accompanied by *infra* note 9), noting that "Congress continued its steady improvement of the national election laws by enacting FECA" (*id*. at 117).
8. Buckley v. Valeo, 424 U.S. 1, 12 (1976).
9. McConnell v. Federal Election Comm'n, 540 U.S. 93, 132 (2003).
10. McConnell v. Federal Election Comm'n, 540 U.S. 93 (2003).
11. In the first of these as-applied challenges in the election law context, which contested the constitutionality of a ban on certain electioneering communications (see § 8), the Court held that, "[i]n upholding [this ban] against a facial challenge, we did not purport to resolve future as-applied challenges" (Wisconsin Right to Life, Inc. v. Federal Election Comm'n, 546 U.S. 410, 411–412 (2006)).

The IRS is of the view that a tax-exempt organization that violates the regulatory requirements of the Federal Election Campaign Act may well "jeopardize its exemption or be subject to other tax consequences."[12]

§ 2 FREE SPEECH PRINCIPLES OVERVIEW

The First Amendment to the U.S. Constitution provides, in part, that "Congress shall make no law . . . abridging the freedom of speech." Inasmuch as various ways in which to participate in federal (and state and local) election campaigns constitute speech, an initial conclusion might be that all statutes regulating the campaign process are unconstitutional. But the courts have never taken this "absolutist" approach. Today, the constitutional power of Congress to regulate federal elections is well established.

(a) General Free Speech Principles in Political Context

Nonetheless, free speech (and other constitutional) principles still obtain. Thus, the constitutional law questions that arise go to the issue of whether the "specific legislation that Congress has enacted interferes with First Amendment freedoms or invidiously discriminates against nonincumbent candidates and minor parties in contravention of the Fifth Amendment."[13]

Indeed, federal election law limitations "operate in an area of the most fundamental First Amendment activities," in that "[d]iscussion of public issues and debate on the qualification of candidates are integral to the operation of the system of government established by our Constitution."[14] The First Amendment affords the broadest protection to such political expression in order to "assure [the] unfettered interchange of ideas for the bringing about of political and social changes desired by the people."[15] Although First Amendment protections are not confined to the "exposition of ideas,"[16] there is "practically universal agreement that a major purpose of that Amendment was to protect the free discussion of governmental affairs, . . . of course include[ing] discussions of candidates."[17] This no more than reflects U.S. society's "profound national commitment to the principle that debate on public issues should be

---

12. Rev. Rul. 2004-6, 2004-1 C.B. 328; IR-2003-146. The federal election law, however, states that "[n]othing in this subsection [concerning electioneering communications] may be construed to establish, modify, or otherwise affect the definition of political activities or electioneering activities (including the definition of participating in, intervening in, or influencing or attempting to influence a political campaign on behalf of or in opposition to any candidate for public office) for purposes of the Internal Revenue Code of 1986." 2 U.S.C. § 434(f)(7).
13. Buckley v. Valeo, 424 U.S. 1, 14 (1976).
14. Id.
15. Roth v. United States, 354 U.S. 476, 484 (1957).
16. Winters v. New York, 333 U.S. 507, 510 (1948).
17. Mills v. Alabama, 384 U.S. 214, 218 (1966).

uninhibited, robust, and wide-open."[18] "In a republic where the people are sovereign," the Court wrote, the "ability of the citizenry to make informed choices among candidates for office is essential, for the identities of those who are elected will inevitably shape the course that we follow as a nation."[19] The Court observed that it can "hardly be doubted that the constitutional guarantee has its fullest and most urgent application precisely to the conduct of campaigns for political office."[20]

The First Amendment protects political association as well as political expression. The constitutional right of association stemmed from the Court's recognition that "[e]ffective advocacy of both public and private points of view, particularly controversial ones, is undeniably enhanced by group association."[21] The First (and Fourteenth) Amendment guarantees "freedom to associate with others for the common advancement of political briefs and ideas," a freedom that encompasses the "right to associate with the political party of one's choice."[22]

The framework for analysis of a campaign finance law is first to determine whether it burdens political speech; then, if it does, to determine whether the burden is justified by a compelling state interest; then, if it is, to determine whether the restriction is sufficiently narrowly tailored to achieve the particular goal.[23] As to the second prong, the Supreme Court has recognized a strong governmental interest in combating corruption and the appearance of corruption.[24] On one occasion, the Court wrote that "[p]reventing corruption or the appearance of corruption are the only legitimate and compelling government interests thus far identified for restricting campaign finances."[25] This rationale, then, is always invoked when limitations on contributions and expenditures are reviewed.[26] A federal court of appeals, however, stated that the Court has "emphasized that the anti-corruption rationale is not boundless,"[27] noting the Court's observation that the core corruption that government may

---

18. New York Times Co. v. Sullivan, 376 U.S. 254, 270 (1964).
19. Buckley v. Valeo, 424 U.S. 1, 14–15 (1976).
20. Monitor Patriot Co. v. Roy, 401 U.S. 265, 272 (1971).
21. NAACP v. Alabama, 357 U.S. 449, 460 (1958).
22. Kusper v. Pontikes, 414 U.S. 51, 56, 57 (1973), quoted in Cousins v. Wigoda, 419 U.S. 477, 487 (1975).
23. NAACP v. Button, 371 U.S. 415, 438 (1963); Williams v. Rhodes, 393 U.S. 23, 31 (1968); Buckley v. Valeo, 424 U.S. 1, 44–45 (1976); Federal Election Comm'n v. Massachusetts Citizens for Life, Inc., 479 U.S. 238, 252 (1986); Austin v. Michigan State Chamber of Commerce, 494 U.S. 652, 660 (1990).
24. E.g., Buckley v. Valeo, 424 U.S. 1, 26–27 (1976); McConnell v. Federal Election Comm'n, 540 U.S. 93, 154 (2003).
25. Davis v. Federal Election Comm'n, 128 S. Ct. 2759 (2008).
26. See § 2(b).
27. EMILY's List v. Federal Election Comm'n, 581 F.3d 1, 6 (D.C. Cir. 2009).

permissibly target with campaign finance regulation is the "financial *quid pro quo*: dollars for political favors."[28]

(b) Contribution and Expenditure Limitations

Campaign contributions and expenditures are forms of *speech* within the protection of the First Amendment. The Supreme Court wrote that "contribution and expenditure limitations operate in an area of the most fundamental First Amendment activities."[29] A federal appellate court wrote that the Court "has never strayed from that cardinal tenet, notwithstanding some passionate objections."[30]

Another overarching principle in this context is that government cannot limit campaign contributions and expenditures to achieve *equalization*—that is, it cannot restrict the speech of some so that others might have equal voice or influence in the electoral process. Thus, the Supreme Court stated that the "concept that government may restrict the speech of some elements of our society in order to enhance the relative voice of others is wholly foreign to the First Amendment."[31] The Court added that the government's interest in "equalizing the relative ability of individuals and groups to influence the outcome of elections" does not justify regulation.[32]

As discussed, the government's interest in precluding corruption is the rationale underlying limitations on contributions and expenditures.[33] This anticorruption interest is, of course, implicated by contributions to *candidates*. Thus, the Court wrote that, "[t]o the extent that large contributions are given to secure a political *quid pro quo* from current and potential office holders, the integrity of our system of representative democracy is undermined."[34] Later, the Court

---

28. Federal Election Comm'n v. Nat'l Conservative PAC, 470 U.S. 480, 497 (1985).
29. Buckley v. Valeo, 424 U.S. 1, 14 (1976). On this point, *Buckley* is the "foundational case." EMILY's List v. Federal Election Comm'n, 581 F.3d 1, 5 (D.C. Cir. 2009).
30. EMILY's List v. Federal Election Comm'n, 581 F.3d 1, 5 (D.C. Cir. 2009). One of these objections is in a concurring opinion in Nixon v. Shrink Missouri Gov't PAC, where it was written that "[m]oney is property; it is not speech" (528 U.S. 377, 398 (2000)).
31. Buckley v. Valeo, 424 U.S. 1, 48–49 (1976).
32. *Id.* at 48. A classic example of this precept occurred when the Supreme Court rendered unconstitutional the so-called *millionaires amendment*, which was applicable in instances where wealthy individuals finance their campaigns. This law provided for a series of staggered increases in otherwise applicable contribution-to-candidate limits if the candidate's opponent spent a triggering amount of his or her personal funds (2 U.S.C. § 441a(i)). Also, coordinated expenditure limits were eliminated in certain circumstances (*id.*). This law was struck down because it "imposes an unprecedented penalty on any candidate who robustly exercises" free speech rights (Davis v. Federal Election Comm'n, 128 S. Ct. 2759, 2771 (2008)). Rich candidates, wrote the Court, must, under this law, "choose between the First Amendment right to engage in unfettered political speech and subjection to discriminatory fundraising limitations" (*id.*).
33. See § 2(a).
34. Buckley v. Valeo, 424 U.S. 1, 26–27 (1976).

stated that, in its 1976 opinion, it "identified a single narrow exception to the rule that limits on political activity were contrary to the First Amendment": The exception relates "to the perception of undue influence of large contributors to a *candidate*."[35]

A federal appellate court wrote that, "[b]ased on the close relationship between candidates and parties and record evidence demonstrating that political parties sold access to candidates in exchange for contributions, the [Supreme] Court has held that the anti-corruption interest also justifies limits on contributions to *parties*."[36] From the outset of the Court's election law jurisprudence, it has taken the position that Congress was "surely entitled" to conclude that "contribution ceilings were a necessary legislative concomitant to deal with the reality or appearance of corruption inherent in a system permitting unlimited financial contributions" (even where adequate disclosure is required).[37] It has written that contribution limitations "in themselves do not undermine to any material degree the potential for robust and effective discussion of candidates and campaign issues by individual citizens, associations, the institutional press, candidates, and political parties."[38] Contribution limits on individuals are constitutional, in that the "weighty interests served by restricting the size of financial contributions to political candidates are sufficient to justify the limited effect upon First Amendment freedoms caused" by such a limit.[39] Contribution limits on political committees are justified; they "serve the permissible purpose of preventing individuals from evading the applicable contribution limitations by labeling themselves committees."[40]

In applying this anti-corruption rationale, the Court has "afforded stronger protection to *expenditures* by citizens and groups (for example, for advertisements, get-out-the-vote efforts, and voter registration activities) than it has provided to their *contributions* to candidates or parties."[41] The Court "has explained that contributions to a candidate or party pose a greater risk of *quid pro quo* corruption than do expenditures."[42] At the same time, the Court "has stated that limits on contributions to candidates or parties pose only a 'marginal restriction upon the contributor's ability to engage in free communication.'"[43]

---

35. Citizens Against Rent Control v. City of Berkeley, 454 U.S. 290, 296–297 (1981).
36. EMILY's List v. Federal Election Comm'n, 158 F.3d 1, 6 (D.C. Cir. 2009), referencing McConnell v. Federal Election Comm'n, 540 U.S. 93, 154 (2003).
37. Buckley v. Valeo, 424 U.S. 1, 28 (1976).
38. *Id.* at 29.
39. *Id.*
40. *Id.* at 35–36.
41. EMILY's List v. Federal Election Comm'n, 581 F.3d 1, 6 (D.C. Cir. 2009).
42. *Id.* at 6–7, referencing Buckley v. Valeo, 424 U.S. 1, 46–47 (1978).
43. EMILY's List v. Federal Election Comm'n, 581 F.3d 1, 7 (D.C. Cir. 2009), referencing Buckley v. Valeo, 424 U.S. 1, 20–21 (1976).

By contrast, expenditure limitations limit "political expression at the core of our electoral process and of the First Amendment freedoms."[44] A "restriction on the amount of money a person or group can spend on political communication during a campaign necessarily reduces the quantity of expression by restricting the number of issues discussed, the depth of their exploration, and the size of the audience reached."[45] Originally, the Court stated that, in order to preserve a limitation on political expenditures, it must be construed to apply only to expenditures for "communications that in express terms advocate the election or defeat of a clearly identified candidate for federal office."[46] In summary, the Court's jurisprudence in this regard reflects a "fundamental constitutional difference between money *spent* to advertise one's views independently of the candidate's campaign and money *contributed* to the candidate to be spent on his campaign."[47]

The Court has been "somewhat more tolerant of regulation of for-profit corporations and labor unions," permitting "statutory limits on contributions that for-profit corporations and unions make from their general treasuries to candidates and parties."[48] Also, the Court has upheld laws that prohibit for-profit corporations and unions from making expenditures for activities expressly advocating the election or defeat of a federal candidate,"[49] permitting these expenditure limits on the ground that they restrain the "corrosive and distorting effects of immense aggregations of wealth that are accumulated with the help of the corporate form and that have little or no correlation to the public's support for the corporation's political ideas."[50]

A federal appellate court summed up this aspect of the law this way:

> In reconciling the competing interests, the Supreme Court has generally approved statutory limits on *contributions* to candidates and political parties as consistent with the First Amendment. The Court has rejected *expenditure* limits on individuals, groups, candidates, and parties, even though expenditures may confer benefits on candidates. And the Court has upheld limits on for-profit corporations' and unions' use of their general treasury funds to make campaign contributions to candidates or political parties or to make expenditures for activities expressly advocating the election or defeat of federal candidates.[51]

---

44. Buckley v. Valeo, 424 U.S. 1, 39 (1976).
45. *Id*. at 19.
46. *Id*. at 44.
47. Federal Election Comm'n v. Nat'l Conservative PAC, 470 U.S. 480, 497 (1985) (emphases added). Also Randall v. Sorrell, 548 U.S. 230, 241–242 (2006).
48. EMILY's List v. Federal Election Comm'n, 44 F.3d 1, 7 (D.C. Cir. 2009).
49. *Id*. at 7–8.
50. Austin v. Michigan State Chamber of Commerce, 494 U.S. 652, 660 (1990). Also McConnell v. Federal Election Comm'n, 540 U.S. 93, 204–205 (2003). Cf. First Nat'l Bank of Boston v. Bellotti, 435 U.S. 765, 776–777 (1978).
51. EMILY's List v. Federal Election Comm'n, 581 F.3d 1, 8 (D.C. Cir. 2009).

§ 3   FEDERAL ELECTION COMMISSION

The Federal Election Commission[52] administers and formulates policy with respect to the federal election campaign laws.[53] The powers of the FEC include the development of implementing rules and forms, conduct of investigations and hearings, rendering of advisory opinions, maintenance of an Internet-based repository of election reports, and initiation of litigation.[54]

§ 4   POLITICAL COMMITTEES

The federal election law addresses the matter of political committees[55] and their organization. A principal requirement is that a political committee must have a functioning treasurer; contributions and expenditures may not occur in the absence of this officer.[56] An expenditure may not be made for or on behalf of a political committee without the authorization of the treasurer or his or her agent.[57] Accounting requirements apply to political committees and authorized political committees,[58] as well as record-keeping and records preservation requirements.[59] Candidates for federal office must designate a political committee to serve as the principal campaign committee of the candidate.[60]

Authorized campaign committees, separate segregated funds, and other political committees are required to timely file statements of organization with the FEC.[61] The law stipulates the contents of these statements[62] and provides a termination procedure.[63] Treasurers of political committees must timely file reports of receipts and disbursements.[64] The types of reports to be filed depends on whether the committee is the principal campaign committee of a candidate for the House of Representatives or Senate, the principal campaign committee of a candidate for the U.S. presidency, or other political committee.[65] The election law stipulates the contents of these reports.[66]

---

52. 2 U.S.C. §§ 431(10), 437c(a)(1). Hereinafter "FEC."
53. 2 U.S.C. § 437c(b)(1).
54. 2 U.S.C. §§ 437d, 437f, 437h, 438, 438a.
55. A *political committee* is (1) a group of persons that receives contributions in excess of $1,000 during a calendar year or that makes expenditures in excess of $1,000 during a calendar year, (2) a separate segregated fund (see § 13), or (3) certain local committees of a political party. 2 U.S.C. § 431(4).
56. 2 U.S.C. § 432(a).
57. *Id.*
58. An *authorized committee* is a political committee authorized by a candidate to receive contributions or make expenditures on behalf of the candidate. 2 U.S.C. § 431(6).
59. 2 U.S.C. § 432(b)–(d).
60. 2 U.S.C. § 432(e).
61. 2 U.S.C. § 433(a).
62. 2 U.S.C. § 433(b).
63. 2 U.S.C. § 433(d).
64. 2 U.S.C. § 434(a)(1).
65. 2 U.S.C. § 434(a)(2).
66. 2 U.S.C. § 434(b).

Every person, other than a political committee, who makes independent expenditures,[67] in an amount or value in excess of $250 in the course of a calendar year, must file with the FEC a statement of contributions received.[68] Every person who makes a disbursement for the direct costs of producing and airing electioneering communications[69] in an amount in excess of $10,000 during a calendar year must timely file a statement with the FEC.[70]

§ 5 LIMITATIONS ON CONTRIBUTIONS

In general, a person[71] may not make contributions[72] to (1) any candidate and his or her authorized political committees with respect to an election for federal office that exceed $2,000; (2) the political committees established and maintained by a national political party, that are not the authorized political committees of a candidate, in any calendar year that exceed $25,000; (3) a political committee established and maintained by a state committee of a political party in a calendar year that exceed $10,000; or (4) any other political committee in a calendar year that exceed $5,000.[73] Other limitations apply with respect to contributions by multicandidate political committees.[74] Some of these limitations are indexed for inflation.[75]

All contributions made by political committees established, financed, maintained, or controlled by a corporation are considered to have been made by a single political committee.[76] In a case where a corporation establishes, finances, maintains, or controls more than one separate segregated fund, all such funds are treated as a single segregated fund for purposes of the limitations on contributions.[77] For contribution limitation purposes, all contributions made by a person, either directly or indirectly, on behalf of a candidate, including contributions that are in any way earmarked or otherwise directed through an

---

67. An *independent expenditure* is an expenditure by a person expressly advocating the election or defeat of a clearly identified candidate, that is not made in concert or cooperation with or at the request or suggestion of the candidate, the candidate's authorized political committee, or a political party committee. 2 U.S.C. § 431(17), (18).
68. 2 U.S.C. § 434(c).
69. See § 8.
70. 2 U.S.C. § 434(f).
71. The term *person* includes an individual, partnership, committee, association, corporation, labor organization, or any other organization or group of persons but does not include the federal government or any authority of the federal government. 2 U.S.C. § 431(11).
72. The term *contribution* generally includes (1) a gift, subscription, loan, advance, or deposit of money or anything of value when made by any person for the purpose of influencing any election for federal office; or (2) the payment by any person of compensation for the personal services of another person that are rendered to a political committee without charge. 2 U.S.C. § 431(8).
73. 2 U.S.C. § 441a(a)(1).
74. 2 U.S.C. § 441a(a)(2).
75. 2 U.S.C. § 441a(c).
76. 2 U.S.C. § 441a(a)(5).
77. *Id.*

intermediary or conduit to such candidate, are treated as contributions from the person to the candidate.[78] The intermediary or conduit must report the original source and the intended recipient of the contributions to the Federal Election Commission and the intended recipient.[79]

Restrictions are placed on the amount of total contributions that can be made over a two-year period. From the period that begins on January 1 of an odd-numbered year and ends on December 31 of the next even-numbered year, an individual may not make contributions to candidates and the authorized committees of candidates aggregating more than $37,500.[80] For that same time period, an individual may not make contributions aggregating more than $57,500, in the case of other contributions, of which not more than $37,500 may be attributable to contributions to political committees that are not political committees of national political parties.[81]

§ 6   CORPORATE CONTRIBUTIONS AND EXPENDITURES

Corporations, including labor organizations,[82] are generally prohibited from making a contribution or expenditure in connection with a federal election.[83] These rules are applicable to tax-exempt, nonprofit advocacy corporations.[84] The Supreme Court, however, held that these financing restrictions are unconstitutional as applied[85] to advertisements that an exempt social welfare organization intended to run before an election because the advertisements were not express advocacy or its functional equivalent.[86]

This prohibition on contributions and expenditures does not extend to communications by a corporation to its stockholders and executive and administrative personnel and their families, or by a labor organization to its members and their families.[87] The prohibition also does not apply with respect to nonpartisan registration and get-out-the vote campaigns by a corporation or labor organization aimed at these classes of persons.[88] Moreover, this prohibition

---

78. 2 U.S.C. § 441a(a)(8).
79. *Id.*
80. 2 U.S.C. § 441a(a)(3)(A).
81. 2 U.S.C. § 441a(a)(3)(B).
82. A *labor organization* is an organization, or employee representation committee or plan, in which employees participate and which exists for the purpose, in whole or in part, of dealing with employers concerning grievances, labor disputes, wages, rates of pay, hours of employment, or conditions of work. 2 U.S.C. § 441b(b)(1). See § 16.1.
83. 2 U.S.C. § 441b(a).
84. Federal Election Comm'n v. Beaumont, 539 U.S. 146 (2003).
85. Cf. with text accompanied by *supra* note 11.
86. Federal Election Comm'n v. Wisconsin Right to Life, 551 U.S. 449 (2007).
87. 2 U.S.C. § 441b(b)(2)(A).
88. 2 U.S.C. § 441b(b)(2)(B).

does not bar a corporation or labor organization from establishing, administering, and soliciting contributions for a separate segregated fund to be utilized for political purposes.[89]

These rules do not prevent a trade association,[90] or a separate segregated fund established by an association, from soliciting contributions from the stockholders and executive or administrative personnel, and their families, of its member corporations, to the extent that the solicitation has been approved by the member corporation and the corporation does not approve a solicitation of this nature by more than one trade association in a calendar year.[91]

§ 7 SOFT MONEY RESTRICTIONS

In general, a committee of a national political party (or its agent) may not solicit, receive, or direct to another person a contribution or other transfer of funds, or expend funds, which are not subject to the limitations, prohibitions, and reporting requirements of the federal election campaign laws (that is, funds that are soft money).[92] State, district, and local party committees may not use soft money for activities that affect federal elections.[93] An amount spent by these committees to raise funds that are used, in whole or in part, for expenditures for a federal election activity[94] must be made from funds that are subject to the federal election campaign laws (hard money).[95]

A national, state, district, or local committee of a political party, or a controlled entity or agent, is not permitted to solicit funds for, or make or direct any contributions to, a tax-exempt organization that engages in electioneering activities.[96]

Federal candidates and officeholders are restricted from receiving, spending, or soliciting soft money in connection with federal elections; they are limited in their ability to do so in connection with state and local elections.[97] The law prevents circumvention of the restrictions on national, state, and local

---

89. 2 U.S.C. § 441b(b)(2)(C). See Chapter 17.
90. See Chapter 14.
91. 2 U.S.C. § 441b(b)(4)(D).
92. 2 U.S.C. § 441i(a).
93. 2 U.S.C. § 441i(b).
94. The term *federal election activity* generally means (1) voter registration activity during the period that starts 120 days before a regularly scheduled federal election; (2) voter identification, get-out-the-vote activity, or generic campaign activity conducted in connection with an election in which a candidate for federal office is on the ballot; (3) a public communication that refers to a clearly identified candidate for federal office and that promotes or supports a candidate for that office, or attacks or opposes such a candidate; or (4) services provided during any month by an employee of a state, district, or local committee of a political party who spends more than 25 percent of his or her compensated time during that month on activities in connection with a federal election. 2 U.S.C. § 431(20).
95. 2 U.S.C. § 441i(c).
96. 2 U.S.C. § 441i(d).
97. 2 U.S.C. § 441i(e).

party committees by prohibiting state and local candidates from raising and spending soft money to fund advertisements and other public communications that promote or attack federal candidates.[98]

These provisions, constituting Title I of the BCRA, are, wrote the Court, Congress's effort to "plug the soft-money loophole."[99] The "cornerstone" of Title I is the first of these provisions,[100] which "prohibits national party committees and their agents from soliciting, receiving, directing, or spending any soft money."[101] This provision, said the Court, "takes national parties out of the soft-money business."[102] The remaining provisions of this body of law "largely reinforce" the restrictions in this first provision.[103]

The Court observed that, since *Buckley*, it has "subjected restrictions on campaign expenditures to closer scrutiny than limits on campaign contributions."[104] Contribution limits, the Court said in *Buckley*, "entai[l] only a marginal restriction upon the contributor's ability to engage in free communication."[105] Contribution limits "may bear more heavily" on the right of association than on the freedom to speak.[106] Limits on contributions also prevent the "actual corruption threatened by large financial contributions" and the "eroding of public confidence in the electoral process through the appearance of corruption."[107]

These restrictions, said the Court, "have only a marginal impact on the ability of contributors, candidates, officeholders, and parties to engage in effective political speech."[108] "Complex as its provisions may be," wrote the Court, this body of law, "in the main, does little more than regulate the ability of wealthy individuals, corporations, and unions to contribute large sums of money to influence federal elections, federal candidates, and federal officeholders."[109]

The relevant inquiry, said the Court, in reviewing § 323, is "whether the mechanism adopted to implement the contribution limit, or to prevent circumvention of that limit, burdens speech in a way that a direct restriction on the contribution itself would not."[110] The Court concluded the mechanism does not do that.

National parties are prohibited from receiving or spending nonfederal (soft) money; state party committees are prohibited from spending nonfederal money on federal election activities. "[N]either provision in any way," wrote the Court,

98. 2 U.S.C. § 441i(f).
99. McConnell v. Federal Election Comm'n, 540 U.S. 93, 133 (2003).
100. 2 U.S.C. § 441i(a).
101. McConnell v. Federal Election Comm'n, 540 U.S. 93, 133 (2003).
102. *Id.*
103. *Id.*
104. *Id.* at 134.
105. Buckley v. Valeo, 424 U.S. 1, 20 (1976).
106. Nixon v. Shrink Missouri Government PAC, 528 U.S. 377, 388 (2000).
107. Federal Election Comm'n v. Nat'l Right to Work Committee, 459 U.S. 197, 208 (1982)
108. McConnell v. Federal Election Comm'n, 540 U.S. 93, 138 (2003).
109. *Id.*
110. *Id.* at 138–139.

"limits the total amount of money parties can spend."[111] Rather, "they simply limit the source and individual amount of donations" and "[t]hat they do so by prohibiting the spending of soft money does not render them expenditure limitations."[112]

The Court concluded that the solicitation provisions,[113] which restrict the ability of national party committees, federal candidates, and federal officeholders to solicit nonfederal funds, "leave open ample opportunities for soliciting federal funds on behalf of entities subject to FECA's source and amount restrictions."[114] The provision[115] that "on its face enacts a blanket ban on party solicitations of funds to certain tax-exempt organizations, nevertheless allows parties to solicit funds to the organizations' federal PACs."[116] That latter section "places no limits on other means of endorsing tax-exempt organizations or any restrictions on solicitations by party officers acting in their individual capacities."[117]

The Court applied the "less rigorous scrutiny applicable to contribution limits" to evaluate the constitutionality of this body of law, noting that Congress enacted this provision "as an integrated whole to vindicate the Government's important interest in preventing corruption and the appearance of corruption."[118]

As noted, national committees of political parties are prohibited from receiving or spending nonfederal (soft) money.[119] The Court said the "main goal" of this section (which was said to be "modest") is to "effect a return to the scheme that was approved in *Buckley* and that was subverted by the creation of the FEC's allocation regime, which permitted the political parties to fund federal electioneering efforts with a combination of hard and soft money."[120]

This section was upheld, against free speech and overbreadth challenges, because of "substantial evidence" that supported Congress's determination that "large soft-money contributions to national political parties give rise to corruption and the appearance of corruption."[121] As noted, state party committees are prohibited from spending nonfederal money on federal election activities.[122] This provision was also upheld.

Another provision, as noted, on its face enacts a blanket ban on party solicitations of funds to certain tax-exempt organizations, yet nevertheless allows

---

111. *Id.* at 139.
112. *Id.*
113. 2 U.S.C. §§ 441i(a), (e).
114. McConnell v. Federal Election Comm'n, 540 U.S. 93, 139 (2003).
115. 2 U.S.C. § 441i(d).
116. McConnell v. Federal Election Comm'n, 540 U.S. 93, 139 (2003).
117. *Id.*
118. *Id.* at 141–142.
119. 2 U.S.C. § 441i(a).
120. McConnell v. Federal Election Comm'n, 540 U.S. 93, 142 (2003).
121. *Id.* at 154.
122. 2 U.S.C. § 441i(b).

parties to solicit funds to the organizations' federal PACs.[123] The government defended this law as being necessary to prevent circumvention of the limits on contributions of soft money to national, state, and local party committees, a justification the Court found "entirely reasonable."[124] The Court wrote that, absent this provision, these committees "would have significant incentives to mobilize their formidable fundraising apparatuses, including the peddling of access to federal officeholders, into the service of like-minded tax-exempt organizations that conduct activities benefiting their candidates."[125] Also: "All of the corruption and appearance of corruption attendant on the operation of those fundraising apparatuses would follow."[126]

This provision, said the Court, is "closely drawn" to prevent political parties from using exempt organizations as "soft-money surrogates."[127] This section restricts solicitations only to tax-exempt groups[128] that make expenditures or disbursements in connection with an election for federal office and to political organizations.[129] Parties remain free to solicit hard-money contributions to an exempt organization's federal PAC and to political organizations that already qualify as federal PACs.

This section also prohibits national, state, and local party committees from making or directing any contributions to qualifying tax-exempt, including political, organizations. This, too, was defended as an anticircumvention measure, as to which the Court agreed "insofar as it prohibits the donation of soft money."[130] The Court "narrowly construe[d]" this provision "to apply only to donations of funds not raised in compliance with FECA."[131] Thus, political parties "remain free to make or direct donations of money to any tax-exempt organization that has otherwise been raised in compliance with FECA."[132]

§ 8 ELECTIONEERING COMMUNICATIONS

The federal election law defines the term *electioneering communication*, which was introduced in 2002.[133] This term means any "broadcast, cable, or satellite communication" that (1) "refers to a clearly identified candidate for Federal office"; (2) is made within (a) 60 days before a general, special, or runoff

---

123. 2 U.S.C. § 441i(d).
124. McConnell v. Federal Election Comm'n, 540 U.S. 93, 174 (2003).
125. *Id*. at 175.
126. *Id*.
127. *Id*. at 177.
128. That is, IRC § 501(c) entities.
129. That is, IRC § 527 entities.
130. McConnell v. Federal Election Comm'n, 540 U.S. 93, 178 (2003).
131. *Id*. at 180.
132. *Id*. at 181.
133. This definition replaced the narrowing construction of the disclosure provisions adopted by the Supreme Court in *Buckley* (see § 2(b)).

election for the office sought by the candidate; or (b) 30 days before a primary or preference election, or a convention or caucus of a political party that has authority to nominate a candidate, for the office sought by the candidate; and (3) in the case of a communication that refers to a candidate other than President or Vice President, is "targeted to the relevant electorate."[134] This type of communication is *targeted to the relevant electorate* if it "can be received by 50,000 or more persons" in the district or state the candidate seeks to represent.[135]

The Court wrote that this term "replace[d] the narrowing construction of FECA's disclosure provisions adopted by this Court in *Buckley*."[136] In that case, the Court "drew a constitutionally mandated line between express advocacy and so-called issue advocacy."[137] This limitation, however, was the "product of statutory interpretation rather than a constitutional [law] command."[138] Thus, this distinction, held the Court, is not a basis for challenging the constitutionality of this term. This term was upheld as being constitutional on its face.[139]

§ 9 DISCLOSURE REQUIREMENTS

Whenever a person makes disbursements totaling more than $10,000 during a calendar year for the direct costs of producing and airing electioneering communications, he or she must file a statement with the FEC identifying the pertinent elections and all persons sharing the costs of the disbursements.[140] If the disbursements are made from a corporation's or labor union's segregated account,[141] or by a single individual who has collected contributions from others, the statement must identify all persons who contributed $1,000 or more to the account or the individual during the calendar year.[142]

The statement must be filed within 24 hours of each *disclosure date*, which is defined to include the first date and all subsequent dates on which a person's aggregate undisclosed expenses for electioneering communications exceed $10,000 for that calendar year.[143] The execution of a contract to make a

---

134. 2 U.S.C. § 434(f)(3)(A)(i). Exceptions to this definition are provided in 2 U.S.C. § 434(f)(3)(B).
135. 2 U.S.C. § 434(f)(3)(C).
136. McConnell v. Federal Election Comm'n, 540 U.S. 93, 189 (2003).
137. *Id.* at 190.
138. *Id.* at 192.
139. *Id.* at 202.
140. 2 U.S.C. §§ 434(f)(2)(A), (B), and (D).
141. Corporations and labor unions are prohibited from funding electioneering communications with money from their general treasuries; they must utilize a separate segregated fund for these expenditures. 2 U.S.C. § 441b(b)(2). See § 13.
142. 2 U.S.C. §§ 434(f)((2)(E), (F).
143. 2 U.S.C. §§ 434(f)(1), (2), and (4).

disbursement is treated as a disbursement for purposes of these disclosure requirements.[144]

§ 10 COORDINATED COMMUNICATIONS AND EXPENDITURES

Disbursements for electioneering communications that are coordinated with a candidate or party are treated as contributions to and expenditures by that candidate or party.[145] An expenditure made by a person in cooperation, consultation, or concert, with, or at the request or suggestion of, a candidate, his or her authorized political committee, or their agents, is considered to be a contribution to that candidate.[146] In 2002, the same rule was added applicable to expenditures coordinated with a national, state, or local committee of a political party.[147] The Court upheld this rule as being constitutional on its face.[148]

§ 11 CORPORATE AND LABOR DISBURSEMENTS FOR ELECTIONEERING COMMUNICATIONS

Corporations and labor unions are prohibited from using funds in their general treasuries to finance advertisements expressly advocating the election or defeat of candidates in federal elections. They are permitted, however, to form and administer separate segregated accounts.[149] The Supreme Court has repeatedly held that use of these funds provides these entities with a constitutionally sufficient opportunity to engage in express advocacy.[150]

In 2002, this rule was extended to all electioneering communications.[151] Thus, corporations and unions may not use their general treasury funds to finance electioneering communications but they remain free to organize and administer separate segregated funds for that purpose.

Also in 2002, the prohibition on the use of general treasury funds to pay for electioneering communications, termed in this context *applicable electioneering communications*, was made applicable to nonprofit corporations.[152] The Court upheld these rules as being constitutional on their face.[153]

---

144. 2 U.S.C. § 434(f)(5).
145. 2 U.S.C. § 441a(a)(7)(C).
146. 2 U.S.C. § 441a(a)(7)(B)(i).
147. 2 U.S.C. § 441a(a)(7)(B)(ii).
148. McConnell v. Federal Election Comm'n, 540 U.S. 93, 203 (2003).
149. 2 U.S.C. § 441b.
150. E.g., Federal Election Comm'n v. Nat'l Right to Work Committee, 459 U.S. 197 (1982).
151. 2 U.S.C. § 441b(b)(2).
152. 2 U.S.C. § 441b(c)(1).
153. McConnell v. Federal Election Comm'n, 540 U.S. 93, 209 (2003).

Nonetheless, the term *applicable electioneering communication* does not include a communication by a tax-exempt social welfare organization[154] or an exempt political organization[155] made in a certain manner[156] if the communication is paid for exclusively by funds provided directly by individuals who are U.S. citizens or nationals or lawfully admitted for permanent residence.[157] The law, however, states that this exception does not apply in the case of a targeted communication made by an organization referenced in the exception.[158] The term *targeted communication* is defined as including all electioneering communications.[159] This exception to the exception thus completely cancels out the exception.

The Supreme Court held that it is constitutional, in application of free speech principles, to bar tax-exempt advocacy corporations from contributing directly to candidates for federal office.[160] The Court also held, however, that the prohibition on corporations from using general treasury funds to make an expenditure in connection with a federal election, and to instead use a separate segregated fund, is unconstitutional as applied to the political activity conducted by the type of tax-exempt corporation involved in the case.[161] This latter organization was formed for the "express purpose of promoting political ideas, and cannot engage in business activities"; did not have any shareholders or other persons "affiliated so as to have a claim on its assets or earnings"; and was not established by a business corporation or a labor union, and it has a policy to not accept contributions from such entities.[162] This exception is not available for tax-exempt chambers of commerce and similar entities.[163]

§ 12   REPORTING OF INDEPENDENT EXPENDITURES

A disclosure requirement is applicable to persons making independent expenditures of $1,000 or more during the 20-day period immediately preceding an election.[164] This provision treats the execution of a contract to make a disbursement as the functional equivalent of a payment for the goods or

---

154. See Chapter 13.
155. See Chapter 17.
156. See 2 U.S.C. § 434(f)(2)(E) or (F).
157. 2 U.S.C. § 441b(c)(2).
158. 2 U.S.C. § 441b(c)(6)(A).
159. 2 U.S.C. § 441b(c)(6)(B).
160. Federal Election Commission v. Beaumont, 539 U.S. 146 (2003).
161. Federal Election Commission v. Massachusetts Citizens for Life, Inc., 479 U.S. 238 (1986).
162. *Id.* at 264.
163. Austin v. Michigan State Chamber of Commerce, 494 U.S. 652 (1990).
164. 2 U.S.C. § 434(g)(1).

services covered by the contract. The Court upheld this rule as being constitutional on its face.[165]

§ 13 ESTABLISHMENT AND MAINTENANCE OF SEGREGATED FUNDS

Corporations can avoid the federal law limits placed on contributions and expenditures[166] by creating a separate segregated fund ("SSF"). The limit against a corporation making contributions or expenditures in relation to an election to a political office does not extend to the "establishment, administration, and solicitation of contributions to a separate segregated fund to be utilized for political purposes by a corporation, labor organization, cooperative, or corporation without capital stock."[167] A corporation can lawfully incur the cost of office space, telephones, salaries, utilities, supplies, legal and accounting fees, fundraising, and other expenses involved in organizing and operating an SSF established by a corporation.[168]

The sponsoring corporation may wholly control the SSF.[169] The SSF, as long as it complies with federal law regarding registration and disclosure of activities, is free to make contributions and expenditures in connection with federal elections.[170] The SSF allows "corporate political participation without the temptation to use corporate funds for political influence, quite possibly at odds with the sentiments of some shareholders or members, and it lets the government regulate campaign activity through registration and disclosure."[171]

Although an SSF can solicit and collect contributions on its own behalf,[172] it is restricted as to from whom it can solicit and collect contributions. The SSF cannot lawfully solicit contributions from any person other than "its stockholders and their families and its executive or administrative personnel and their families."[173] A corporation, or an SSF established by a corporation, can make two written solicitations for contributions during the calendar year from any stockholder, executive or administrative personnel, or employee of a corporation or the families of these persons.[174] A corporation without capital stock, or

---

165. McConnell v. Federal Election Comm'n, 540 U.S. 93, 212 (2003).
166. See § 6.
167. 2 U.S.C. § 441b(b)(2)(C).
168. 11 C.F.R. §114.1(b).
169. Federal Election Comm'n v. Beaumont, 539 U.S. 146, 149 (2003). An SSF is sometimes referred to as a PAC in reflection of the political action committee that operates it.
170. Federal Election Comm'n v. Beaumont, 539 U.S. 146, 149 (2003).
171. *Id*. at 163.
172. 11 C.F.R. 102.6(b)(4).
173. 2 U.S.C. § 441b(b)(4)(A)(i). These individuals are defined as a *restricted class*.
174. 2 U.S.C. § 441b(b)(4)(B). This solicitation must be made only by mail addressed to stockholders, executive or administrative personnel, or employees at their residence, and must be so designed that the corporation or SSF conducting the solicitation cannot determine who makes a contribution of $50 or less as a result of the solicitation and who does not make a contribution.

an SSF established by a corporation without capital stock, can solicit contributions to the SSF from members of the corporation.[175] Therefore, a tax-exempt organization that establishes an SSF should have members from which it may solicit contributions. When soliciting an employee for a contribution to a SSF, the employee, at the time of solicitation, must be informed of the political purposes of the fund and that the employee has the right to refuse to contribute without reprisal.[176]

§ 14   USE OF FACILITIES

Subject to the rules and practices of a corporation, stockholders and employees of the corporation may make "occasional, isolated, or incidental use" of the facilities of the corporation for individual volunteer activity in connection with a federal election.[177] The stockholders and employees will be required to reimburse the corporation to the extent that the overhead and operating costs of the corporation are increased.[178] *Occasional, isolated, or incidental use* generally means:

- When used by employees during working hours, an amount of activity during any particular work period that does not prevent the employee from completing the normal amount of work that the employee usually carries out during the work period; or

- When used by stockholders other than employees during the work period, the use does not interfere with the corporation in carrying out its normal activities; but

- Any such activity that does not exceed one hour per week or four hours per month, regardless of whether the activity is undertaken during or after normal working hours, shall be considered as occasional, isolated, or incidental use of the corporate facilities.[179]

If a stockholder or an employee makes more than occasional, isolated, or incidental use of corporate facilities in connection with a federal election, the stockholder or employee must reimburse the corporation within a commercially reasonable time for the normal and usual rental charge.

Any person who uses the facility of a corporation to produce materials in connection with a federal election is required to reimburse the corporation within a reasonable time for the normal and usual charge for producing the materials in the commercial market.[180] Persons, other than stockholders or

---

175. 2 U.S.C. § 441b(b)(4)(C).
176. 2 U.S.C. § 441b(b)(3).
177. 11 C.F.R. § 114.9(a)(1)
178. *Id.*
179. *Id.*
180. 11 C.F.R. § 114.9(c).

employees of the corporation, who make any use of the corporate facilities for activity in connection with a federal election are required to reimburse the corporation within a commercially reasonable time in the amount of the normal or usual rental charge.[181]

A candidate, candidate's agent, or person traveling on behalf of a candidate who uses an airplane owned or leased by a corporation for travel in connection with a federal election must, in advance, reimburse the corporation.[182] For travel to a city served by regularly scheduled commercial service, the amount of reimbursement is the amount of first-class airfare.[183] For travel to a city not served by regularly scheduled commercial service, the amount of reimbursement is the usual charter rate.[184] A candidate, candidate's agent, or person traveling on behalf of a candidate who uses other means of transportation owned or leased by a corporation must reimburse the corporation at the normal and usual rental charge within a commercially reasonable time.[185]

§ 15   HOSTING DEBATES

A tax-exempt charitable or social welfare organization that does not endorse, support, or oppose political candidates or political parties may stage candidate debates.[186] If the exempt organization chooses to host a candidate debate, the debate must include at least two candidates, and the exempt organization must not structure the debate to promote or advance one candidate over another.[187] The exempt organization must use preestablished objective criteria in determining which candidates may participate in the debate.[188] The exempt organization cannot use nomination by a particular political party as the sole objective criterion to determine whether to include a candidate in a general election debate.[189] For a debate held prior to a primary election, caucus, or convention, the exempt organization can restrict candidate participation to candidates seeking the nomination of one party, and need not stage a debate for candidates seeking the nomination of any other political party or independent candidates.[190] The exempt organization also may accept funds donated from a corporation or labor organization to stage candidate debates.[191]

---

181. 11 C.F.R. § 114.9(d).
182. 11 C.F.R. § 114.9(e).
183. 11 C.F.R. § 114.9(e)(1)(i).
184. 11 C.F.R. § 114.9(e)(1)(ii).
185. 11 C.F.R. § 114.9(e)(2).
186. 11 C.F.R. § 110.13(a).
187. 11 C.F.R. § 110.13(b)(1), (2).
188. 11 C.F.R. § 110.13(c).
189. *Id*.
190. *Id*.
191. 11 C.F.R. § 114.5(f).

Table of Cases

Table of IRS Revenue Rulings

TABLE OF IRS REVENUE RULINGS

Revenue Rulings	Book Sections	Revenue Rulings	Book Sections
60-193	4.3(c), 13.3(b), 20.3(c)(iii), 23.2(c), 23.5(b)	64-231	7.6(d)
		64-246	19.12
60-228	24.4(g) 24.5(e)(ii)	64-274	7.8
60-243	7.14	64-275	8.4
60-323	15.2, 20.10	64-286	7.13
60-324	15.2	64-313	13.1(b)
60-351	8.5, 8.6	65-1	6.3(e), 9.2, 20.5(h)
60-367	28.5	65-2	7.11, 8.4
60-384	4.1(a), 7.14	65-5	19.12
61-72	7.6(d)	65-6	19.6
61-87	7.8, 8.6	65-60	9.2
61-137	19.6	65-61	11.3
61-153	13.1(a)	65-63	15.2
61-158	13.1(b)	65-64	15.6
61-170	14.2(c)(ii), 20.5(h), 24.5(e)(iv)	65-99	19.5(a), 19.5(b)
		65-164	14.1(d), 25.5(e)(iv)
61-177	14.1(c)(ii), 14.1(d), 22.6	65-174	19.5(b)
62-17	16.1	65-191	7.8, 8.4
62-23	8.3(a)	65-195	13.1(a)
62-66	7.14	65-201	13.2(a), 19.5(a), 19.5(b)
62-71	20.3(c)(iii)	65-219	15.2
62-113	28.2(e)	65-244	14.2(c)(ii)
62-167	13.1(a), 15.1(b)	65-270	7.12, 8.4
62-191	16.1, 24.4(g), 24.5(f)	65-271	7.12
63-15	7.13	65-298	6.3(a), 8.4, 9.2, 9.4
63-20	7.14	65-299	7.3(a), 13.1(a)
63-190	13.1(a), 15.1(b)	66-46	7.12
63-208	7.13	66-47	24.4(g),
63-209	7.13	66-59	19.3
63-220	7.8, 8.6	66-79	28.2(e)
63-234	8.6	66-102	19.2(a)
63-235	7.7, 25.9(a)	66-103	7.8, 7.12
63-252	28.2(e)	66-104	6.3(e), 8.6
64-108	4.6,	66-105	16.2
64-109	19.6	66-108	19.12
64-117	7.8	66-146	7.7, 7.11
64-118	7.8, 15.1(b)	66-147	8.5, 9.4
64-128	8.3(a)	66-148	13.1(a)
64-174	7.12	66-149	15.2
64-175	7.12	66-150	13.1(b), 15.1(b), 19.2(a)
64-182	4.5(a), 4.7, 7.13, 24.5(d)	66-151	13.1, 13.2, 24.4(g), 24.5(e)(i), 24.5(e)(ii), 24.5(e)(iv)
64-187	13.4		
64-192	8.5	66-152	19.12
64-193	19.5(a)	66-177	4.1(a)
64-194	19.4(a)	66-178	7.12
64-195	8.4, 20.3(c)(iii)	66-179	7.7, 8.5, 11.1(a), 13.1(a), 15.1(b), 16.3
64-217	19.6		

Revenue Rulings	Book Sections	Revenue Rulings	Book Sections
66-180	19.3	67-219	14.1(d), 24.5(d)
66-212	18.3	67-223	19.12
66-219	4.1(a)	67-249	15.1(b)
66-220	7.10, 8.5, 8.6	67-250	7.11, 8.5
66-221	24.1	67-251	20.9
66-222	20.9	67-252	16.2
66-223	14.1(d)	67-253	19.12
66-225	20.10	67-264	14.1(b)
66-255	8.5	67-265	19.5(a), 19.5(b)
66-256	8.5, 23.2(c)	67-284	19.20
66-257	6.3(a), 7.1	67-290	7.14
66-258	13.3(b), 20.3(c)(iii), 23.2(c),	67-291	7.8
	23.5(b)	67-292	7.7, 7.15(a), 8.3(c)
66-259	20.3, 20.5(g)	67-293	13.3(a), 22.2, 22.5
66-260	§ 14.1(d)	67-294	13.1(a)
66-273	13.1(a)	67-295	14.1(d)
66-295	19.2(a), 27.13	67-296	20.9, 24.5(d), 24.5(e)(iv)
66-296	27.13	67-302	15.2
66-323	7.6(i), 24.2(e), 24.2(f),	67-325	5.5(a), 6.2(b)(ii), 6.3, 6.3(a),
	26.4(g)	67-327	8.4
66-338	14.2(c)(ii), 24.5(e)(i)	67-342	8.5
66-354	13.1(a), 14.2(c)(ii), 16.1, 18.3	67-343	14.1(b)
66-358	6.3(b), 7.7, 20.7	67-344	14.1(d)
66-359	11.1	67-346	19.12
66-360	13.1(b)	67-367	6.3(a), 20.5(h)
67-4	6.3(b), 7.8, 7.13, 8.5	67-368	13.3(b), 23.5(b)
67-5	20.5(b)	67-390	27.1(b)
67-6	7.4, 7.11, 13.2(a), 13.3(a), 22.5	67-391	7.7, 8.5
67-7	16.1	67-392	7.12, 8.4
67-8	15.1(b), 20.5(b)	67-393	14.1(f)
67-71	13.3(b), 23.2(b)(iv), 23.5(b)	67-394	14.1(f)
67-72	7.8, 8.4, 20.11(a)	67-422	19.12
67-77	14.1(c)(ii)	67-428	15.1(b), 15.2
67-109	13.1(a), 24.4(a)	67-429	19.12
67-128	19.12	67-430	19.12
67-138	7.4, 7.11, 8.5	68-14	7.7, 8.5, 13.2(a), 20.11(a)
67-139	8.5, 15.1(b)	68-15	7.7, 7.11, 8.5
67-148	8.4	68-16	7.8, 8.4
67-149	7.8, 7.13	68-17	7.4, 7.11, 8.4
67-150	7.1, 8.4	68-26	4.5(a), 7.10, 10.2(a), 10.2(b),
67-151	11.1		27.13
67-152	19.12	68-27	22.1(c), 7.6(e)
67-170	6.3(d), 19.6	68-45	13.1(b)
67-175	14.1(d)	68-46	14.1(b), 24.4(g)
67-176	24.5(e)(ii)	68-70	7.11, 8.5
67-182	14.2(c)(ii)	68-71	8.4, 8.5
67-216	8.5, 16.2	68-72	7.10, 8.4
67-217	7.8, 8.6	68-73	7.6(i)

TABLE OF IRS REVENUE RULINGS

Revenue Rulings	Book Sections	Revenue Rulings	Book Sections
68-75	19.5(b)	68-638	15.2
68-76	19.12	68-655	7.4, 7.11
68-104	24.5(l)	68-656	13.3(a), 22.5
68-117	7.1, 28.2(c)	68-657	14.1(d)
68-118	13.1(a)	69-51	24.4(g), 24.5(e)
68-119	20.10	69-52	19.12
68-123	10.8, 24.4(g)	69-66	20.5(g)
68-164	8.5	69-68	15.1(b)
68-165	7.1, 8.4, 28.2(e)	69-69	24.4(g), 27.1(a), 27.1(h)
68-166	7.1	69-80	28.2(e)
68-167	4.4, 7.1, 8.6	69-96	3.4
68-168	20.10	69-106	14.1(d)
68-175	8.3(a)	69-144	18.3
68-182	14.1(c)(ii)	69-160	11.4
68-217	27	69-161	7.1
68-222	19.2(a)	69-162	24.6(g)
68-224	13.1(a)	69-174	7.1
68-225	24.5(d)	69-175	20.5(i)
68-263	20.3(c)(iii), 23.2(c)	69-176	20.5(j)
68-264	14.2(c)(ii), 14.2(c)(iv)	69-177	8.6
68-265	14.1(d), 14.2(c)(iv)	69-217	15.2
68-266	15.1(b)	69-219	15.2
68-267	24.4(g)	69-220	15.2, 15.5, 24.1
68-296	29.1(a), 30.7	69-222	19.12
68-306	7.10	69-232	15.5, 15.6
68-307	8.5	69-247	21.15
68-371	19.2	69-256	4.3(a), 4.3(b), 20.5(h)
68-372	8.3(b)	69-257	7.8
68-373	9.2, 11.3, 20.5(h), 24.6(l)	69-266	4.6, 7.6(i), 19.4(j)
68-374	26.4(b)(ii)	69-267	24.5(b)(i)
68-375	24.5(b)(ii)	69-268	24.5(b)(i), 24.5(c), 24.7(b)
68-376	24.5(b)(i)	69-269	24.5(b)(i)
68-422	6.3(a), 20.5(f)	69-278	19.2(a)
68-438	7.4, 7.11, 8.5	69-279	4.3(a), 4.3(b)
68-455	13.1(b)	69-280	13.2(a)
*68-489	4.7, 6.3(a), 27.17	69-281	13.2(a), 15.1(b)
68-490	19.2(a)	69-282	19.7
68-496	19.12	69-283	19.1, 19.7
68-504	6.3(a), 8.4, 20.11(a)	69-381	19.2(a)
68-505	24.3(b), 24.4(g), 24.7(e)	69-383	20.3
68-534	16.1	69-384	13.1(a)
68-535	20.10	69-385	13.1(b), 13.4
68-538	8.6	69-386	16.1
68-550	24.4(d)	69-387	14.1(f)
68-563	7.10, 10.2(a)	69-400	7.8, 8.4
68-564	19.5(b)	69-417	19.12
68-581	24.5(a)	69-441	7.1, 7.3(a), 8.5
68-609	31.8(b)	69-459	7.14

TABLE OF IRS REVENUE RULINGS

Revenue Rulings	Book Sections	Revenue Rulings	Book Sections
69-463	24.5(b)(ii)	70-590	7.6(i), 8.5, 24.2(e)
69-492	8.3(a)	70-591	14.1(d)
69-526	7.6(i), 9.1, 9.2	70-604	13.2(a)
69-527	15.1(b)	70-640	4.6, 8.5
69-528	7.13, 27.13	70-641	7.6(g), 8.5, 14.1(b), 14.1(e)
69-538	7.8	71-29	7.7
69-545	7.1, 7.6, 7.6(a), 7.6(e), 31.7(b)	71-97	7.8
69-572	6.3(b), 7.13, 23.2(g)	71-99	7.7
69-573	7.8, 15.1(b)	71-100	19.12
69-574	24.2(g)	71-131	7.14, 19.19(c)
69-575	19.12, 29.2	71-132	7.14
69-632	6.3(e), 9.1, 14.1(c)(iii), 14.1(f)	71-155	14.1(d), 14.2(c)(ii), 24.5(e)(ii)
	20.5(h)	71-156	18.4
69-633	3.5, 7.13, 11.4, 24.4(g), 24.7(f)	71-276	27.1(b)
69-634	14.1(f)	71-300	19.6
69-635	15.1(b)	71-311	29.3
69-636	20.10	71-395	7.12, 20.5(h)
69-637	19.6	71-413	7.8
69-651	19.12	71-421	15.1(b)
70-4	7.11, 13.1(a)	71-447	6.2(b)(ii)
70-31	14.1(a)(ii)	71-460	4.1(a), 28.2(e)
70-32	15.1(b)	71-504	14.1(e)
70-48	20.10	71-505	14.1(e)
70-79	7.7, 7.11, 8.5, 20.3(c)(iii)	71-506	8.5, 9.4, 14.1(e)
70-81	14.3	71-529	7.8, 7.13, 8.6, 24.2(e), 27.12(b)
70-129	7.8	71-544	19.2(a)
70-130	19.5(b)	71-545	8.3(c)
70-186	6.3(b), 7.7, 7.15(a), 20.5(h),	71-553	7.13
	20.11(a)	71-580	7.10, 20.5(h)
70-188	18.4	71-581	24.7(c), 27.13
70-189	18.4	72-16	7.6(i), 8.4, 24.5(b)(v)
70-202	19.3	72-17	19.6
70-244	14.1(b)	72-36	19.5(a), 19.5(b)
70-270	12.1(g)	72-37	19.7
70-321	7.8, 8.5, 23.2(c)	72-50	19.12
70-372	16.2	72-51	19.12
70-411	18.3	72-52	19.12
70-449	22.3(c)(iii)	72-101	7.8, 8.3(a), 20.11(a)
70-533	4.5(b), 7.1, 8.3(a), 20.7	72-102	13.2(a), 19.14
70-534	8.4, 24.5(i)	72-124	6.3(a), 6.3(c), 7.6(d), 24.2(e)
70-535	13.1(b)	72-147	20.5(h)
70-536	18.4	72-209	7.6(i)
70-562	7.14	72-211	14.1(f), 14.2(c)(i)
70-566	19.13	72-228	7.11, 8.5
70-583	7.1, 7.7, 8.4	72-355	3.5, 17
70-584	7.7, 7.8, 8.4, 13.3(b), 23.5(b)	72-369	4.4, 4.5(a), 4.6, 7.13, 24.5(j)
70-585	7.1, 7.4, 7.11	72-391	16.1, 16.2, 20.5(h)

TABLE OF IRS REVENUE RULINGS

Revenue Rulings	Book Sections	Revenue Rulings	Book Sections
72-430	8.3(a)	73-569	8.5
72-431	24.4(g), 24.5(h)(i), 24.7(k)	73-570	19.12
72-512	23.2(b)(i)	73-587	24.4(g)
72-513	22.3(c)(i), 23.2(b)(iv)	74-13	19.20
72-542	27.13	74-14	7.14
72-559	4.6, 6.3(b), 7.1	74-15	7.14
72-560	7.7, 8.5	74-16	8.4
72-589	19.12	74-17	13.2(a), 19.14
73-45	7.12, 24.2(e)	74-18	18.3
73-59	19.12	74-21	3.5, 17
73-93	19.12	74-23	17
73-104	24.5(c)	74-30	15.1(b)
73-105	4.4, 4.5(a), 24.5(c)	74-38	24.5(g)
73-126	20.5(f)	74-81	14.2(c)(ii), 24.5(e)(i)
73-127	8.6, 24.4(b)	74-99	13.2(a)
73-128	6.3(b), 7.1, 8.4, 8.6, 24.2(b)	74-116	14.1(c)(iii)
73-148	19.12	74-117	23.2(b)(iv)
73-164	27.13	74-118	16.2
73-165	19.4(a)	74-146	6.3(e), 7.8, 7.13, 20.7
73-192	19.4(a)	74-147	14.1(c)(iii), 14.1(f)
73-193	24.6(g)	74-148	15.1(b), 20.10
73-247	19.12	74-167	16.1
73-248	19.12	74-168	15.2
73-285	7.10, 7.11	74-194	11.1
73-306	13.1(b)	74-195	16.2
73-307	18.4	74-196	19.9(c)
73-308	19.12	74-199	3.5, 17, 19.14
73-313	4.6, 6.3(e), 7.6(g), 7.6(i)	74-224	10.4
73-349	13.1(b)	74-228	14.2(c)(ii)
73-364	27.2(b)(ii)	74-246	7.7
73-370	19.4(b)	74-281	19.3
73-386	24.4(b)	74-287	12.2(b)
73-407	21.7	74-308	14.2(c)(ii)
73-411	14.3, 14.4	74-318	3.5
73-422	25.3(b), 27.1(b)	74-319	3.5
73-424	24.3(a), 24.5(g)	74-327	19.12
73-434	8.3(a)	74-361	7.7, 13.1(a), 13.4, 24.5(d) 24.7(a)
73-439	20.5(i)	74-362	19.5(b)
73-440	22.2(a)	74-368	12.1(g)
73-452	14.1(f)	74-399	24.4(h), 24.5(c)
73-453	19.5(g)	74-443	11.4
73-454	19.6	74-450	12.1(b)
73-455	12.2(a)	74-475	17
73-504	25.3(a)	74-488	16.2
73-520	15.1(b)	74-489	15.2
73-543	8.3(a)	74-490	27.1(b)
73-567	7.6(g), 8.7, 14.1(g)	74-493	11.4

TABLE OF IRS REVENUE RULINGS

Revenue Rulings	Book Sections	Revenue Rulings	Book Sections
74-518	16.2	75-388	19.12
74-523	28.2(e)	75-434	7.10, 28.2(e)
74-553	7.6(g), 9.2, 14.1(g)	75-436	7.14
74-563	13.2(a)	75-470	7.11, 8.3(b)
74-567	19.12	75-471	6.3(e), 7.12
74-572	7.6(a)	75-472	7.6(i), 8.4, 24.4(f), 24.5(b)(v)
74-574	23.2(b)(iv), 23.2(c)	75-473	16.1
74-575	7.10, 20.7	75-492	8.3(a)
74-587	7.11, 7.15(e)	75-494	13.2(a), 15.1(b), 20.10
74-595	8.5	76-4	8.5, 20.7
74-596	16.1	76-18	12.4(a)
74-600	8.3(b)	76-21	7.1
74-614	7.8, 7.13, 24.2(e)	76-22	7.1
74-615	8.5	76-31	16.1
75-4	19.12	76-33	24.5(a), 24.5(b)(v)
75-5	19.12	76-37	7.8
75-38	4.3(a), 12.1(g)	76-38	14.2(c)(ii)
75-42	21.7	76-81	13.3(a), 22.5, 24.5(e)(ii)
75-65	28.2(e)	76-91	31.8(b)
75-74	7.1, 7.15(d)	76-93	24.5(g)
75-75	7.15(d)	76-94	24.4(b)
75-76	7.15(d)	76-147	7.11, 13.2(a)
75-97	19.12	76-152	7.3(b), 7.12
75-110	19.12	76-167	8.3(a), 8.3(b)
75-196	6.3(a), 6.3(e), 8.3(c), 8.4, 20.11(a)	76-204	7.8, 7.9, 7.15(a), 16.2
75-197	7.6(i)	76-205	7.10, 7.11, 8.5
75-198	6.3(a), 7.1, 7.6(d), 7.6(i)	76-206	7.12, 20.1, 20.9
75-199	12.1(a), 19.4(a)	76-207	14.1(d), 14.3
75-200	20.5(g)	76-233	19.12
75-201	24.5(g), 24.5(h)(ii)	76-241	16.2
75-207	7.15(a)	76-244	6.3(a), 7.1
75-215	8.3(a)	76-296	9.3, 26.4(g), 24.6(l)
75-228	19.12	76-297	24.6(g)
75-231	6.2(b)(ii)	76-298	19.12
75-258	3.5, 6.6	76-323	10.8, 24.4(g)
75-282	7.6(b), 7.10, 7.13, 25.9(a)	76-335	19.2(a)
75-283	7.1	76-336	7.8
75-284	7.4, 7.8	76-337	24.10
75-285	7.11, 8.5	76-341	24.4(g)
75-286	7.7, 13.2(a), 20.11(a)	76-354	24.12(c)
75-287	14.1(f), 16.2	76-366	8.6
75-288	16.1	76-384	8.3(a)
75-290	25.2(a)	76-388	19.12
75-359	7.13, 7.14	76-399	16.2
75-384	6.3(i), 7.7, 13.1(a)	76-400	14.1(c)(ii), 14.1(d)
75-385	6.3(a), 7.1	76-402	24.4(d)
75-387	12.3(b)(iv)	76-408	7.11

TABLE OF IRS REVENUE RULINGS

Revenue Rulings	Book Sections	Revenue Rulings	Book Sections
76-409	14.2(c)(ii)	77-272	6.2(e), 7.8, 8.4
76-410	14.1(f)	77-283	23.2(b)(iv)
76-417	8.3(a)	77-290	24.4(g)
76-418	7.7	77-295	10.7
76-419	7.11	77-331	21.7
76-420	16.1	77-365	6.2(d), 8.4, 24.2(d)
76-440	12.3(b)(i), 12.3(b)(iv)	77-366	4.4, 7.10, 8.4
76-441	20.5, 31.7(b), 31.8(b)	77-367	8.3(b), 20.7
76-442	6.3(e)	77-381	10.5
76-443	8.5	77-384	19.12
76-452	7.6(a)	77-407	25.3(b)
76-455	9.2	77-416	31.7(b)
76-456	23.2(c)	77-429	19.2, 19.2(a)
76-457	19.4(b)	77-430	7.10
76-495	19.14	77-436	24.4(g)
76-549	19.19(b)	77-440	19.12
76-550	19.19(b)	77-469	27.1(b)
77-3	7.1	78-41	7.6(c). 7.13, 25.9(a), 28.2(d)
77-4	8.5	78-42	7.8, 16.1
77-5	16.1	78-43	24.5(i)
77-42	7.1	78-50	13.1(a)
77-43	18.4	78-51	26.4(e)(i)
77-46	16.1	78-52	24.5(e)(i)
77-68	7.6(i), 7.8, 8.4	78-68	7.7, 13.1(a)
77-69	7.6(g)	78-69	7.7, 13.1(a)
77-70	19.6	78-70	14.4
77-71	24.12(b)	78-82	8.3(a)
77-72	24.12(c)	78-84	7.15(b)
77-111	4.6, 7.11, 7.15(e)	78-85	6.3(e), 13.2(a)
77-112	14.1(a)(i)	78-86	4.6, 12.1(a)
77-114	25.2(a)	78-87	19.4(a)
77-116	25.3(b)	78-88	24.2(g), 24.12(c)
77-121	27.13	78-95	12.3(b)(i)
77-124	27.13	78-98	24.4(d)
77-153	16.2	78-99	8.5
77-154	16.1	78-100	10.7
77-159	27.1(b)	78-131	7.2, 13.1(a)
77-160	21.7	78-132	13.1(b)
77-162	27.2(a)(vii)	78-143	19.6
77-165	7.14, 19.19(b)	78-145	7.6(i), 24.2(e), 24.2(f), 26.4(g)
*77-206	20.11(a), 20.11(a-1)	78-160	23.2(c)
77-207	25.3(a)	78-188	10.2(a)
77-208	25.3(a), 27.1(b)	78-189	10.2(a)
77-214	3.5	78-190	10.2(a)
77-232	7.14, 14.1(e)	78-225	14.3
77-246	6.3(a), 7.1	78-232	10.2(c), 20.5(g)
77-261	19.19(b)	78-238	19.5(b)

TABLE OF IRS REVENUE RULINGS

Revenue Rulings	Book Sections	Revenue Rulings	Book Sections
78-239	19.11(a)	80-124	18.4
78-240	24.7(f)	80-130	20.10
78-248	23.2(b)(iii), 23.2(c)	80-200	7.15(f)
78-287	16.1	80-205	13.1(a)
78-288	16.1	80-206	13.1(b)
78-289	27	80-215	7.11
78-305	8.2	80-259	25.2(a), 25.2(b)
78-309	8.3(a)	80-278	6.3(b), 7.15(a), 23.2(g)
78-310	7.8, 7.13, 8.4	80-279	6.3(b), 7.15(a), 23.2(g)
78-315	12.1(b)	80-282	23.2(b)(iii), 23.2(c)
78-316	19.19(b), 27.2(b)(iii)	80-286	7.8, 7.15(f), 8.4, 28.2(e)
78-384	7.8, 7.9, 7.15(a)	80-287	14.2(c)(ii)
78-385	7.10, 8.5, 10.2(a), 24.4(g)	80-294	20.9, 24.5(a), 24.5(e)(iv)
78-426	9.2, 11.3	80-295	24.5(a)
78-427	7.6(i)	80-296	24.5(a)
78-428	7.1, 24.2(e)	80-297	24.4(d)
78-434	19.9(c)	80-298	24.4(d)
78-435	24.5(b)(i)	80-301	20.5(h)
79-11	17.1(a)	80-302	20.5(h)
79-12	17.1(a)	80-309	7.6(i)
79-13	17.1(a)	80-316	11.4
79-17	7.1, 7.2, 24.2(e)	81-19	24.7(b), 25.9(a)
79-18	6.3(a), 7.1, 7.2. 24.2(e), 24.2(e)	81-27	24.5(e)(iv)
79-19	7.1, 7.2, 24.2(e), 24.5(b)(v)	81-28	7.1, 7.6(i)
79-26	7.8, 8.2	81-29	6.3(b), 6.3(e), 7.8, 7.13, 20.7,
79-31	24.2(f)		24.2(e), 25.5(b)(i)
79-99	6.2(b)(ii)	81-58	13.1(b), 19.4(a)
79-128	19.3	81-59	16.2
79-130	8.3(a)	81-60	16, 20.9
79-222	24.9	81-61	24.4(f)
79-316	13.1(b), 13.2(b)	81-62	24.4(g)
79-323	7.14	81-68	18.4
79-358	7.1, 7.6(i)	81-69	15.5
79-359	7.10	81-75	24.5(e)(i)
79-360	7.6(h), 24.5(b)(iv)	81-94	10.2(c), 20.5(g)
79-361	24.4(g), 24.5(b)(v)	81-95	13.3(b), 17.6, 23.5(a)
79-369	7.12, 8.5	81-96	19.12
79-370	26.5(g)	81-101	26.5(g)
80-21	8.3(a)	81-108	19.2(b)
80-63	13.2(a)	81-109	19.5(b)
80-86	19.5(b)	81-116	4.6, 13.1(a)
80-103	17.5	81-117	19.4(b)
80-106	20.7, 27.13	81-138	14.3
80-107	13.1(b)	81-174	14.2(b)(i), 14.2(c)(ii)
80-108	3.2, 25.2(a), 23.3(a)	81-175	14.2(b)(i), 14.2(c)(ii)
80-113	25.3(a)	81-177	25.2(b)
80-114	7.6(i)	81-209	7.14

TABLE OF IRS REVENUE RULINGS

Revenue Rulings	Book Sections	Revenue Rulings	Book Sections
81-276	6.3(e), 7.6(g), 7.7, 12.3(b)(i)	86-75	19.4(a)
81-284	7.11, 7.15(e)	86-95	23.2(c)
81-291	19.5(b)	86-98	13.1(a), 13.1(b), 14.2(c)(ii)
81-295	19.20	87-2	7.14, 19.19(c)
82-138	14.1(a)(ii), 24.5(e)(iv)	87-119	17.1(a)
82-139	24.5(e)(i)	87-126	13.1(b)
82-148	19.3	88-56	19.14
82-216	17	88-115	17.3(a)
83-43	19.5(a)	89-74	10.2(c)
83-74	19.14	89-94	19.1, 27.2(b)(ii)
83-104	6.2(b)(i)	90-36	19.23
83-140	8.3(a)	90-42	19.12
83-153	12.3(b)(i), 12.3(b)(iv)	90-74	18.17
83-157	7.6(a)	90-100	25.2(a), 25.3(a), 25.6
83-164	14.1(c)(iii)	93-73	10.2(a)
83-166	11.4, 19.8	94-16	19.20
83-170	13.1(a), 15.1(b), 19.5(f)	94-65	19.20
84-48	19.4(a)	94-81	19.20
84-49	19.4(a)	95-8	24.12(c)
84-55	24.5(i)	97-21	20.4(c)
84-81	19.12	98-15	4.5(c), 20.11(b), 30.3(b)
84-140	19.11(a)	2000-44	27.5(a)
85-1	7.7	2002-43	12.4(a)
85-2	7.7	2002-55	19.5(b), 29.2
85-109	24.5(b)(iii), 24.7(b)	2003-38	24.5(m)
85-110	24.5(b)(iii)	2003-49	25.8, 27.5
85-115	17.5	2003-64	15.6, 24.10
85-160	4.3(a)	*2004-6	17.4, App. H § 1
85-173	25.2(b)	2004-51	30.4
85-184	28.5	2004-112	24.5(m), 24.7(f)
85-199	18.3	2006-27	6.3(b), 7.1,7.5
86-49	7.11	2007-41	23.2(b)(iii)

Table of IRS Revenue Procedures

Revenue Procedures	Book Sections
59-31	28.2(e)
67-37	19.12
68-14	25.1(b)
71-17	15.2
72-5	25.1
72-16	19.12
72-17	19.12
72-54	6.2(b)
73-29	27.2
73-39	19.12
75-13	7.15(d)
75-50	6.2(b)(ii), 6.2(d)
76-9	27.2(a)(ix)
76-34	25.3(a)
78-9	26.2(a)
79-2	27.2(a)(ix)
79-6	27.7
79-8	27.2(a)(vii)
79-63	26.2(b)(ii)
80-27	25.1, 25.6
80-28	26.2(c)
80-30	25.1
81-7	12.3(b)(iv)
82-2	4.1(a), 4.3(b)
82-39	26.4
83-23	27.2(b)(iii)
84-47	25.2(a)
84-86	26.4
85-58	27.2(a)(ix)
86-43	8.2
87-51	27.12(b)

Revenue Procedures	Book Sections
90-27	17.6, 25.1, 25.1(a), 25.1(a)(i), 25.1(a)(ii), 25.1(b), 25.1(c), 25.2(a), 25.3(a), 25.6, 26.1, 26.2, 26.2(b)(i), 26.2(b) (ii), 27, 27.1(a)
90-29	19.12
91-20	10.6
92-59	7.15(d)
92-85	25.2(a)
93-28	25.2(a)
94-17	27.2(b)(iii)
95-21	24.5(e)(iii)
95-35	22.6(c)
96-32	7.4, 30.5
96-40	25.6
97-12	24.5(e)(iii)
*2003-40	26.6A
2003-21	27.2(b)(iii)
2006-53	22.6(a), 24.7(j), 24.7(l)
2007-1	25.1
2007-2	25.1
2007-4	25.1
2007-7	25.1
2007-8	25.1(d)
2007-27	27.5(a)
2009-6	25.1
2009-8	25.1
2009-9	2.2(b), 3.2, 25.1, 25.1(a), 25.1(a)(i), 25.1(a)(ii), 25.1(b), 25.1(c), 25.1(d), 25.2(a), 25.6, 25.7, 25.8, 26.1, 26.2, 26.2(b), 26.2(b)(i), 26.2(b)(ii), 26.3, 26.7, 27.1(a), 27.8(a)(ii), 27.9(a)
2009-50	22.6(a), 24.7(j), 24.7(l)

Table of IRS Private Determinations Cited in Text

PRIVATE LETTER RULINGS, TECHNICAL ADVICE MEMORANDA, EXEMPTION DENIAL AND REVOCATION LETTERS, GENERAL COUNSEL MEMORANDA, AND CHIEF COUNSEL ADVICE MEMORANDA

Private Letter Rulings and Technical Advice Memoranda

Private Determinations	Book Sections	Private Determinations	Book Sections
7740009	10.7	7944018	16.1
7741004	24.6(g)	7946001	24.5(h)(i)
7742008	17.1(a)	7946009	17.7
7806039	24.7(a)	7948113	24.5(a), 24.5(g)
7816061	24.4(f)	7951134	7.13, 20.7
7820007	11.3	7952002	20.11(b), 30.2(a)
7820057	30.7	8004011	26.4(b)(i)
7820058	20.11(b), 30.2(a)	8020010	24.4(d)
7823048	24.1	8024001	24.4(d)
7823062	26.4(e)	8025222	24.5(a)
7826003	24.4(d)	8032039	7.13
7833055	24.12(b)	8037103	11.2
7838028	10.8	8040014	8.3(b), 24.7(a)
7838108	15.4	8041007	24.7(a), 24.7(b)
7839042	24.4(g)	8107006	24.4(f)
7840014	24.5(e)(ii)	8109002	19.5(b)
7840072	24.4(d)	8112013	24.5(e)(i)
7845029	24.5(a)	8116095	24.7(c)
7847001	24.5(e)(ii)	8119061	19.19(b)
7851003	24.5(a)	8120006	24.4(f)
7851004	24.5(a)	8122007	24.7(c)
7902006	24.5(e)(i)	8127019	2 h.5(h)(i)
7903079	28.5	8128072	21.7
7905129	24.3(a)	8141019	15.3
7908009	24.4(d)	8145011	19.2(a)
7919053	24.5(a)	8147008	17.7
7921018	20.11(b)	8147009	17.1(a)
7922001	14.1(d), 24.4(f), 24.5(a)	8202019	17.7
7924009	24.6(1)	8203134	24.3(b), 24.5(h)(i)
7926003	24.6(g)	8204057	31.7(b)
7930005	11.3	8211002	24.7(a)
7930043	24.5(a)	8216009	24.5(h)(i)
7935043	7.14	8226019	24.4(g)
7936006	24.6(l)	8232011	24.5(h)(i)
7937002	19.4(a), 24.5(e)(ii)	8234084	20.5(c), 31.7(b)

TABLE OF IRS PRIVATE DETERMINATIONS CITED IN TEXT

Private Determinations	Book Sections	Private Determinations	Book Sections
8234085	31.7(b)	8503103	24.5(e)(iv)
8242003	15.3	8505002	7.6(h), 24.4(f), 24.5(b)(iv)
8244114	31.1(b)	8505044	29.3(a)
8303001	24.4(g)	8505047	24.5(e)(iv)
8303078	24.5(a)	8511082	24.4(g)
8304112	29.1(a)	8512058	18.3
8306006	9.5	8512084	9.5, 24.4(f)
8309092	10.4	8516001	17.7
8317004	4.9(b)	8518067	25.2(a)
8326008	24.5(c)	8518090	24.4(f)
8337092	15.6	8519069	31.7(b)
8337094	27.2(d)	8521055	30.1(b)
8338127	30.2(a)	8523072	24.4(f)
8347010	30.7	8524006	14.2(c)(i), 14.2(c)(iv), 24.5(e)(i)
8349051	24.4(f)		
8349072	24.4(f)	8530043	24.4(g)
8351160	24.4(f)	8539091	19.11(a)
8402014	10.5	8541008	15.3
8409055	11.3	8541108	30.2(b)(i)
8416065	10.5	8542003	15.3, 15.4
8417003	24.5(e)(i)	8602001	24.7(h)
8418003	24.5(e)(iv)	8605002	24.5(c)
8422168	24.4(f)	8606056	9.5, 29.2
8422170	14.1f	8606074	24.4(f)
8426001	15.3, 15.4	8621059	30.1(b)
8427105	24.5(b)(i)	8623081	24.4(f)
8429010	16.2, 24.5(f)	8624127	24.4(f)
8429049	19.14	8626080	24.4(f), 26.4(b)(v)
8432004	24.5(c)	8628001	17.7
8433010	24.4(g), 24.7(a)	8628049	24.4(f)
		8633034	24.4(f)
8433077	19.14	8634001	8.3(b)
8437014	24.4(g)	8638131	29.5
8442064	4.10	8640007	24.4(f)
8442092	24.5(d)	8640052	31.2(b)
8443009	24.5(d)	8643049	24.4(f)
8444097	8.3(b)	8643091	24.4(f)
8446004	24.4(g)	8650001	17.1(a)
8446008	15.3	8705041	19.2(a), 28.5
8446047	27.1(b)	8706012	29.1(a)
8450006	24.4(f)	8709051	29.3(a)
8452011	24.5(b)(vi)	8709072	24.4(f)
8452012	24.5(b)(vi)	8715055	30.7
8452074	24.4(g)	8719004	21.7
8452099	24.5(b)(vi)	8725056	24.5(h)(i)
8501002	24.4(f)	8730060	24.5(e)(iv)
8502003	17.5	8736046	24.5(b)(vi)

TABLE OF IRS PRIVATE DETERMINATIONS CITED IN TEXT

Private Determinations	Book Sections	Private Determinations	Book Sections
8737090	19.19(b)	9105002	17.7
8739055	28.2(c)	9110041	19.5(b)
8747066	24.5(h)(i)	9111001	19.5(b)
8749085	24.4(f), 24.5(b)(vi)	9114025	21.7
8802079	24.5(e(iv))	9128003	14.2(c)(iv), 24.4(g)
8814004	24.4(g)	9130002	20.1, 20.5(c), 20.5(d),
8817039	30.1(b)		30.2, 31.7(b)
8818008	30.1(b)	9130008	17.1(a)
8820061	24.4(f)	9137002	24.4(f)
8820093	20.6	9141050	25.10(d), 33.3(b)
8822065	26.4(b)(vi)	9145002	24.4(g)
8823109	24.5(h)(i)	9147007	24.3(d), 24.5(a)
8824018	24.4(f)	9216033	18.3
8826012	28.5	9217001	7.12
8828011	24.5(e)(ii)	9220010	13.1(a)
8833038	30.1(g)	9231047	20.6
8836038	27.12(g)	9233037	20.6
8836040	28.5	9237034	6.3(e)
8842071	19.19(a)	9237090	24.5(b(vi))
8851039	31.1(a)	9241055	24.5(b)(v),
8910001	6.2(g)(iii)		24.5(b)(vi)
8925092	30.6	9242002	19.2(a), 28.2(d)
8936002	23.2(d)(iv), 23.2(g)	9242035	24.4(f)
8938001	30.2	9242038	29.3(b)
8938072	31.7(b)	9242039	29.3(g)
8939002	29.5	9243008	9.5
8942099	20.6	9244003	17.3
8944007	21.7	9245031	29.2, 29.3(a)
9003045	14.1(f)	9246004	27.12(b)
9010073	31.7(g)	9246032	28.3
9012045	31.2(a)	9249001	24.4(f)
9014061	7.8	9252037	24.4(f)
9016003	21.7	9302023	24.7(a)
9016072	29.1(a)	9303030	31.3, 31.4
9017003	28.2(a)	9305026	29.3(a), 29.6
9019004	28.2(d)	9308047	29.1(a), 29.3(c)
9023081	24.5(e)(i)	9309037	31.3
9027003	8.4	*9314058	7.2A
9029047	24.5(e)(ii)	9314059	31.3
9032005	14.1(f)	9315001	27.11
9036025	24.5(a)	9316032	24.2(h), 24.2(c)
9042004	17.7	9316052	9.5, 20.4(i)
9042036	19.14	9317054	31.3
9042038	24.6(i)	9320042	24.4(c)
9043001	24.4(g)	9325062	24.4(f)
9050002	14.1(f)	9329041	7.6(h), 24.5(b)(iv)
9105001	17.7	9335001	30.2

TABLE OF IRS PRIVATE DETERMINATIONS CITED IN TEXT

Private Determinations	Book Sections	Private Determinations	Book Sections
9335061	24.5(b)(v), 24.5(b)(vi)	9538026	31.7(b)
9345004	24.5(e)(iii)	9538031	31.7(b)
9346015	31.3	9539015	24.4(f)
9352030	29.5	9539016	20.4(a)
9401031	24.4(f)	9540002	4.6, 24.5(i)
9401035	19.5(b)	9540042	21.7
9403022	24.4(f)	9542002	11.4
9404029	24.5(b)(i)	9544029	24.7(a)
9405004	24.5(b)(i)	9545014	31.7(a), 31.7(b)
9408002	24.5(e)(i)	9548019	31.3
9414002	19.2	9550001	14.1(d), 14.2(c)(i) 24.4(g),
9414044	18.3		24.5(e)(i), 24.5(j)
9416002	24.5(e)(iii)	9550003	26.5(c)
9417003	31.1(b)	9551009	31.3
9425030	24.3(a)	9603019	24.12(g)
9425032	17.5	9608003	24.5(j)
9426040	31.1(b)	9608039	12.3(b)(i), 12.3(b)(iv),
9428029	18.5		30.2(a)
9428030	18.5	9609007	23.2(b)(iv)
9429016	20.8(a)	9610032	21.7
9434041	7.6(b)	9612003	24.2(g)
9436002	24.4(g)	*9615030	6.3(b), 20.11(a.1)
9438029	29.8	9615045	24.6(h)(iii)
9438030	30.2(b)(i), 31.1(b)	9619069	24.6(j)
9440001	24.5(e)(i)	9627001	21.7
9441001	24.5(e)(ii)	9629030	24.6(j)
9442025	7.6(g)	9631004	6.3(a)
9448036	20.9	9633044	24.5(e)(iv)
9451001	20.4(b), 31.1(b)	9635003	23.2(c) 23.3
9451067	12.4(d)	9637050	29.1 (b)
9502009	24.7(k)	9637051	29.6
9509002	24.6(g)	9641011	24.5(j)
9516006	17.1(a)	9645004	24.2(f), 24.4(d),
*9516047	7.2A		24.7(b)
9522022	31.3	9645007	27.12(b)
9522039	18.17	9645017	29.6, 29.8
9527031	9.5	9646002	8.3(b)
9527043	28.1, 31.2(a)	9651046	24.4(f)
9530024	7.7	9651047	7.6(f), 24.5(j)
9530008	31.3	9652026	17.1(a), 17.14,
9530032	20.5		22.3(g)
9530036	31.3	9702004	8.4, 24.2(f), 24.5(l)
9533015	15.3, 15.4,	9703020	21.7
	31.3	9703028	28.2(e)
9535023	24.4(b), 25.5(b)(vi),	9709014	30.3(a)
	24.7(b)	9710030	7.6(a)
9535043	12.2(b)	9711002	24.5(j)
9535050	24.4(f)	9711003	4.7, 24.1

Private Determinations	Book Sections	Private Determinations	Book Sections
9711004	25.6	9847006	17.5
9712001	24.3(d)	9848002	24.5(e)(iv)
9715031	29.2, 30.3(a)	9849027	24.5(j), 27.13
9719002	24.2(b)	9850025	17.6
9720002	24.5(c)	9851001	20.5(d)
9722006	19.5(b), 29.2	9851054	24.5(b)(iii)
9726006	21.7	9853026	24.4(f)
9728004	26.1	199905027	24.4(f)
9730002	28.2(e)	199905031	24.5(e)(i)
9732022	16.2	199909056	24.4(f)
9732032	7.6(h), 8.5, 24.5(a),	199910053	24.4(f)
	24.5(b)(iv)	199910060	24.5(j)
9733015	28.5	199910061	24.4(f)
9736047	7.6(h)	199912033	13.1(b), 15.3, 15.4
9738055	31.3	*199914040	7.2A
9738056	31.3	199914051	31.3
9739043	26.4(b)(iii)	199916053	31.3
9740032	24.6(h)(i)	*199917079	7.2, 7.2A
9802045	21.4(a)	199920041	24.4(f)
9808037	17.1(a)	199922055	24.4(f)
9809054	28.4	199925051	17.1(a)
9809055	19.5(b)	199929049	24.4(f)
9810038	24.4(f)	199938041	28(1)(a)
9811001	24.5(j)	199939049	21.7
9812001	23.2(b(iv))	199943053	24.5(b)(vi)
9812037	19.17(c)	199945062	24.4(f)
9814051	24.4(f)	199946036	24.5(b)(vi)
9821049	24.4(f)	199946037	24.5(b)(vi)
9821063	24.5(b(vi))	199949045	24.4(f)
9821067	24.4(g)	200003053	18.3
9822004	24.5(j)	200009051	18.3
9822006	24.4(g)	200011063	24.10
9822039	24.5(b)(vi)	200020056	14.1(a)(iii)
9824048	24.4(f)	200020060	20.4(b)
9825001	21.7	200021056	4.4, 4.11(a)(ii), 4.11(b),
9825030	24.4(f)		8.6, 24.1, 24.2(d), 24.2(f),
9835001	20.3		24.4(a), 24.4(h), 24.5(c)
9835003	20.7, 25.1(f), 27.1(a)	200022056	24.5(j)
9837031	24.5(b)(i)	200030027	24.4(f)
9839039	24.5(j), 28.9, 30.7,	200030028	31.3
	31.5	200030033	24.4(f)
9839040	24.5(b)(vi)	200033046	22.1(c)
9840050	16.8	200033049	24.2(f), 26.4(f), 26.4(g)
9840051	28.4	200037050	24.5(j)
9840053	31.3	200037053	11.8(d)
9840054	31.3	200041034	28.3
9841049	24.7(b)	200044038	23.2(b)(iv)
9847002	24.5(j), 28.9	200044039	27.12(b)

TABLE OF IRS PRIVATE DETERMINATIONS CITED IN TEXT

Private Determinations	Book Sections	Private Determinations	Book Sections
200044040	31.5	200223067	14.1(b)
200047049	24.2(b), 24.2(h), 24.2(i), 24.4(g)	200223068	24.10
		200225041	18.3
200051046	15.6	200225044	24.4(f)
200051049	7.6(h), 24.1	200225046	29
200101034	24.5(j)	200227007	29.3(a)
200101036	24.5(b)(iv))	200230005	24.7(c), 28.5
200102056	18.5	200233024	7.6(i)
200102051	24.5(g)	200233032	24.12(c)
200102052	31.5	200234071	28.3, 31.3
*200103083	20.11(a.1)	200238001	19.19(a)
200103084	23.2(b)(iv), 33.1(d)	200241050	26.4(f)
200108045	24.5(j)	20024307	27.15(e)
200111046	18.3	200244028	21.4(a), 21.9(b)
200114040	20.11(a)	200245064	7.6(e)
200117043	31.5	200246032	24.6(j)
200118054	30.1(b), 30.4, 31.5	200247055	21.4(a)
200119061	24.2(h), 24.6(j)	200249014	24.5(a), 31.6
200124033	31.6	200301047	18.3
200126033	24.4(f)	200301048	24.4(f)
200126034	18.3	200302052	18.3
200128059	24.5(h)(ii)	200303051	31.8(c)
200131034	26.4(g), 24.5	200303062	24.5(f), 24.5(m), 24.8
200132040	29.2, 31.1(d)	200304041	30.1(b), 31.5
200133036	15.3	200304036	24.5(a), 31.6
200134025	4.1(b)(ii), 25.2(c), 27.2(c)	200305032	31.3
200147058	24.9	200307065	19.19(c)
200149043	29.2	200307094	24.5(m)
200150032	24.4(f)	200311034	19.17(c), 31.5
200150038	24.4(f)	200313024	19.17(c), 24.5(a)
200151045	11.4, 30.2, 30.2(b)(ii)	200314024	19.19(d)
200151047	24.4(f)	200314030	15.6
200151060	23.2(b)(iv), 28.3	200314031	24.5(j), 24.6(h)(iii)
200201024	31.6	200325003	31.5
200202077	31.6	200326035	9.5, 29
200203069	29	200328042	24.2(i)
200204045	18.3	*200332018	21.4(a), 21.5(f)
200204051	24.4(f)	200333008	31.8(c)
200206056	18.4	200333031	31.5
200210024	19.19(c)	200335037	21.4(a), 21.7
200211053	18.3	200341023	31.6
200211051	24.5(b)(i)	200343027	4.5(a)
200213027	24.4(f)	200345041	24.4(f)
200217044	31.8(c)	200348029	31.3
200220028	24.4(f)	200349008	24.4(f)
200222030	8.3(b), 8.6, 24.5(c)	200351033	30.1(b), 30.4, 31.6
200222031	28.5(b)(vi)	200352017	24.4(f)

Private Determinations	Book Sections	Private Determinations	Book Sections
200402003	31.8(c)	200522022	14.2(c)(ii), 14.2(c)(iii)
200404057	24.6(h)(iii)	200524024	27.17
200405016	29.2	200525020	4.11(b)
200411044	31.5	200528008	19.23
200413014	21.9(b)	200528029	4.5(c), 30.1
200421010	21.4(a)	200530016	19.19(d)
200425050	29	200530028	10.3(a), 10.3(b)
200425052	31.3	200530030	19.7
200427016	19.19(c)	200531024	27.2(a)(vii)
200428021	19.19(d)	200531025	13.1(a)
200431018	31.6	200532052	28.2(c)
200432026	24.12(b)	200532056	15.6
200435005	29.8	200532058	7.7
200435018	21.4(c)	200534022	7.4
200436022	30.4, 31.6	200534023	15.3
200437040	5.2, 10.3(a), 10.3(b), 21.16, 23.3, 29.4	200535029	5.2, 20.1, 25.1(a)(i)
		200536021	25.1(a)(i)
200439043	7.6(g), 8.7, 24.5(n)	200536023	14.2(c)(ii)
200444024	7.4, 7.5	200536024	7.15(c)
200444044	29	200536025	19.16(a)
200446025	20.1, 20.5	200536026	14.1(c)(iii)
200446033	23.2(b)(iv), 23.3, 28.3	200537038	7.15(e), 24.12(b)
		200538026	8.3(a)
200447046	7.3(c)	200538027	24.6(h)(iii), 24.12(b)
200447050	20.11(c)	200539027	4.11(b)
200450037	7.3(c)	200540012	19.11(a)
200450038	7.4	200541042	31.13
200450041	4.1(a), 4.3, 4.3(d), 4.4, 15.1(b)	200544020	13.2(a)
		200602039	29.2, 29.7(c)
200452036	3.3(h), 7.3(c)	200602042	23.2(b)(iii), 23.2(b)(iv), 23.3
200501020	13.4		
200502044	10.3(b)	200603029	6.2(e)
200503027	18.3	*200606042	6.3(b), 19.11(c), 20.11(a-1)
200504035	19.5(b)		
200505024	14.1(c)(iii)	200607027	4.1(a), 5.4(e)(i)
200506024	4.5(a)	200611033	7.7
200506025	24.4(f)	*200614030	19.11(c), 20.11(a-1)
200508016	14.2(d)	200619024	24.2(h)
200508019	4.3	200620036	8.3(a)
200509027	20.1, 20.5	200621023	4.4
200510030	31.6	200621025	6.3(a)
200511019	4.11(b)	200622055	5.6(f), 6.3(h), 8.3, 30.1(c)
200511022	16	200623068	12.3(b)(ii)
200512023	4.11(b), 13.4	200623069	24.6(n)
200512027	4.11(g)	200623072	15.2
200519084	19.11(a)	200623075	7.5
200520035	19.9(a)	200624068	7.7
		200634036	7.7

TABLE OF IRS PRIVATE DETERMINATIONS CITED IN TEXT

Private Determinations	Book Sections	Private Determinations	Book Sections
200634040	296.1	200841038	19.12
200635018	20.11(a), 20.11(b)	200842047	4.3(b)
200644043	16.2	200842050	29.2
200646020	4.5(a)	200843051	20.4(i)
200702042	20.11(b)	200842055	11.2
200703037	24.2(b)	200843035	14.2(a)
200703039	6.2(b)(ii)	200843040	31.3
200706014	13.2(a)	200843052	5.6(n)
*200708087	20.11(a-1), 20.11(c)	200844022	26.3
200709070	14.1(c)(iii)	200844029	8.6
200709072	24.4(a)	*200845053	5.6(n), 20.11(d)
200713024	24.7(f)	200845054	14.2(a)
200716034	29.7(b)	*200846040	5.6(o)
200717019	24.6(h)(iii)	*200849017	20.11(a-1)
200717020	19.5(b)	*200849018	4.4, 7.15(c)
200717031	24.4(a)	*200851033	25.1(a)(i)
200721075	7.5	*200851040	4.4
200722028	24.6(j.1)	*200852036	9.2
200723029	14.1(d), 20.9, 31.3	*200902013	30.1(b)
200723030	24.5(b)(ii), 31.6	*200905028	4.4
200724034	7.7	*200905029	4.4
200727020	7.7	*200905033	20.11(a-1)
*200727021	10.3(a), 10.3(b)	*200906057	4.4
200728044	24.2(h)	*200908050	23.10
200733030	24.4(f)	*200909064	6.2(c)
200736037	5.1(b), 20.11(d)	*200909072	4.4
200737044	5.6(n), 20.11(d)	*200910060	11.3
200739012	7.7	*200911037	18.3
200742022	13.1(b), 14.2(c)(ii)	*200912039	10.3(b)
200752043	26.3	*200915053	15.1(b)
200810025	26.3	*200916035	5.6(o), 20.11(d)
200815035	4.11(b), 25.1(a)(i)	*200917042	20.9
200819017	21.14	*200926033	7.2A
200825046	4.7	*200926036	10.3(b)
200826038	15.6	*200926037	5.6(o)
200826043	6.2(a)	*200926049	10.3(b)
200828029	5.6(n)	*200929019	7.7
200829029	13.2(b)	*200930049	4.4
200830025	19.9(a)	*200931059	28.2(e)
200830028	1.2, 5.6(n), 20.11(d)	*200931064	24.4(a)
*200832027	4.11(c), 24.2(g), 24.5(j)	*200941038	11.6
200833021	23.5, 23.5(a)	*200943042	22.3(d)
200837035	14.1(c)(iii), 14.2(a)	*200944053	20.11(a-1)
*200839034	6.3(a), 7.2, 7.2A	*200944055	20.4(b)
200839037	7.8	*200947064	7.6(a)

Exemption Denial and Revocation Letters

Ex. Den. and Rev. Ltrs.	Book Sections
20042701E	15.1(b)
20042702E	14.2(d)
20042705E	7.6(a)
20042708E	7.15(c)
20044001E	14.3
20044002E	4.5(a)
20044008E	13.4, 20, 20.11(c), 23.5(b)
20044010E	23.1
20044016E	15.2
20044018E	30.1(c)
20044044E	7.3(c)
20044045E	7.3(c)

General Counsel Memoranda

GCM	Book Sections
14407	19.19(b), 19.19(c)
31433	7.6(i)
32453	20.4(c)
33207	4.3(b)
33912	23.2(b)(vii), 29.2, 31.4
34608	14.2(c)(iii)
34631	23.2(b(vii))
35719	29.2, 31.4
35811	24.5(a)
35855	20.7
35862	16.1
35869	20.5(f)
35921	19.5(b)
36078	25.2(b)
36918	20.4(c)
37126	4.3(b)
37158	31.7(b)
37257	24.2(e)
37351	19.2(a)
37458	25.2(b)
37726	16.1
37783	31.7(b)
37789	20.11(b), 30.2(b)(ii), 31.7(b)
37858	6.2(a), 23.2(g)
37942	16.1
38104	24.5(g)
38168	24.5(g)

GCM	Book Sections
38205	24.5(g)
38248	10.1(b)
38283	4.10, 21.4(b)
38437	8.3(a)
38444	23.2(c)
38458	14.2(c)(ii)
38459	6.3(b), 7.9, 8.4, 20.1, 20.3, 24.2(e)
38497	7.15(e)
38577	11.3
38699	10.3(a)
38735	7.6(e)
38827	10.7, 10.8
38878	29.7(b)
38881	7.3(a)
38905	21.4(b)
38949	24.5(c)
38954	21.5(f)
38982	10.3(a)
39005	20.11(b), 30.2, 30.2(a), 30.2(b)(i), 30.2(b)(ii)
39082	6.2(e)
39105	14.2(c)(iii)
39107	21.7
39108	24.1
39115	15.4
39212	19.4(a)
39288	6.3(b)
39326	29.2, 31.4
39341	19.2(a)
39343	15.2
39357	19.3
39389	27.2(a)(viii)
39411	14.2(c)(ii)
39444	20.11(b), 30.2(b)(i), 30.2(b)(ii)
39498	20.3, 20.4(c)
39508	7.6(i)
39510	19.4(a)
39524	6.2(b)(iii)
39525	6.2(b)(iii)
39546	20.11(b), 30.2, 30.2(b)(i), 30.2(b)(ii)
39574	6.2(b)(ii)
39598	29.2, 29.5
39612	6.3(b)

GCM	Book Sections
39613	8.8
39622	8.8
39633	4.3(a)
39670	20.3, 20.4(c)
39674	20.4(c), 20.5(f), 21.4(c)
39692	11.4
39694	23.2(a), 23.4
39703	27.12(b)
39715	24.4(f)
39717	24.5(l)
39721	14.1(e)
39727	24.5(h)(i)
39732	20.11(b), 30.2(b)(ii), 33.3(b)
39744	24.5(l)
39757	6.2(b)(ii), 8.8
39762	31.7(b)
39775	11.2
39776	11.5
39792	6.2(e)
39806	24.5(l)
39809	27.2(a)(viii)
39811	17.6, 23.2(f), 27

GCM	Book Sections
39813	26.4(a), 26.4(b)
39817	18.3
39828	7.6(e), 27.12(b)
39830	25.9(a)
39837	17.7
39862	20.1, 20.6, 20.7, 20.11(b), 30.1(b), 30.2(b)(ii)
39865	24.3(b)
39872	8.8
39873	18.3
39877	17.5
39891	24.3(b)

Chief Counsel Advice Memoranda

CCAM	Book Sections
200431023	7.3(c), 7.3(d), 21.4(a), 21.11
200504031	7.2, 27.16
*200620001	7.3(c), 8.3
*200936027	19.11(a)

Table of IRS Private Letter Rulings, Technical Advice Memoranda, and General Counsel Memoranda

The following citations, to pronouncements from the Internal Revenue Service issued in the context of specific cases, are coordinated to the appropriate footnotes (FN) in the suitable chapters.

Citations are to IRS private letter rulings, technical advice memoranda, and general counsel memoranda, other than those specifically referenced in footnotes, directly pertinent to the material discussed in the text. Seven-number and nine-number items are either private letter rulings or technical advice memoranda; five-number items are general counsel memoranda.

While these pronouncements are not to be cited as precedent (IRC § 6110(k)(3)), they are useful in illuminating the position of the IRS on the subjects involved.

FN	Private Letter Rulings, etc.
Chapter 3	
90	39782
98	8337006
Chapter 4	
13	8705078, 8709069, 8810048
17	9014063, 9629020
46	200150027
57	200740012
62	200508020, 200508022, 200508031, 200509028, 200509031
64	8936050, 9526033
92	30808
93	200151045
95	39736
105	8501082
124	200634041
147	200447047, 20044015E, 20055035E
165	20044041E
171	9132005
176	8142024, 8204016, 32689, 34682, 36130, 37596, 38686
177	39684
*199	20044002E, 20044003E, 20044011E, 20044012E, 20044015E, 20044035E, 20044039E, 20044047E, 200443033, 200447048, 200447049, 200449035, 200449044, 200452035, 200503028, 200505023, 200508017, 200511018, 200511020, 200511021, 200511025,

FN	Private Letter Rulings, etc.
199 cont'd	200516017, 200519088, 200520030, 200520032, 200531021, 200535029, 200536021, 200549010, 200646019, 200646020, 200717018, 200724035, 200726032, 200728046, 200728047, 200732030, 200739013, 200742030, 200742023-200742025, 200744022, 200748019, 200748022, 200748023, 200802036, 200803025, 200804028, 200805024, 200810033, 200810034, 200812025, 200814027, 200814028, 200817045, 200817055, 200817057, 200822029, 200824025, 200825046, 200829033-200829035, 200829038, 200829043-200829046, 200829049-200849051, 200829054, 200829056, 200837033, 200837043, 200837050, 200850036, 200903081
*200.1	200728047, 200748023, 200749024, 200803029, 200807020, 200808032, 200810029, 200811024-200811027, 200817044, 200817046, 200817060, 200829037, 200834023, 200837040, 200837052, 200840047, 200842045, 200844027, 200846026, 200844027, 200846026, 200846036
209	39288, 39716
232	9036001, 200606045
244	200634046
260	9243008, 9316052
422	9243008, 9316052
434	20044033E

FN	Private Letter Rulings, etc.	FN	Private Letter Rulings, etc.
*444	20044006E, 20044038E, 200502046, 200505023, 200508017, 200511019, 200520032, 200534021, 200636105, 200651037, 200702042, 200709064, 200724035, 200732034, 200733027, 200743038, 200802036, 200807022, 200809037, 200809040, 200815035, 200817042, 200821037, 200824025, 200824027, 200825051, 200827041, 200837033, 200844029, 200845053, 200847018, 200847019, 200944053	111 cont'd	200514021, 200523024, 200528028, 200536022, 200538028, 200538040, 200549010, 200601034, 200602036, 200605012, 200606041, 200606044, 200611035, 200614031, 200625043, 200628041, 200631026, 200634045, 200637039, 200642010, 200642012, 200649033, 200649035, 200649036, 200733034, 200808036, 200808038, 200825047; 200835037, 200837036, 200837047, 200846023, 200851024, 200915059, 200919053, 200936038, 200936043, 200941039, 20044044E, 20044045E, 20044046E
455	20044038E		
456	200534021		
Chapter 6		115	9411037, 20044048E
52	200826043, 200829048	119	20044048E
69	39800	125	200721025
70	200527021	134	9204033
93	35986, 37462	*140	200534021, 200540013, 200545013, 200610021, 200610029, 200623071, 200623074, 200625036, 200634042, 200643007, 200645025, 200704041, 200711040, 200718034, 200718035, 200732020, 200733031, 200736034, 200739014, 200743034, 200743035, 200747024, 200749025, 200807021, 200809039, 200817051, 200817058, 200819022, 200821038, 200833024, 200842044, 200842053, 200844020, 200844030, 200846025, 200846029, 200851027, 200901034, 200911043, 200915060, 200920062, 200921042, 200940033, 200941039
98	7851096, 8327066, 33752, 37462, 39082, 39117		
122	8910001, 39792		
140	37858		
177	8024109		
178.1	200839035, 200839036, 200839038		
181	9307027		
185	8736046		
186	8405083		
187	8827074		
*190	9631004, 200851037		
198	9351027, 38050		
199	9718034, 20044035E	141	9043059, 9535023
201	9214031	142	20042706E
210	37257, 37787, 38459	152	200233024
222	9408026	155	8633038
Chapter 7		157	9241055, 9242002
6	9718034	158	8251089, 8251096, 8736046, 8936045, 8936046, 9527035
7	9752064		
14	8801067, 9311034, 9411037	167	9307027
18	8637141	173	9412002
23	9325061	174	9246004, 38735, 39057, 39487, 39799, 39828, 39829, 39830
74	20044045E, 20044046E		
99	20044044E–20044046E, 200447046, 200450037, 200450039, 200450042–200450045, 200452306, 200506038, 200510031, 200510044, 200514021, 200523024, 200528028, 200536022, 200538028, 200538040, 200549010, 200611035, 200614031, 200625043	178.1	200819023
		190	9714011, 9716021, 9721031, 9722042, 9738038–9738054
		207	38686, 38894, 39120
		209	8237052, 8509044, 8509073, 8511082, 8625081, 9408026, 39340
		218	32896, 36827
*111	200450037, 200450039, 200450042-200450045, 200452036, 200506038, 200510031, 200510044,	219	9325061
		225	9210032, 9735048
		229	9001011

FN	Private Letter Rulings, etc.	FN	Private Letter Rulings, etc.
240	9411037, 9541003, 9629002	463	8425019, 8425031, 8425032, 8425038, 8425064, 8426029, 8429012, 8429028, 8430026, 8430044, 8431024, 8431025, 8432038, 8432050, 8435027, 8435028, 8435080, 8435089, 8435102, 8436042, 8437021, 8437038, 8437040, 8437041, 8437068, 8437082, 8437095, 8438019, 8441014, 8442081, 8443031, 8443077, 8444019, 8444053, 8445027, 8447013, 8447059, 8447084, 8447102, 8448020, 8448021, 8450009, 8452018, 8501077, 8502026, 8502037, 8502071, 8503031, 8505010, 8506035, 8506048, 8507018, 8507034, 8514019, 8516027, 8516048, 8516093, 8517026, 8517027, 8518072, 8522024, 8524111, 8534020, 8534056, 8536027, 8536037, 8537014, 8537040, 8541025, 8542010, 8543014, 8544015, 8544027, 8546060, 8603034, 8607010, 8607040, 8609020, 8609033, 8610025, 8611036, 8620036, 8621085, 8622034, 8639024, 8639039, 8650008, 34704
241	8723052, 9243008, 9246032, 9246033, 9629002, 200606047, 200611033, 200634036, 38693, 39347, 39348, 39682, 39685, 39852		
242	9047049, 39348		
248	200724034		
253	9249026		
255	9530025, 9530026, 9537035–9537053		
259	9408026		
262	39733		
263	7823052		
264	9731038		
268	199932052		
274	8629045, 9802045		
275	8429102, 8629045, 9048046, 9237027		
288	39562		
290	9118012		
302	9539013		
307	9247030	464	8342022, 8412064
309	9002036, 9025073, 9306034	467	7823052, 9526033
310	9002036, 9306034	469	39055
311	39360	480	200505032
316	38050	486	8429051, 9240001, 39047, 39883
317	9407005, 9526033	487	9048046, 9539015
345	9014063	489	39633
357	8705078	500	200521029
358	37518	**Chapter 8**	
359	37518	92	8705078
362	8536099, 9014063, 35936, 35966, 37180, 38401, 38322	96	8823088
377	9210026	101	9325061
385	8334001, 8849072	113	9211002, 9211004
386	20044014E, 20044037E	116	8645017
388	8734007	118	200333034
390	8906062, 35945	119	200333034
393	7816061, 7905129, 7951134	134	8909004
394	7902019, 8920084	136	8846002
403	7816061	145	9414003
409	8753049, 9242002, 9635037, 39562	152	9019046
429	8839024	176	8751007, 8811021, 9036025, 9851052
435	8351103	177	9210026
439	8448020, 8717020, 8721022, 8921061, 9347001	202	9048046, 9237027
440	7909026, 7935043, 8347031, 8348025, 8944068	223	20044015E
		226	8930052
446	8630021	228	9638001
452	8349017, 8438027, 8511032	246	9335061, 39622
461	8836056	**Chapter 9**	
		14	8723061–8723064, 200714026
		15	9240001, 39883

FN	Private Letter Rulings, etc.
18	7852997, 8028004
19	9627023
29	9346006
50	8512084
51	9017052
52	9311032, 9722032

Chapter 10

FN	Private Letter Rulings, etc.
116	37622, 37503, 37391, 37247
131	8626100, 8626101, 8627044, 8628077, 8629051, 8641069–8641072, 8643055
133	8422171, 8422174, 8423078, 8423079, 8424056, 8424098, 8425058, 8425076, 8425115, 8425118, 8425123, 8425130–8425135, 8426022, 8426023, 8426045, 8426047, 8426068, 8426091, 8426107–8426109, 8427096–8427099, 8427103, 8427104, 8428108, 8428115, 8428110–8428113, 8429065–8429068, 8429106, 8429107, 8429110, 8430073, 8431067–8431069, 8431075, 8431081–8431083, 8432068–8432070, 8432076–8432078, 8432110, 8433053, 8433054, 8433111 8434064–843067, 8435047, 8435086, 8435158–8435161, 8435168, 8435171–8435174, 8435090–8435098, 8436036, 8436037, 8436039, 8436040, 8436050, 8437070, 8437076, 8437090, 8437101, 8437102, 8437104, 8437112, 8437114, 8438045, 8438061, 8438062, 8438066, 8439014, 8439015, 8439081, 8439097, 8439102, 8439103, 8440092, 8440093, 8440097–8440100, 8441046, 8441065, 8442065–8442073, 8442075, 8442093, 8442097–8442101, 8442110, 8442132, 8442134–8442141, 8443049–8443051, 8443081, 8443090–8443092, 8444085, 8444087–8444089, 8444095, 8444096, 8445074–8445078, 8445080, 8445101–8445107, 8446033, 8446037, 8447066, 8447067, 8447088–8447090, 8448041–8448043, 8448045, 8448049, 8448055–8448058, 8448070, 8449068, 8450072–8450074, 8451051, 8452070–8452073, 8452075, 8452081–8452084, 8453096–8453101, 8501061, 8501062, 8502062, 8502063, 8502076–8502078, 8502085–8502090, 8502096, 8502101, 8503040, 8503042, 8503071, 8503078–8503082, 8504052, 8504057, 8504081, 8505061–8505064, 8505077, 8506067, 8506078–8506080, 8506084, 8506101, 8506103, 8506119, 8508082–8508085, 8508100, 8508104, 8509068, 8509101, 8510041, 8510042, 8510058–8510060, 8510090, 8510091, 8511051–8511053, 8511069, 8511070, 8512075, 8512076, 8512080, 8512091, 8512092, 8514056–8514059, 8514061,

FN	Private Letter Rulings, etc.
133 cont'd	8514062, 8514078, 8514083, 8514084, 8514086, 8514096, 8514097, 8515065, 8516059, 8516097, 8516102, 8516108, 8516109, 8516115, 8516136, 8516137, 8517059–8517061, 8517065, 8518055, 8510856, 8518081–8518086, 8518091, 8518092, 8519035, 8519036, 8520047, 8520052, 8520064, 8520067, 8520071, 8520118, 8520119, 8521013, 8521100, 8521104, 8521105, 8522080–8522083, 8522085, 8523082, 8523087, 8523091, 8523094, 8523095, 8523101, 8523104, 8523106–8523111, 8524065–8524069, 8525076, 8525088–8525090, 8526083, 8527045, 8527049, 8527067, 8529051, 8529052, 8529098, 8529105, 8530054–8530058, 8530134, 8531051, 8531066, 8531067, 8532014, 8532015, 8532024, 8532044, 8532047, 8532060, 8532069, 8532095–8532097, 8533020, 8533079, 8534062, 8534086, 8534087, 8535060, 8535061, 8535119, 8536089, 8536090–8536094, 8537059, 8537060, 8537102–8537107, 8538067, 8539090, 8540032, 8540083, 8540089, 8541106, 8541109, 8541110, 8542059, 8542066, 8542096, 8542097, 8543048, 8543057–8543063, 8543090, 8544087, 8546100–8546106, 8546113, 8546114, 8546116, 8546124, 8546130, 8546132, 8546136, 8546137, 8547059, 8547060, 8547068–8547073, 8548081, 8549064, 8550048, 8550049, 8550052, 8550054–8550056 8550074–8550076, 8551049–8551050, 8551052–8551059, 8551067–8551070, 8551078–8551080, 8551081, 8552108, 8601056, 8601057, 8601059–8601062, 8601064, 8601065, 8601068–8601072, 8602048, 8602065, 8603089–8603095, 8603097, 8603107–8603109, 8603122–8603124, 8604081, 8604083, 8604084, 8604090, 8604091, 8604094, 8605048, 8605050, 8606070, 8606071, 8606073, 8606076, 8608081, 8608082, 8609070, 8609071, 8610079, 8610080, 8610084, 8611047, 8611049, 8611080–8611083, 8614045, 8615045, 8615047, 8615049, 8615058–8615062, 8615088–8615090, 8616057, 8616062–8616065, 8616096, 8618045, 8618046, 8618066, 8619048–8619050, 8619054–8619060, 8619063–8619066, 8620059–8620063, 8620081, 8620083, 8621102, 8621114, 8622046–8622048, 8622052–8622054, 8622057, 8622061, 8623045, 8623052, 8624080–8624083, 8624091, 8624093, 8624094, 8624128, 8624152, 8624166, 8624168, 8625089, 8625102–8625105, 8626100, 8626101, 8627044, 8628077, 8629051, 8631061, 8631072, 8631073,

TABLE OF IRS PRIVATE LETTER RULINGS

FN	Private Letter Rulings, etc.	FN	Private Letter Rulings, etc.
133 cont'd	8631080, 8631083, 8631092, 8631093, 8631097–8631099, 8631107, 8631108, 8631110, 8631111, 8631113–8631117, 8633037, 8634061, 8634064, 8635056, 8635057, 8638124, 8641069–8641072, 8833001, 9624001, 36078, 36993, 37116	176	37853
		178	9124004, 200528008
		182.1	200833031, 200843034, 200843043, 200844025
168	9448017, 39614	185	8826004
175	200437040, 200712046, 200712047, 200830028	188	20044007E, 20044031E, 20044043E
		189	200505024, 200536025, 200538039, 200601032
181	9518021	190	20042707E, 200606046, 200827040
199	9434002	196	20044001E, 200444024
209	7838029–7838036	207	9429002, 9429003
211	33574, 36254, 36787, 37503	**Chapter 15**	
Chapter 11		15	200728048, 200817064, 200837042, 200846033
7	9851001		
16	9211004, 39459, 39560, 39775	18	39773
19	9129040, 39459, 39560	36	200449045, 200531026, 200540018
32	39799, 9851054	37	20042701E, 200449045, 200519085, 200520031, 200520033, 200531026, 200531027
38	20044009E		
61	36738, 39598		
Chapter 12		42	9533015
188	200807019	*43	200919052
189	200731035	49	20044016E, 20044017E, 20044019E, 200511023, 200534023, 200540011
Chapter 13		66	9043019
1	9149004, 9201039, 39574, 39866	*68	200540011, 200623072, 200624069, 200625042, 200628040, 200631027, 200636106, 200735028, 200735030; EDRLs 20044016E, 20044017E, 20044019E, 200702044, 200729040, 200729041, 200732024, 200735028, 200735030, 200811023, 200825048, 200829041, 200846034, 200850035, 200915055, 200915061, 200919072
9	200531025		
24	8923001		
34	20042708E, 37518		
39	200511024, 200714027		
60	9044060		
63	9811003, 9815061		
73	200720026		
80	200809035	69	200133037, 200134021
90	200716035	79	200507014
102	39763	*80	200910067
121	200511024	82.1	200723032
128	8829072	90	9212002
133	8828058, 8838052	91	39688
Chapter 14		98	8809087, 8812006, 9043003, 9044022, 39717
5	200020056		
8	9517036	100	8729001
57	20044041E	109	39658
59	200601035	110	8816004
72	9029035	117	8905002, 8920002, 8922067, 8943009, 9043019, 200625034, 39773
91	39721		
106	9349022	118	8728002, 9246043
127	20044043E, 20044007E, 20044031E, 20044042E	126	200451031
		127	8737060, 8738075, 8919062, 8951062, 9025001, 9027044, 9040018, 9307004, 9608002, 9629032, 9630001, 9824045,
166	20044043E		

FN	Private Letter Rulings, etc.	FN	Private Letter Rulings, etc.
127 cont'd	9844012, 200427031, 200451035, 200638026, 200826038, 200837045	64	200225041
		65	200413013, 200450040
		67	200126035
128	8724045, 8740002	69	200327063, 200327066
129	9225001	70	20006056
*140	200916036	71	9410048, 9413042
Chapter 16		72	9213029
3	200552019	74	8936070, 200003054
7	39698, 200649029	78	9214032, 9233027, 9242014, 9325054, 9351042, 9401033, 9410048, 9508032, 9640024, 9640025, 9646034, 9649037, 200308055
*13	200921041		
82	8739066, 39672		
Chapter 17		80	200609025
13	8850014	81	8717062, 8833039, 8937038
17	8650001, 9249002, 9652026, 9725036, 39694	92	8937038
		93	9402034, 200006056
19	9320002	97	8951061, 9645022
38	200511003	98	8721092
50	9622002	104	9522023
64	9409003	107	9402034, 9403023
70	9603017	108	8629086, 8929087, 9403023
77	9433001	109	9403023
90	7903079, 9042004, 9245001		
92	8901050	**Chapter 19**	
93	39694	3	39859
94	8852037	20	8038024, 8207007, 8217023, 8312127, 8534101, 9605001, 9642054, 200003038
Chapter 18			
30	9802038	25	9213027, 200449034
31	9507009	28	8751006, 9130008
32	9413042	31	200214035, 200214036
35	9147059, 9325041, 9332044, 9438017, 9641034, 20042704E. 200651036	37	9308047
		39	200449304
36	9437016, 200511003	43	200449034
38	9145031, 9145032, 200537036, 39834	45	200615026
41	39817	55	9721034, 200503029, 200509026, 200705036
46	200549008		
47	200602037, 200602038	75	9113038, 200519087, 200520034, 200808039, 39735
48	199930040		
50	9641034, 200028007, 39879	82	200818022
53	9139003, 200451032, 39621, 39879	92	39575
56	8822089, 8925091, 8936070, 9006051, 9014065, 9115035, 9252038, 9446036, 9720034, 200023052, 200024054, 200503027, 39801	100	200847017
		107	200634044
		108	9539003, 9542039, 9551010, 9551036
57	200638027	*122	200602043, 200907040
59	9505019, 9551007, 200038054	123	8812016, 9149007, 9715045, 200644039, 200803021, 200842046
60	9401033, 9438017		
61	200203073–200203075, 200338023, 200431020, 200450040	125	200504035
		127	200601031
62	200111047, 200111048	131	200849016

FN	Private Letter Rulings, etc.	FN	Private Letter Rulings, etc.
133	200721020, 200721021, 200806014, 200806017, 200806018	346 *cont'd*	8831043, 8910024, 8934038, 8940025, 8944029, 9003091, 9007022, 9035045, 9030014, 9042045, 9045019, 9102008, 9133024, 9201022, 9201022, 9214020, 9233025, 9242018, 9250023, 9315020, 9348018, 9406032, 9413046, 9735021, 9816008, 9850011, 199931045, 200034006, 200203027, 200344017, 200511001, 200652004, 200701009, 200752004
139	199908001		
140	9110041, 9111001		
145	8816004, 39724		
147	9510066		
149	9510066, 9722006		
152	9111001		
164	200805025, 200806022	359	8524011, 9038018
165	8639074, 9231045	373	200538039
168	39865	402	9825035, 200030030, 200024055, 200123065, 200134032, 200214032, 200231020, 200232035
173	8902003, 9626021		
179	200834022		
181	9102015	409	9130026
208	39885	413	9130036, 9611044
*212.1	200837044, 200851026, 200851035, 200903082, 200903089, 200903093, 200903094, 200910066, 200911044, 200913069, 200915054, 200915058, 200915062, 200919051	416	7821037, 8107117, 8147094, 8313060, 8314050, 8342022, 8425032, 8453038, 8603034, 8609020, 8621085, 8633034, 8650008, 8721061, 8728057, 8728058, 8728073, 200008024, 200008039
214	200810031, 200829053, 200831028, 200842052, 200842058	417	9348021, 9515014, 200428021, 200430008
*219	200529008, 200531019, 200531022, 200531023, 200531028, 200550044, 200550045, 200644047, 200705030, 200715012, 200723027, 200724036, 200736033, 200803022, 200807018, 200808034, 200809034, 200809045, 200822040, 200824024, 200824028, 200824029, 200837041, 200842049, 200850040, 200909062	418	9244003, 200428021, 200430008
		422	8719023, 9109030, 9149007
		*428	8639024, 8645036, 8705015, 8705038, 8705054, 8710016, 8713030, 8719023, 8721022, 8721061, 8722030, 8725010, 8725024, 8725033, 8728057, 8728058, 8729038, 8733018, 8737090, 8738036, 8740015, 8743032, 8747010, 8748017, 8748031, 8748024, 8749030, 8751017, 8752011, 8752022, 8753008, 8803020, 8803022, 8803033, 8803035, 8803057, 8804028, 8804058, 8806028, 8806062, 8809038, 8809047, 8809051, 8810060, 8810062, 8810084, 8814018, 8815009, 8815010, 8815027, 8816022, 8816040, 8819046, 8819055, 8820030, 8821030, 8821046 8823034, 8823035, 8824015, 8825034, 8825081, 8825087, 8825096, 8825100, 8826026, 8826037, 8826048, 8829041, 8829062, 8831047, 8832020, 8832047, 8832056, 8832066, 8832067, 8834031, 8835034, 8836056, 8836038, 8839014, 8839024, 8839039, 8839083, 8842070, 8842071, 8847032, 8849023, 8850037, 8850038, 8850063, 8920056, 8920023, 8920037, 8921024, 8921055, 8923024, 8925010, 8925014, 8925015, 8925028, 8926078, 8927058, 8928061, 8929039, 8930036, 8931008, 8931061, 8931068, 8931069, 8932031, 8933011, 8934009, 8934026, 8934052, 8935012, 8936028, 8938018, 8938044, 8939047, 8940032, 8940034, 8941052, 8942037, 8943051, 8943053, 8944008, 8944031, 8944032, 8944068, 8948057, 8948060, 8950050, 8951048, 8951057, 8951012,
220	199914052		
225	39864		
237	9747003, 199924057–199924059, 200011050, 200850037		
238	8741004, 9315002		
243	200519084, 200531018,		
244	9315002		
261	8807025, 8811003, 9034043, 9229011		
287	8626002		
289	9310031		
293	9217003, 9314001		
298	8750002		
303	39522		
310	39819		
325	9309012		
327	9132038		
329	200728045		
331	9021013		
346	8627011, 8644065, 8729071, 8801003, 8804009, 8815019, 8824029, 8827054,		

FN	Private Letter Rulings, etc.	FN	Private Letter Rulings, etc.
*428 cont'd	8952016, 8952036, 9002016, 9004034, 9012031, 9015057, 9017052, 9025062, 9026015, 9026054, 9026055, 9027025, 9027028, 9027038, 9028033, 9032012, 9033062, 9034041, 9035013, 9035024, 9037019, 9037046, 9038036, 9041054, 9041070, 9042059, 9042060, 9043017, 9043035, 9043047, 9043067, 9045021, 9046039, 9046042, 9046060, 9049025, 9050052, 9050055, 9103009, 9106007, 9106023, 9106026, 9107032, 9109020, 9110004, 9110022, 9110062, 9113021, 9114055, 9115016, 9115037, 9129043, 9137019, 9140046, 9140050, 9140070, 9142019, 9143057, 9145042, 9149011, 9151026, 9201027, 9205020, 9206012, 9212010, 9217032, 9218014, 9238011, 9238024, 9240024, 9243044, 9245007, 9247014, 9247015, 9248024, 9249015, 9342029, 9347001, 9401003–9401006, 9401010, 9402028, 9403025, 9405024, 9409040, 9410034, 9411017, 9412027, 9421008, 9421009, 9423038, 9424007, 9425029, 9435031, 9436048, 9436052, 9440012, 9443032, 9443034, 9505015, 9506037, 9507019, 9522043, 9523008, 9524028, 9530017, 9530018, 9533040, 9540007, 9541030, 9544024, 9545015–9545017, 9546012, 9546014, 9549030, 9552045, 9605006, 9609034, 9613007, 9622019 (withdrawn by 9631011), 9624013, 9627016, 9630018, 9631008, 9635017, 9637037, 9646018, 9646026, 9627016, 9706006, 9706007, 9722029, 9723042, 9725022, 9731023, 9740005, 9741002, 9742003, 9746035, 9746057, 9809013, 9819023, 9819029, 9823012, 9829024, 9830006, 9831025, 9835045, 9836014, 9844029, 9845018, 9846029, 9848025, 9849003, 9852019, 9852020, 9852043, 9853022, 199905026, 199909048, 199911047, 199913041, 199916045, 199916050, 199924046, 199924063, 199928011, 199928035, 199930028, 199931042, 199942008, 199952049, 199952083, 200003052, 200019023, 200022019, 200031045, 200040016, 200007015, 200003052, 200008024, 200008039, 200023022, 200109002, 200116069, 200127033, 200151015, 200201001, 200210025, 200214026, 200243023, 200301025, 200318058, 200326012, 200327024, 200334021, 200337006, 200351006, 200403026, 200406024, 200416005, 200418018, 200418044, 200426010, 200426017, 200428015, 200428021, 200430008, 200439033, 200449018, 200453009, 200505013, 200506004, 200510016, 200521005, 200537006, 200538004, 200539006, 200606007, 200610001, 200626027, 200630001, 200637031,	*428 cont'd	200702022, 200704007, 200727002, 200730019, 200736022, 200738008, 200743011, 200807001, 200808025, 200811010, 200814014, 200817014, 200822019, 200823020, 200827004, 200828026, 200839005, 200839006, 200839009, 200841013, 200841018, 200841019, 200852017, 200908011, 200908013, 200909019, 200915022, 200919022, 200921024, 200924015, 200925032, 200937023, 200942021, 200943025, 39761
		433	9439008, 200238001
		435	200026013, 200303025, 200314024
		441	200243040
		*443	9627016, 9809013, 9822011, 9823029, 9852018, 199906036, 199928011, 199923029, 200116017, 200210024, 200222007, 200243040, 200403026, 200427016, 200827004
		444	200551034
		Chapter 20	
		13	200446025
		*32	200605012, 200606041, 200625043, 200645025, 200708089, 200712045, 200730031, 200733028, 200738032, 200740013, 200740014, 200742029, 200801040, 200801041, 200814028, 200817014, 200817043, 200817055, 200837033, 200840048, 200840049, 200844021, 200844022, 200845053, 200846039, 200850036, 200850038, 200850039, 200850041, 200850042, 200850050, 200850059, 200912038, 200914063, 200914064, 200926036, 200926037, 200926049, 200928045, 200928046, 200943047
		*33	200646018, 200649037, 200707161, 200710012, 200725040, 200726032, 200730031, 200732017, 200732019, 200736031, 200736032, 200748019, 200748021, 200752043, 200801040, 200801041, 200809032, 200809033, 200840048, 200844021, 200844022, 200844029, 200846031, 200850038, 200850039, 200850041, 200850042, 200850050, 200850059, 200908051, 200909070, 200930055, 200937039
		65	9525056
		89	9112006, 9201035
		110	20044013E
		120	8731032
		124	38394
		127	35638
		144	9231045, 9621035
		146	200447047, 200508021, 200532051

FN	Private Letter Rulings, etc.	FN	Private Letter Rulings, etc.
147	20042703E, 20044004E, 20044032E, 200511016	152	9117001
		*153	200903080
150	8838047	155.1	200843033
157	20044033E		
191	8807081, 8808070	**Chapter 24**	
193	200511016	23	9338043, 200417035
195	8807081, 8808070	34	9120029
196	9025089, 37180, 38283, 39670	39	200027056
197	32518, 35865	*59.2	200704035, 200704036, 200710013–200710016, 200711025–200711039, 200723031, 200732021, 200732022, 200733032, 200733033, 200749023, 200803019, 200803020, 200806019, 200807017, 200810026–200810028, 200810030, 200816034, 200816035, 200817038, 200818025, 200818026, 200821034, 200821035, 200824021, 200824023, 200850048, 200850049, 200904025, 200904037, 200905030, 200905031, 200906053–200906056, 200913063, 200913065, 200919055–200919057, 200922061, 200951037, 200952059
*219	20044004E, 20044032E, 200447050, 200851037		
272.1	200723032		
279	9428035		
308	39876		
320	9530024–9530026		
*323.6	200852036		
339	200635018		
*367	20044004E, 20044032E, 200511017, 200524029, 200606040, 200606041, 200649034, 200711041, 200729042, 200736037, 200737044, 200749026, 200803026, 200806021, 200810025, 200817041, 200817048, 200817049, 200818023, 200818028, 200819021, 200822034, 200822044, 200839040, 200840050, 200841039, 200842057, 200845053, 200936039, 200944053		
		66	9242035
		69	8722082, 9735047, 32896, 36827
		70	9217001
		74	9325061
		83	9401031
		88	36827
Chapter 21		90	9720035
57	200435019–200435022	95	8822057
Chapter 22		96	8840020, 8841041
15	39694	97	8806056, 9318047
25	200449035	104	9042038
67	39694	121	9438040, 9505020, 9509041, 9510039, 200148085
70	9244003		
108	9622002	122	200328045, 200328046, 200328048
118	9507020	127	8651086, 8708052, 8841041
119	9507020	128	8829003, 8932004, 9309002
121	9332042	130	8717002, 8717063, 8733037, 8734005, 8901064, 8934050, 8936013, 9003059, 9017058, 9018049, 9240937, 9337027, 9340061, 9340062, 9349022
142	9332042, 9347034		
212	9510047, 9534021, 9602026, 9636016		
215	199919038		
		131	9425031
Chapter 23		147	8922064, 9407005, 9413020
4	9809062	149	9417003
*5	20044010E, 2004040E, 200724033, 200748021, 200809038, 200928045	152	9137002, 9417003, 9509002, 9721001
		154	199941048
36	200830027	158	8641001
45	39694	163	9302023
105	8906062	169	9539005
119	200437040	170	8819005, 9723046
136	9433001		

FN	Private Letter Rulings, etc.	FN	Private Letter Rulings, etc.
172.2	200709073, 200710017, 200710019, 200717029-200717031, 200717033, 200717034, 200725049, 200725052, 200725055, 200725056	395	200041030
		396	8809092, 8817017
		404	199917084
172.3	200725046-200725048, 200725050, 200725051, 200725053, 200725054, 200725057	406	8626102, 8640052–8640054, 8640056, 8640057, 8645064, 8833002
		409	8949093
175	9535023	411	8814001, 9138003
180	9750056	414	8641060
181	9641011, 9728034, 9715041	425	9428035
183	8732029, 9041045, 9350045	427	9349024
206	9014069	434	9645027
213	9107030, 9110012, 9137002	435	8815002
218	8743081, 8743086, 8743087, 9347036	439	8432003
221	9110042,9329041, 200203070	446	9147054, 9550001, 9527001
222	8643091	453	8707003, 8842002, 9037063, 9548001, 39723
228	9149002	454	9220054
230	8643049, 9141053, 9150052, 9152039	455	9220054, 9306030, 9318005, 9535004 (withdrawn by 9542046), 9612003, 39827
235	9107030		
261	200147059, 200149044, 200216036, 200222032, 200230004	457	8841003
		469	8734004, 39735
266	200150033, 200150035	471	9550001
276	200352018, 200352019	475	9029047
277	9321072, 9321087, 9323035, 9812031, 9814048, 200234071, 200242041, 200243056, 200444030, 200446011, 200528030, 200532058, 200536024, 200804026, 200807016	489	9847001
		495	9428035
		497	8852002
		498	9128003
285	9137049	507	9325003
304	9853001	508	9128002
305	200752042, 200833022	517	9137002, 9147054, 9205037, 200448048, 39860
306	9138003, 9145002, 9147005, 9320050, 9323035, 200501017, 200512025, 39864	518	8947002, 9044071, 9234002, 9304001, 9345004, 9724006
317	8025222		
337	9137002, 39860	522	9023003, 199914035
342	8641090	523	9302035
346	9231001	525	8932004
348	8650083	530	8726069, 9302023
349	9014069	539	9023001, 9023002, 9204007, 9402005
351	39843	542	9247001
352	39762	543	8834006, 8835001, 9023001, 9023002, 9217002, 9402005, 9419003, 9734002
355	8735004, 8815031, 8817066, 9730941, 9739042	544	8403013
357	8736046	546	9248001
362	8736046, 8817017, 9445024	572	9623035
372	8721103, 8809092, 8921091, 8941082, 9023041	575	8725058
		576	9736046
378	9736047	578	9315001, 9321005
380	9750056, 9803001	587	9250001
381	9110042, 9226055	602	200844029
388	9750056	613	9822004

FN	Private Letter Rulings, etc.	FN	Private Letter Rulings, etc.
615	9521004	759	9108034, 9108043, 9127045, 9128030, 9132040, 9132061, 9144032–9144035, 9150047, 9204048, 9247038, 9252028, 9547040, 9551021, 200637041
616	8846002		
630	9608003, 9711002, 9718029		
632	9752023, 200108048	761	9619068
*632.1	200910061	762	9616039, 9619068, 9619069, 9630031, 9631025, 9631029, 9652028, 9704010, 9745025, 200246032
636	9839039, 200031057, 200033050, 200108048, 200216037		
637	9814039, 9819049, 9839042, 9853026, 199924065, 199943049, 199949038, 200032046, 200036049, 200108048, 200108045, 200108051, 200132139, 200134027, 200215057-200215060, 200233025, 200238051, 200245057	764	9108034, 9108043, 9128030, 9132040, 9132061, 9144032, 9144035, 9150047, 9252028 (modified by 9428037), 9308040, 9316032, 9319044, 9401029, 9407005, 9411018, 9411019, 9412039, 9414002, 9432019, 9629032, 9651014, 9803024, 9826046, 9844004, 9853034, 199952071, 200041038, 200151046, 200151062, 200219037, 200237027, 200510029, 200530029, 200532057
638	200108048		
641	200108046, 200108047, 200108049		
711	9012058		
713	199914042, 199928042, 200518081	775	8201024
714	9042038	779	199928042, 199952086, 200315028, 200315032, 200315034
715	8708031, 8836037, 9442035, 9826046, 200715015		
		780	9043039
716	200315028, 200315032, 200315034	781	8641061, 8831007, 8932004, 8942070, 9033056, 9302023, 9544029, 9605001, 9704012,
721	9030048		
727	9231045		
729	9151001, 9309002, 9306030, 39827	781	199952086, 200251016–200251018
733	8839016	806	200628039
735	9346014	811	39786
737	8827017	813	8832043, 39752
738	8222066, 8645050, 8717066, 8717078, 8721102, 8728060, 8808002, 8808003, 8810097, 8824054, 8828011, 8845073, 8846005, 8922084, 8941011, 8941062, 8948023, 9015038, 9023091, 9024026, 9043039, 9108021, 9316045, 9316052, 9319042, 9319043, 9404003, 9404004, 9417036, 9417042, 9417043, 9419033, 9436001, 9440001, 9441001, 9450028, 9503024, 9552019, 9703025, 9705001, 9709029, 9714016, 9723001, 9724006, 9810030, 9816027, 200046039, 200149035, 200149043, 20019037, 200225046, 200601033, 39615	827	8736046, 9241055
		834	200628039
		845	8915005, 9217001
		846	8728080
		852	200531020
		857	39734
		867	9302035, 9303030
		873	9232003
		874	8920084
		881	9726030
		886	9652004
939	9139029, 9212030, 9231045, 9234043, 9551019, 200601033, 200621031, 200637041, 35957, 39568	908	200029055
		950	9319044, 9750056
		955	9847002
740	9450045, 200041031, 200147058, 200148057, 200148074	958	9145003, 9328003
		960	9141003, 9141004, 9145031, 9145032, 9147059, 9216033, 9242014, 9247039
741	8950072, 9139029, 9141051, 9146047, 9702003		
		962	9247039, 9517035, 9841003
742	8445005, 8720005, 8802009, 8925029, 39825	963	8905002, 8943009, 9721034, 9310034, 9344028, 9628022, 199932050, 39773,200003036
746	8713072, 8822096, 8932042, 9245036, 9246032, 9246033, 9301024, 9315021, 9703025, 9850020, 200532058		
		966	8728008, 8728009, 8925091, 9016039, 9310034, 9351042, 9410048, 9413042, 9818001
749	200032050		
754	9136037		

FN	Private Letter Rulings, etc.
970	200301030
*971.1	200852037
986	8708031, 8717066, 200003048
988	8738006, 9144044, 199952089
989	8522040, 8651091, 8906003, 8935058, 9147058, 9204048, 9726005
993	200821036
998	9246032, 9246033
1001	8950073, 9047040
*1002	200852037
1003	200125096
1004	9241052, 200537037
1005	9651001
1007	8044023, 8104098, 8107114, 8110164, 8338138, 8738006, 8807082, 9031052, 9407023, 9703026, 200041038, 200233032
1009	9010025, 9431001, 9533014
1012	8822057
1014	9042043, 9108021, 9110012, 9527033, 9743054, 200150040, 200233023, 200449033, 39826
1015	9012001
1018	8818008, 8923077, 9031052, 9047069, 9218006, 9218007, 200534025
1020	9450045, 200137061
1022	9508031, 200318076
1031	9128020
1034	9002030
1035	200224014, 200351032
1040	8721104, 8721107, 9042038
1043	9619077
1044	9637053, 9642051
1046	9717004
1059	9147008, 9149006, 39863
1061	9324002

Chapter 25

FN	Private Letter Rulings, etc.
21	200846040
25	200540016,
28	20044034E, 200536021, 200845053
*53	200930049
103	9145001
151	8906008
152	8649001
165	9145039
175	39833
228	39830
229	39830

Chapter 26

FN	Private Letter Rulings, etc.
139	9408066
296.1	200634047, 200636102, 200636104, 200646018, 200649037, 200650027, 200651035, 200714028, 200720028, 200723028, 200743039, 200749027, 200751036, 200752039-200752041, 200802034, 200802037, 200802038, 200803023-200803025, 200803027, 200803028, 200805024, 200808033, 200808035, 200808037, 200808040, 200808041, 200809036, 200817047, 200817052-200817054, 200817063, 200822030-200822033, 200822035-200822039, 200822043, 200829036, 200829039, 200829040, 200829042, 200829047, 200829052, 200829055, 200833019, 200833020, 200833023, 200833025, 200833026, 200834023, 200837034, 200837037-200837039, 200837048, 200837049, 200837051, 200837053, 200842054, 200842056, 200844018, 200844019, 200844023-200844026, 200844031, 200846027, 200846030, 200846032, 200846035, 200850043, 200850044, 200850047

Chapter 27

FN	Private Letter Rulings, etc.
2	9141050
3	8935063
4	9446033, 9446034
19	8906008
120	8728057, 8728058, 8728073
121	200606039, 200649037, 200709071, 200720027, 200720029, 200720030, 200725041, 200725042, 200732018, 200735031, 200738031, 200740015, 200746020, 200746021, 200748020, 200749027, 200751306, 200802034, 200802037, 200802038, 200803023, 200803028, 200805024, 200817047, 200817050, 200817052-200817054, 200817056, 200817057, 200817061-200817063, 200840051, 200844017, 200844028, 200844029, 200846027, 200846030-200846032, 200846035
132	8642083, 8709049, 8724057, 8738039, 8747032, 8818046, 8819037, 8819057, 8819071, 8825044, 8834010, 9040038, 9103047, 9253044, 9310045, 9510068, 9518021, 9619024, 200545047, 200615027
135	9803015
144	9152046
148	8710016, 8715013, 8725010, 8725024, 8738077, 8823091, 8926078, 8932031,

FN	Private Letter Rulings, etc.
148 cont'd	8944068, 9029043, 9150055, 9348021, 9401010, 9409040, 9421009, 9436052, 9540007, 200049035, 200049036
151	9411011
152	9825030, 200436019, 2005198083, 200527019, 200549009, 200601036–200601039, 200607022, 200607024, 200607025, 200612016, 200612017, 200616034, 200616036, 20061307, 200622054
308	9042043, 39826
330	8725056, 9201039, 200449033, 39718, 39737, 39799, 39828, 39829, 39866
333	39761
335	9752023
337	9645007
338	39829
342	39655, 39764
344	9108021, 9110012, 9743054, 200449033
374	39778
389	39684, 39874
392	9527035
410	9033056
433	9010011
464	200315024
548	100441012, 100441016,
*548.1	200931059
*549	200931059

Chapter 28

FN	Private Letter Rulings, etc.
10	8626102, 8627056–8627060, 8627104, 8628052, 8628069, 8639089, 8642062, 8645063, 8645083, 8649081, 8650061, 8709051, 8710083, 8712062, 8712068, 8714053, 8715007, 8715048, 8715058, 8717045, 8717076, 8718066, 8718074, 8718075, 8719030, 8720048, 8721072–8721075, 8721087, 8722066, 8722067, 8722072, 8722081, 8722091, 8722093–8722098, 8722109, 8723037, 8723071, 8723079, 8724070, 8725049, 8725072–8725074, 8725087, 8727074, 8727075, 8727081, 8728070, 8728075, 8728076, 8729082, 8729084, 8730055–8730057, 8730068, 8732044, 8732092, 8735043, 8735044, 8735069–8735071, 8736041, 8737086, 8737101, 8741085, 8742068, 8742074, 8742082, 8744059, 8744062, 8744064, 8744065, 8745044, 8746053, 8746071, 8747033, 8747057–8747060, 8747077, 8748050, 8748061, 8749064, 8750070, 8752051, 8752056, 8752088, 8752090, 8752095, 8753044, 8753049, 8753052, 8753053, 8753056, 8802012, 8802085, 8803009, 8803072, 8803083, 8803084,
10 cont'd	8806009, 8806055, 8806070, 8806080, 8807007, 8807010, 8807049, 8808007, 8808073, 8808082, 8809093, 8809100, 8810033, 8810077, 8811015, 8812076, 8814008, 8814046, 8814047, 8816020, 8817051, 8818005, 8818038, 8818041, 8819057, 8819069, 8819071, 8820074, 8820091, 8821062, 8822092, 8823044, 8823059, 8823087, 8824004, 8825018, 8825077, 8825104, 8827006, 8827016, 8827028, 8827059, 8827060, 8828010, 8830005, 8830005, 8830038, 8830083, 8831010, 8834089, 8807007, 8837016, 8837042, 8837053, 8837062, 8839005, 8839019, 8841004, 8841011, 8845020, 8845027, 8846004, 8846019, 8846057, 8847009, 8849080, 8850026, 8850054, 8850069, 8901051, 8901052, 8901065, 8903017, 8904038, 8904039, 8907060, 8909056, 8912042, 8913051, 8914057, 8917073, 8918079, 8920021, 8920054, 8920055, 8920085, 8921060, 8922065, 8922079, 8925049, 8925069, 8925089, 8925090, 8926083, 8926086, 8929009, 8929038, 8929050, 8932010, 8932012, 8934004, 8934030, 8934031, 8935040, 8940012, 8941007, 8941012, 8941015, 8941061, 8941073, 8941083, 8942102, 8943008, 8943049, 8944014, 8944059, 8945062, 8947041, 8948022, 8950052, 8950070, 8951071, 9001041, 9002037, 9003036, 9003060, 9008088, 9009009, 9011049, 9013049, 9014016, 9014050, 9016053, 9022055, 9024034, 9028075, 9030039, 9034073, 9104023, 9109057, 9110018, 9112025, 9128037, 9134025, 9135054, 9136031, 9138056, 9139025, 9142035, 9151041, 9151049, 9152040, 9203041, 9215047, 9216035, 9217042, 9226044, 9233042, 9234042, 9235054, 9235056, 9238041, 9243045–9243047, 9231041, 9318048, 9318049, 9326055, 9333046, 9343024, 9347031, 9347032, 9350037, 9401034, 9403029, 9404027, 9408024, 9409038, 9424027, 9425006–9425009, 9426040, 9435030, 9438039, 9438046, 9442035, 9447051–9447053, 9448027–9448029, 9450034, 9501037, 9501040, 9503021, 9511035, 9511036, 9511038, 9511046, 9513003, 9517052, 9519057, 9521014, 9527013, 9527043, 9531005, 9533007, 9535017, 9535018, 9538026–9538031, 9541007–9541014, 9542009, 9542039, 9542043, 9542044, 9544028, 9544033–9544036, 9551006, 9551039, 9552021, 9608006, 9608037, 9608038, 9615031, 9630013, 9635028, 9635029, 9635037, 9636026, 9646032, 9651015, 9651026, 9740001–9740002, 9747029–9747032, 9750054–9750056, 9751020, 9752062, 9804054, 9804061,

FN	Private Letter Rulings, etc.
10 cont'd	9805038, 9809054, 9814040, 9814042, 9814043, 9817034, 9819047, 9839038, 9839042, 9842030, 9842037, 9844032, 9847033, 9848038
17	9740001–9740004
25	200714026
35	9002036, 9014061
44	9119069, 9547013
45	9828032, 199943045, 200004041, 200622049–200622051, 200622059, 200634039
47	9629020
51	9135003
52	8714050
56	9031051
77	9119069, 9242002
78	9246033
96	199924065, 199949038
97	9839038, 9839042
103	8810048
104	8417019, 9335022
112	7903079, 9042004

Chapter 29

7	9308047
17	8606056, 8705087, 8706012, 8709071, 8720048, 8749058, 8749059, 8805059, 8810082, 8811003, 8819034, 8821044, 8833002, 8840056, 8846053, 8901012, 8901050, 8903083, 8909029, 8925051, 8934064, 8952076, 9005068, 9024068, 9024026, 9024086, 9030063, 9033069, 9108016, 9119060, 9131058, 9245031, 9308047, 9311031, 9316052, 9341024, 9346013, 9402031–9402933, 9408026, 9417036, 9417042, 9417043, 9421006, 9438041, 9447043, 9523027, 9528020, 9530009, 9535022, 9539014, 9542045 (amended by 9720036), 9547039, 9626021, 9630014, 9637051, 9705028, 9721038, 9726010, 9720031, 9722032, 199941048, 200425050 (reissued as 200444044)
27	8934064, 9242038, 9408026, 9421006, 199941051
30	199929006
33	39598, 39646, 39866
34	39776
38	8625078, 8720048, 8732040, 8743070, 8840056, 8934064, 9027050, 9305026, 9734026, 9734027, 9734036, 9734037, 9734039, 9734040, 199938041, 200037050, 200130048, 200130049, 200130055, 200132040, 200149043, 200405016
47	200602040, 200602041
50	8839002

FN	Private Letter Rulings, etc.
51	8709051, 9305026
69	9105029, 9303030, 9305026, 39866
93	8729005, 8832084, 8833002, 8903083, 8922047, 9010073, 9027051, 9045003, 9108016, 9308047, 9404004, 9438029, 9535022, 9547039, 9705028, 200132040
111	200602040, 200602041
117	200139006
119	8849072, 9136032, 9148051

Chapter 30

27	8925052, 8945063
30	8621060, 8903060, 8912003, 8925052, 8936073, 8945063, 9029034, 9035072, 9105029, 9105031, 9215046, 9308034, 9323030, 9352030, 9407022, 9518014, 9517029, 200206058
33	200304042, 200448048
38	20044018E, 20044020E, 20044030E
39	8925051, 9547039
45	20044020E–20044030E
49	9230001, 9350044
65	8628049, 8705089, 8715039, 9715040, 8717057, 8723065, 8724060, 8727080, 8806057, 8807012, 8814047, 8817039, 8818008, 8820093, 8833009, 8901054, 8909036, 8912003, 8912041, 8915065, 8917055, 8931083, 8936047, 8936077, 8938002, 8939024, 8940039, 8941006, 8942099, 8943050, 8943064, 9021050, 9029034, 9109066, 9122061, 9122062, 9122070, 9147058, 9318033, 9319044, 9323030, 9345057, 9349032, 9352030, 9438030, 9502035 (updating 8528080), 9603839, 9642051, 9736039, 9736043, 9739001, 9709014, 9718036, 9722032, 39732
66	200211052

Chapter 31

18	9451001
28	199913044–199913046
32	8944017
40	8640054, 8640056, 8640057
51	200236049
53	9435029, 9752062, 9752063, 9752065, 9752067, 9839032, 200027057, 200108048
54	9425009, 200704032, 200843037–200843039
56	200702035
58	9623057, 9623059, 9623060, 9738055, 9738056, 9620027, 200150026
59	20003029, 200124021

TABLE OF IRS PRIVATE LETTER RULINGS

FN	Private Letter Rulings, etc.
62	200541043, 200541044
63	200714020–200714024
63.1	200843041
71	200149035, 200418047, 200446011, 200831032, 200831033
81	200044040, 200218037
85	200325003, 200325004, 200327065, 200327067
86	200102053

FN	Private Letter Rulings, etc.
93	200325004
95	200333032, 200333033, 200510030
97	200333032, 200333033
103	8921203, 8932085, 8941006, 8949034, 9001030, 9521013
117	200606047
155	8219066, 9538026–9538031

Table of Cases Discussed in *Bruce R. Hopkins'*
Nonprofit Counsel

The following cases, referenced in the text, are discussed in greater detail in one or more issues of the author's monthly newsletter, as indicated.

Case	Book Sections	Newsletter Issue
Abortion Rights Mobilization, Inc. v. Regan	26.5(a), 26.5(b)	Aug. 1986
Abortion Rights Mobilization, Inc. v. United States Catholic Conference	26.5(b)	Aug. 1988
Arlie Found., Inc. v. United States	20.3, 26.2(b)	July 1993, Nov. 2003
Alpha Medical, Inc. v. Comm'r	20.4	July 1999
Alabama Cent. Credit Union v. United States	24.12(c)	June 1987
Alive Fellowship of Harmonious Harmonious Living v. Comm'r	10.9, 26.2(b)	May 1984
Allen v. Wright	6.2(b), 26.5(b)	Aug. 1984, July 1985
Alumni Ass'n of the University of Oregon, Inc. v. Comm'r	24.5(h), 24.6(g)	Dec. 1999
Amend 16 Robert Wirengard v. Comm'r	4.10	May 2005
American Academy of Family Physicians v. United States	24.2(a), 24.2(b), 24.2(g)	June 1995, Oct. 1996
American Ass'n of Christian Schs. Voluntary Employees Beneficiary Ass'n Welfare Plan Trust v. United States	13.1(b), 18.3, 27.12(a)	Oct. 1996
American Campaign Academy v. Comm'r	4.5(a), 4.5(b), 8.3(a), 8.4, 20.3, 20.11(a), 20.11(c)	July 1989, June 2001, Feb. 2005
American Civil Liberties Union Found. v. Crawford	1.4, 10.1(b)	June 2002
American College of Physicians v. United States	4.9, 24.5(g)	Oct. 1984, June 1986
American Hosp. Ass'n v. United States	24.5(g)	May 1987
American Medical Ass'n v. United States	24.1, 24.5(g)	Oct. 1987, Nov. 1987, Jan. 1990
American Plywood Ass'n v. United States	14.2(b), 14.2(c)	Apr. 2008
American Postal Workers Union, AFL-CIO v. United States	16.1, 24.5(g)	Feb. 1990, Apr. 1991
AmeriDream, Inc. et al. v. Jackson	7.5	Jan. 2008
American Society of Ass'n Executives v. United States	22.9	Jan. 1999, Jan. 2000, July 2000
Anclote Psychiatric Center, Inc. v. Comm'r	20.5, 21.4, 26.2(b), 31.7(b)	June 1992, Sept. 1998
Ass'n of the Bar of the City of N.Y. v. Comm'r	23.2(c)	Nov. 1987, Nov. 1998
At Cost Services, Inc. v. Comm'r	4.8, 4.11(b), 24.1	Jan. 2001
Atlanta Athletic Club v. Comm'r	15.5, 15.6	Mar. 1993
Beiner, Inc. v. Comm'r	20.4(b)	Dec. 2004
*Bellco Credit Union v. United States	19.7, 2	Apr. 2009
Bethel Conservative Mennonite Church v. Comm'r	4.3(b), 4.4, 27.12(a)	Dec. 1984
Bluetooth SIG, Inc. v. United States	14.2(b), 14.2(c)	Apr. 2008
Bob Jones Univ. Museum and Gallery, Inc. v. Comm'r	28.1	Aug. 1996

Case	Book Sections	Newsletter Issue
Bobo v. Christus Health	6.3(j)–(m)	Aug. 2005
Boy Scouts of America v. Dale	1.7, 6.2(d)	Nov. 1999, Aug. 2000
Branch Ministries v. Richardson	21.1(e), 23.2(b)	Sept. 1997
Branch Ministries v. Rossotti	23.2(b), 23.3	June 1999, July 2000
Brentwood Academy v. Tennessee Secondary Schools Athletic Ass'n	4.9(a)	Apr. 2001
Brook, Inc., v. Comm'r	15.3, 15.5	Oct. 1986
Brown Shoe Co. v. Comm'r	15.3	Oct. 2001
Budlong v. Graham	10.1(a)	June 2006
Buder v. United States	7.15(b)	Dec. 1993
Burton v. William Beaumont Hosp.	6.3(j)–(m)	Feb. 2005
Calhoun Academy v. Comm'r	6.2(b)	Apr. 1990
Camps Newfound/Owatonna, Inc. v. Town of Harrison	1.1, 1.1(a), 12.3(b)	July 1997
Caracci v. Comm'r	20.5(c), 21.1, 21.4(a), 21.11, 31.7(b)	Feb. 2000, July 2002, Sept. 2006
*Catholic Answers, Inc. v. United States	23.3	June 2009, Dec. 2009
Chicago Metro. Ski Council v. Comm'r	24.5(g)	May 1995
Chief Steward of the Ecumenical Temples & Worldwide Peace Movement v. Comm'r	4.3(b), 4.5(a), 25.1(a)	May 1985
*Christian Coalition of Florida, Inc. v. United States	23.5	June 2009
Christian Coalition International v. United States	27.8(a)	Nov. 2002
Church by Mail, Inc. v. Comm'r	20.5, 20.11(b)	Oct. 1984
Church of Ethereal Joy v. Comm'r	10.2(c), 20.11	Sept. 1984
Church of Spiritual Tech. v. United States	4.6, 25.1(a), 26.2(b)	Dec. 1989
*Citizens United v. Federal Election Comm'n	App. H	June 2009, Aug. 2009, Nov. 2009
Cleveland Athletic Club, Inc. v. United States	15.3, 15.5	Feb. 1986
CNG Transmission Management VEBA v. United States	18.3, 24.10	Jan. 2009
Colorado State Chiropractic Soc'y v. Comm'r	4.3(a), 26.2(b)	Dec. 1989
Columbia Park Recreation Ass'n, Inc. v. Comm'r	13.2(a), 20.3	Feb. 1987
Common Cause v. Schultz	26.5(a)	Aug. 1999
*Community First Credit Union v. United States	19.7, 24	Mar. 2008, July 2009
CORE Special Purpose Fund v. Comm'r	24.5(g), 24.14	May 1985
CRSO v. Commissioner	12.3(c), 27.13	July 2007
Credit Union Ins. Corp. v. United States	14.1(a), 19.8	July 1995, Sept. 1996
Cutter v. Wilkinson	10.1(a)	May 2005, Sept. 2005
Davenport v. Washington Education Ass'n	15.1	Mar. 2007
Davis v. Federal Election Commission	23.11(i)	Aug. 2008
*Democratic Leadership Council, Inc. v. United States	13, 20.11, 26.3	June 2008, Aug. 2008, Mar. 2009
Devine Brothers, Inc. v. Comm'r	20.4(b)	Mar. 2003
Dexsil v. Comm'r	20.4(b)	Aug. 1998, Jan. 2000
Disabled Am. Veterans v. Comm'r	24.1(a)	Apr. 1990
Doe v. Kamehameha Schools/ Bernice Pauahi Bishop Estate	6.2(e)	Oct. 2005, Feb. 2007, July 2007
Dzina v. United States.	21.1	Jan. 2005
Easter House v. United States	4.4, 4.10, 4.11(b)	Aug. 1987
Ecclesiastical Order of the Ism of Am. v. Comm'r	4.11(a), 10.2(c), 24.5(h)	Dec. 1985
E.J. Harrison Sons, Inc. v. Comm'r	20.4(b), 20.4(g)	Sept. 2005, Sept. 2006
Elk Grove Unified School District	10.1(a)	Mar. 2004, May 2004

Case	Book Sections	Newsletter Issue
Laborer's Int'l Union of North Am. v. Comm'r	24.2(a), 24.2(b), 24.2(c), 30.1(c)	Oct. 2001
Lapham Foundation, Inc. v. Comm'r	12.3(c)	Feb. 2005
Lehrfeld v. Richardson	27.8(a)	Mar. 1998
Lima Surgical Assocs., Inc., Voluntary Employees' Beneficiary Ass'n Plan Trust v. United States	18.3	Sept. 1990, Dec. 1991
Lintzenich v. United States	21.15	Dec. 2005
Littriello v. United States	4.1(b)	Sept. 2005, July 2007
Living Faith, Inc. v. Comm'r	4.5(a), 4.11(b), 23.7, 24.4(b), 24.4(h)	Nov. 1990, Feb. 1992
Locke v. Davey	10.1	Apr. 2004
Louisiana Credit Union Leage v.	4.10, 8.6, 14.2(c), 24.1, 24.2(b), 24.4(a)	Apr. 2005
Lutheran Social Servs. v. United States	10.3, 10.4, 10.5	May 1984, June 1985
Manning Ass'n v. Comm'r	4.5(a), 8.4, 20.5(h), 24.1	Jan. 1990
Massachusetts v. EPA	26.5(b)	June 2007
McConnell v. Federal Election Commission		Feb. 2004, Sept. 2007
McCreary County v. American Civil Liberties Union	10.1(a)	Sept. 2005
Mellon Bank v. United States	6.2(a), 7.15(f), 19.6	Aug. 1984, July 1985
Menard, Inc. v. Comm'r	20.4(b)	Nov. 2004
Meredith v. Jefferson County Board of Education	6.2(b)	Feb. 2007, Sept. 2007
Michigan v. United States	19.19(c)	Dec. 1994
Miller & Son Drywall, Inc. v. Comm'r	20.4(b)	Aug. 2005
Missall v. Comm'r	4.1(a)	Jan. 2009
Mobile Republic Assembly v. United States	27.5(a)	Mar. 2004
Morganbesser v. United States	16.1	Mar. 1992
Music Square Church v. United States	26.2	Sept. 2000
Mutual Aid Ass'n of the Church of The Brethren v. United States	13.1(b), 27.12(a)	June 2005
Myers v. Loudoun County Public Schools	10.1(a)	Oct. 2005
National Ass'n of Am. Churches v. Comm'r	24.5(h), 25.1(a)	Feb. 1984
National Ass'n of Postal Supervisors v. United States	16.1, 24.5(f)	Oct. 1990, April 1991, Dec. 1991
National Collegiate Athletic Ass'n v. Comm'r	24.3(b), 24.3(d)	Apr. 1989, Sept. 1990, Oct. 1990, Nov. 1990
National Federation of Republican Assemblies v. United States	25.8, 27.5(a), 20.4(c)	Nov. 2002
National Found., Inc. v. United States	4.5(a), 20.4(c)	Jan. 1998
National League of Postmasters v. United States	24.5(e)	Sept. 1996
National Paralegal Inst. Coalition v. Comm'r	26.2(b)	Mar. 2006
National Prime Users Group, Inc. v. United States	14.1(c)	Oct. 1987
National Water Well Ass'n, Inc. v. Comm'r	24.5(e)	Mar. 1989
Nehemiah Corporation of America v. HUD	7.5	Nov. 2007
Neonatology Associates, P.A. v. Comm'r	18.3, 27.15(e)	Sep. 2002
New Concordia Bible Church v. Comm'r	25.1(a)	Mar. 1985
New Dynamics Found. v. United States	11.8(a)	June 2006
New York State Club Ass'n v. New York City	6.2(c)	Aug. 1988
Newdow v. U.S. Congress et al.	10.1(a)	Aug. 2002
Nonprofits' Ins. Alliance v. United States	4.11(b), 7.13, 27.12(b)	Dec. 1994
North Carolina Citizens for Business & Indus. v. United States	24.5(g)	Oct. 1989
North Ridge Country Club v. Comm'r	15.3, 15.5	Nov. 1987, Aug. 1989
*Ohio Disability Ass'n v. Comm'r	5.1(b), 5.2, 20.11	Jan. 2010

Case	Book Sections	Newsletter Issue
Ohio Farm Bureau Fed'n, Inc. v. Comm'r	24.3(b)	June 1996
Oregon State Univ. Alumni Ass'n v. Comm'r	24.5(h)	Apr. 1996, Dec. 1999
PNC Bank, N.A. v. PPL Electric Utilities Corp.	16.5	Sept. 2006
Paratransit Ins. Corp. v. Comm'r	4.11(b), 27.12(b)	Aug. 1994
Parents Involved in Community Schools v. Seattle School District No. 1	6.2(b)	Feb. 2007, Sept. 2007
People of God Community v. Comm'r	20.2, 20.4(c)	Feb. 1984
Peters v. Comm'r	6.3(a), 6.3(i), 20.4(b), 21.4(c), 26.4(a)	Dec. 2000
Peterson v. Fairview Health Services	6.3(j)–(m)	Aug. 2005
Phi Delta Theta Fraternity v. Comm'r	8.5, 15.5	June 1988
Planned Parenthood Federation of America, Inc. v. Comm'r	24.6(g)	Aug. 1999
*Pleasant Grove City, Utah v. Summum	10.1(a)(iii)	May 2009
*Polm Family Found. v. United States	12.3(c)	Nov. 2009
Portland Golf Club v. Comm'r	1.4, 15.1(a), 15.5	Jan. 1991
Presbyterian & Reformed Publishing Co. v. Comm'r	4.10, 4.11(a), 26.3	Oct. 1984
Professional Ins. Agents of Wash. v. Comm'r	8.6, 24.5(e)	Mar. 1987
Quality Auditing Co. v. Comm'r	20.11(c), 31.1(d)	Sept. 2000
Rameses School of San Antonio Texas v. Commissioner	20	July 2007
Rapco, Inc. v. Comm'r	20.4(b)	Aug. 1996, Jan. 2000
Redlands Surgical Services v. Comm'r	20.11, 20.11(a),20.11(b), 30.3(b)	Sept. 1999, June 2001
Research Consulting Assocs., Inc. v. Electric Power Research Inst.	26.5(a)	Mar. 1986
Roberts, Acting Comm'r, Minn. Dep't of Human Rights v. United States Jaycees	6.2(c)	Aug. 1984
St. David's Health Care System, Inc. v. United States	20.11(b), 30.3(b), 31.1(b)	Aug. 2002, Jan. 2004, July 2004, Aug. 2004
St. Louis Science Fiction, Ltd. v. Comm'r	7.12, 8.4, 20.11(c)	July 1985
Salvation Navy, Inc. v. Comm'r	4.5(a), 4.8	Jan. 2003
Self-Realization Bhd., Inc. v. Comm'r	10.2(c)	Sept. 1984
Senior Citizens of Mo., Inc., v. Comm'r	20.4(h)	Mar. 1989
Service Bolt & Nut Co. Profit Sharing Trust v. Comm'r	24.9	Apr. 1984
Shays & Meehan v. Federal Election Commission	17	Nov. 2004, Nov. 2005, Feb. 2006, Oct. 2007
Sherwin-Williams Co. Employee Health Plan Trust v. Comm'r	18.3, 24.10	Jan. 2001, Aug. 2003, Jan. 2009
Sierra Club, Inc. v. Comm'r	24.5(h), 24.6(g), 24.7(k)	July 1993, Oct. 1994, Aug. 1996, May 1999
Skillman Family Reunion Fund, Inc., The v. United States	15.4	June 2002
Sklar v. Comm'r	10.2(a)	April 2002
Smith v. United States	4.4, 19.6	May 1985
Solution Plus, Inc. v. Comm'r	4.8, 7.3	April 2008
South Community Ass'n v. Comm'r	24.7(a)	Feb. 2006
*Southern Faith Ministries, Inc. v. Geithner	26.6(c)	Dec. 2009
Spiritual Outreach Soc'y v. Comm'r	10.3	Apr. 1991
*Stahl v. United States	10.7	Feb. 2010
State Police Ass'n v. Comm'r	24.5(g)	Nov. 1997
Stichting Pensioenfonds Voor de Gezondheid v. United States	Jan. 1998	16.1
Sunrise Constr. Co. v. Comm'r	18.3	May 1987

Case	Book Sections	Newsletter Issue
Tax Analysts v. Internal Revenue Service	27.8(b)	Nov. 2002, Feb. 2004, Mar. 2005, May 2006
Tax Analysts v. IRS and Christian Broadcasting Network, Inc.	27.8(b)	Sept. 2005
Tennessee Baptist Children's Homes, Inc. v. United States	10.5	July 1985
Texas Apartment Ass'n v. U.S.	24.5(d)	Apr. 2005
Texas Farm Bureau v. United States	24.5(e)	Aug. 1995
Texas Learning Technology Group v. Comm'r	23.7(a)	May 1992
Texas Medical Ass'n Ins. Trust v. United States	14.6, 19.23	Mar. 2006
Triune of Life Church, Inc. v. Comm'r	4.10	Sept. 1985
Trust U/W Emily Oblinger v. Comm'r	24.5, 30.1	May 1993
Tualatin Valley Builders Supply, Inc. v. United States	App. A	July 2008
Tupper v. United States	16.1	Mar. 1998
Twin Oaks Community, Inc. v. Comm'r	10.7	Jan. 1987
United Cancer Council, Inc. v. Comm'r	4.7, 4.11(b), 20.3, 20.11(c), 21.8, 26.2, 26.3	Jan. 1998, Apr. 1999
United States v. American Bar Endowment	8.6, 24.2(b), 24.5(h), 26.4(a)	Apr. 1984, Aug. 1986
United States v. Chicago, Burlington & Quincy Railroad Co.	15.3, 26.4(a)	Oct. 2001
United States v. Church of Scientology	26.6(a)	Sept. 1990
*United States v. Hovind	4.1(a)	Oct. 2009
*United States v. Living Word Christian Center	26.6(c)	Jan. 2009, Feb. 2009, Apr. 2009, June 2009
United States Catholic Conference & Nat'l Conference of Catholic Bishops, In Re	26.5(b)	Oct. 1989, Nov. 1989
University Med. Resident Servs., P.C. v. Comm'r	7.7, 7.8	Oct. 1996
Van Orden v. Perry	10.1(a)	Sept. 2005
Variety Club Tent No. 6 Charities, Inc. v. Comm'r	20.1, 20.3, 20.5(k), 21.8, 24.7(h)	Mar. 1998
Veterans of Foreign Wars, Dep't of Mich. v. Comm'r	24.2(a), 26.5(g)	Aug. 1987
Veterans of Foreign Wars, Dep't of Mo., Inc. v. United States	24.5(h)	Dec. 1984
Vigilant Hose Co. of Emmitsburg v. United States	4.8, 24.2(a), 24.4(g), 30.1(c)	Aug. 2001
*Vision Service Plan v. United States	13.2(a)	Feb. 2006, Apr. 2008, Apr. 2009
Washington v. Washington Education Ass'n	15.1	Mar. 2007
Wayne Baseball, Inc. v. Comm'r	4.4, 7.15(c), 8.4	Dec. 1999
Wendy L. Parker Rehabilitation Found., Inc. v. Comm'r	6.3(a)	Nov. 1986
West Va. State Med. Ass'n v. Comm'r	15.5, 24.2(b), 24.14	Nov. 1988
Westward Ho v. Comm'r	4.6, 4.8	June 1992
Wiccan Religious Cooperative of Florida, Inc., The v. Zingale	8.1(b)	June 2005
Woodrum v. Integris Health, Inc.	6.3(j)–(m)	Mar. 2005
Zimmerman v. Cambridge Credit Counseling Corp.	1.1(a)	Aug. 2005

Table of IRS Private Determinations Discussed in *Bruce R. Hopkins' Nonprofit Counsel*

The following IRS private letter rulings and technical advice memoranda, referenced in the text, are discussed in greater detail in one or more issues of the author's monthly newsletter, as indicated.

Private Determination	Book Sections	Newsletter Issue	Private Determination	Book Sections	Newsletter Issue
8306006	9.5	Dec. 1993	9619069	25.6(j)	Aug. 1996
8505044	29.3(a)	May 1985	9635001	24.7(k)	Nov. 1996
8512084	9.5, 24.2(f)	Dec. 1993	9635003	23.2(ce), 23.3	Nov. 1996
8606056	9.5, 29.2	Apr. 1986	9637050	29.1(b)	Nov. 1996
8621059	30.1(b)	Aug. 1986	9637051	29.6	Apr. 1997
8706012	29.1(a)	Apr. 1987	9641011	24.5(j)	Dec. 1996
9017003	28.2(a)	July 1990	9645004	24.2(f), 24.4(d), 24.7	Jan. 1997
9029047	26.5(e)	Sept. 1990			
9042038	24.6(i)	Jan. 1991	9645017	29.6, 29.8	Feb. 1997, Apr. 1997
9130002	20.1, 20.5(c), 20.5(d), 30.2, 31.7(b)	Nov. 1991	9651047	7.6(f), 24.5(j)	Jan. 1997
			9652026	17.1(a), 17.4	Jan. 1998
9242002	19.2(a) 28.2(d)	Dec. 1992	9702004	8.4, 24.2(f), 24.5(i), 28.2(e), 31.8(g)	Mar. 1997
9243008	9.5	Dec. 1992			
9305026	29.3(a), 29.6(b)	Apr. 1993, Apr. 1997			
9316052	9.5, 20.4(a)	Dec. 1993	9710030	7.6(a)	July 1997, Sept. 1997
9345004	24.5(e)	June 1994	9711002	24.5(j)	May 1997
9416002	24.5(e)	June 1994	9711003	4.7, 24.1	June 1997
9425032	17.5	Aug. 1994	9711004	25.6	June 1997
9434041	7.6(b)	Oct. 1994	9712001	24.3(d)	June 1997
9438029	29.8	Nov. 1994	9720002	24.5(c)	Sept. 1997
9438030	30.2(b), 31.1(b)	Nov. 1994	9722006	19.5(a), 29.2	Feb. 1999, Nov. 2002
9448036	20.9	Jan. 1995	9732022	16.2	Oct. 1997
9506046	31.3	Mar. 1995	9732032	7.6, 8.5, 24.5(a), 24.5(b)	Oct. 1997
9530024	7.7	Nov. 1995			
9542002	11.4	Dec. 1995			
9550001	14.1(d), 14.2(c), 24.5(j), 24.4(g), 24.5(e)	Feb. 1996	9739043	24.5(b)	Dec. 1997
			9740032	24.1(h)	Dec. 1997
			9747003	19.11(a)	Jan. 1998
			9750056	31.3	Feb. 1998
9603019	24.12(b)	Mar. 1996	9803001	4.11(b) 7.6(a), 24.5(b)	Apr. 1998
9608003	24.5(j)	Apr. 1996			
9615030	6.3(b), 20.11(a)	June 1996	9805001	13, 24.8	Mar. 1998
			9811001	24.5(j)	May 1998
9615045	24.6(h)	July 1996	9812001	23.2(b)	May 1998

Private Determination	Book Sections	Newsletter Issue	Private Determination	Book Sections	Newsletter Issue
9815061	13, 15, 19.4, 19.11(a), 27.17	July 1998	200133037	15.3	Oct. 2001
			200132040	29.2, 31.1(d)	Nov. 2001
			200134025	4.1(b), 25.2(c)	Nov. 2001
9816027	24.6(g)	June 1998	200147058	24.9	Jan. 2002
9821049	24.4(f)	Aug. 1998	200151060	23.2(b), 28.3	Mar. 2002
9821063	24.5(b)	Aug. 1998	200152048	19.6, 29	Mar. 2002
9821067	24.4(g)	Aug. 1998	200203069	29	May 2002
9822004	24.5(j)	Oct. 1998	200204051	24.4(f)	Apr. 2002
9822006	24.4(g)	Oct. 1998	200217044	31.8(c)	July 2002
9822039	24.5(b)	Oct. 1998	200222030	8.3(b), 8.6, 24.5(c)	Sept. 2002
9825030	24.4(f)	Aug. 1998			
9835001	20.3	Nov. 1998	200225044	24.4(f)	Sept. 2002
9835003	20.7, 25.1(f), 27.1(a)	Nov. 1998	200225046	29	Oct. 2002
			200230005	24.7(c), 28.5	Oct. 2002
			200243057	27.15(e)	Dec. 2002
9839039	24.5(a), 28.9, 30.7, 31.5	Dec. 1998	200244028	21.4(a), 21.9(a)	Jan. 2003
9841003	18.3	Jan. 1999			
9847002	24.5(j), 28.9 28.9	Mar. 1999	200247055	21.4(a)	Feb. 2003
			200303051	31.8(c)	Mar. 2003
9847006	17.5	Jan. 1999	200303062	24.5(g), 24.5(m), 24.8	Mar. 2003
9849027	24.5(j), 27.13	Mar. 1999			
9853001	24.4(g)	Mar. 1999	200304041	30.1(b), 31.5	Apr. 2003
199901002	24.4(g)	Mar. 1999	200305032	31.3	Apr. 2003
199932052	7.7	Oct. 1999	200311034	19.17(c), 31.5	May 2003
199938041	28.1(a)	May 2000	200313024	19.17(c), 24.5(a)	June 2003
200020056	14.1(a)	July 2000			
200020060	20.4(b)	Aug. 2000	200314031	24.5(j)	June 2003
200021056	4.4, 4.11(a), 4.11(b), 8.6, 24.1, 24.2(d), 24.2(f), 24.4(a)	Aug. 2000		24.5(h)	Aug. 2003
			200325003	7.6(a), 30.1(b)	Sept. 2003
			200326035	9.2, 9.5, 20.11(b), 24.4, 24.6(g), 29.7	Sept. 2003
200022056	24.5(j)	July 2000, May 2001			
			200333031	31.5	Oct. 2003
200026013	19.19(d)	Aug. 2000	200333034	8.5	Nov. 2003
200027056	14.1, 24.6(j), 29	Sept. 2000	200335037	21.4(a), 21.7	Nov. 2003
			200341023	31.6	Dec. 2003
200037053	11.8(d)	Dec. 2000	200343027	4.5(a)	Dec. 2003
200044038	23.2(b)	Jan. 2001	200345041	24.4(f)	Jan. 2004
200044039	27.12(b)	Jan. 2001	200347009	9.5	Jan. 2004
200051046	15.6	Feb. 2001	200347023	12.4	Jan. 2004
200051049	7.6(h), 24.1	Feb. 2001	200348029	31.3	Feb. 2004
200108045	24.5(j)	May 2001	200350022	12.4(a)	Feb. 2004
200114040	20.11(a)	June 2001	200352021	12.4(a)	Mar. 2004
200117043	31.5	July 2001	200402003	31.8(c)	Mar. 2004
200118054	30.1(b), 30.4	July 2001	200405016	29.2	Apr. 2004
200119061	24.2(h), 24.6(j)	Aug. 2001	200411044	31.5	May 2004
200128059	24.5(h)	Sep. 2001	200413014	21.9(b)	June 2004
200133036	15.3	Oct. 2001	200421010	21.4(a)	July 2004

Private Determination	Book Sections	Newsletter Issue	Private Determination	Book Sections	Newsletter Issue
200427016	19.19(d)	Nov. 2004	200528008	19.23	Sept. 2005
200428021	19.19(d)	Nov. 2004	200528029	4.5(c), 30.1(b)	Sept. 2005
200431018	31.6	Oct. 2004	200530028	10.3(a), 10.3(b)	Oct. 2005
200432026	24.12(b)	Oct. 2004	200530029	24.2(h), 24.6(j)	Oct. 2005
200435018	21.4(c)	Nov. 2004	200531020	14.1, 24.7(f)	Dec. 2005
200435019	21.4(c)	Nov. 2004	200531024	27.2(a)	Oct. 2005
200435020	21.4(c)	Nov. 2004	200532052	28.2(c)	Dec. 2005
200435021	21.4(c)	Nov. 2004	200532056	15.6	Oct. 2005
200435022	21.4(c)	Nov. 2004	200532058	7.7	Dec. 2005
200436019	27.2(b)	Nov. 2004	200534022	7.4	Nov. 2005
200436022	4.1(b), 7.6, 30.4, 31.6	Nov. 2004	200535029	5.2, 20.1, 25.1(a)	Dec. 2005
200437040	5.1(d), 10.3(a), 21.4(c), 21.16, 23.2(b), 29.4	Nov. 2004	200536023	14.2(c)	Dec. 2005
			200536024	7.15(c)	Dec. 2005
200439043	7.6(g), 8.7, 24.5(n)	Dec. 2004	200536025	19.16(a)	Dec. 2005
20044008E	4.5, 13, 20.11(c)	Feb. 2005	200536026	14.1(c)	Dec. 2005
200446033	23.2(b), 23.3, 28.3	Jan. 2005	200536027	12.4(a), 12.4(e)	Dec. 2005
200450037	7.3(c)	Feb. 20005 Mar. 2005	200537037	24.12	Feb. 2006
			200537038	7.15(e), 24.12(b)	Dec. 2005
200450038	7.4	Feb 2005	200538026	8.3(a)	Feb. 2006
200450041	4.1(a), 4.3, 4.3(d), 4.4, 15.1(b)	Mar. 2005	200538027	24.6(h), 24.12(b)	Dec. 2005
			200539027	4.11(b)	Feb. 2006
200501017	24.4(g), 29	Mar. 2005	200541042	31.13	Dec. 2005
200501021	12.4(a), 24.6(d)	Mar. 2005	200542037	12.4(a)	Feb. 2006
200501022	12.4(a), 24.6(d)	Mar. 2005	200544020	4.11(b), 13, 20.11(a)	Feb. 2006
200504035	19.5(b)	Apr. 2005	200549009	12.3(c), 27.2(b)	Feb. 2006
200505024	14.1(c)	Apr. 2005			
200505032	7.15(d)	Apr. 2005	200552013	26.3	Mar. 2006
200506024	4.5(a)	Apr. 2005	200601030	20.4(c)	Mar. 2006
200506025	24.4(f)	Apr. 2005	200601033	24.6(g)	Mar. 2006
200510029	24.2(h), 24.6(j)	May 2005	200601035	14.1(b), 14.1(c)	Apr. 2006
200510030	31.6	May 2005	200602039	28.6, 29.7	Apr. 2006
200511003	18.3	May 2005	200606042	7.6, 20.1, 20.11, 24.4	May 2006
200511023	4.11(b), 13.4	June 2005			
200511024	13, 27.17	May 2005	200607027	4.1(b), 27.2, 27.9	Apr. 2006
200512023	4.11(b), 13.4	June 2005	200611033	7.7, 24.4	May 2006
200512025	24.2(f)	June 2005	200614030	8.3(a), 12.3(c), 20.11(b)	July 2006
200512027	4.11(b)	June 2005			
200513030	12.3(b)	July 2005	200619024	24.2(h)	Sept. 2006
200520035	19.9(a)	Aug. 2005	200621023	4.4, 13	Aug. 2006
200522022	14.2(c)	Sept. 2005	200621025	6.3(a)	Aug. 2006
200525020	4.11(b)	Sept. 2005			

Private Determination	Book Sections	Newsletter Issue	Private Determination	Book Sections	Newsletter Issue
200622055	5.6(f), 8.3, 30.1(c)	Aug. 2006	200830028	5.6(n), 20.11(d)	Oct. 2008
200623069	24.6(n)	Aug. 2006	*200832027	4.11, 24.2(d), 24.2(e), 24.4(h), 24.5(j)	Mar. 2009
200623072	4.4, 15.2	Aug. 2006			
200623075	7.5	Aug. 2006	200833021	23.5	Dec. 2008
200624068	7.7, 13.1(a)	Nov. 2006	200837035	14.1(c)(iii)	Dec. 2008
200625033	19.5(b)	Nov. 2006	200841038	19.12	Jan. 2009
200625035	24.5(a), 24.7(b)	Sept. 2006	200843032	5.6(n), 20.11	Jan. 2009
200634036	7.7	Feb. 2007	200843036	24.12(b)	Jan. 2009
200635018	20.11(a), 20.11(b)	Nov. 2006	200844021	20	Feb. 2009
			200844022	12.3(c), 20.11, 26.3	Feb. 2009
200638027	18.3, 20.1	Nov. 2006			
200642009	7.4, 31.6	Dec. 2006	*200845053	5.6(p), 20.11	Feb. 2009
200648031	24.2, 24.6(h)	Feb. 2007	200846040	25.1(a)(i)	Feb. 2009
200649034	20	Apr. 2007	200849016	19.5(b)	Feb. 2009
200702042	20	Apr. 2007	200849017	4.11, 9.2, 12.3(c)	Feb. 2009
200703037	24.2, 24.5(j)	Mar. 2007	200849018	11.2	Feb. 2009
200708087	20.11	June 2007	*200851031	4.3, 4.5(a), 20	Feb. 2009
200709064	4.11(a), 20.5	June 2007			
200709065	7.13, 12.4(c)	June 2007	*200851037	6.3(a), 20	Feb. 2009
200709070	14.2(c)	June 2007	*200851040	6.3(a), 10.2, 20.11, 24.2(e)	Feb. 2009
200709072	19.7, 24	June 2007			
200713024	24.6(g), 24.7(f)	June 2007	*200902013	30.1	Apr. 2009
200716026	14	July 2007	*200903081	4.5, 12.3(c), 20	Mar. 2008
200716034	24.4(b), 29.7	July 2007	*200904026	25.1(a)(i)	May 2009
200717019	27.7	July 2007	*200905028	4.3(b), 4.5(a), 10.2, 20	May 2009
200717020	19.5(b)	July 2007			
200721025	7.5	Aug. 2007	*200905029	8.1, 15.1, 19.4(a)	May 2009
200722028	24.4	Aug. 2007			
200727021	10.3	Oct. 2007	*200905033	9.2, 20	Apr. 2009
200731034	12.3(c)	Oct. 2007	*200906057	15.1(b), 15.2	Apr. 2009
200736037	5.1(b), 20.11(a)	Nov. 2007	*200908050	23.10	May 2009
			*200909064	6.2(b), 8.3(a)	May 2009
200750020	12.2(e), 12.4(a)	Feb. 2008	*200909072	13, 15	May 2009
			*200910060	11.3	May 2009
200752043	12.3(c), 20.11, 26.3	Feb. 2009	*200912039	10.3	Aug. 2009
			*200913067	20	July 2009
200810025	12.3(c), 20.11, 26.3	Feb. 2009	*200916035	5.1(b), 20.11(a)	July 2009
200815035	4.11(b), 25.1(a)(i)	June 2008	*200917042	14, 20.1	July 2009
			*200926033	7.2	Sep. 2009
200819017	21.14	July 2008	*200926036	10.3, 20	Sep. 2009
200825046	4.7	Aug. 2008	*200926037	10.3, 20	Sep. 2009
200826038	15.6	Aug. 2008	*200926049	10.3	Sep. 2009
200826043	6.2(a)	Aug. 2008	*200928045	23.2(b), 26.6(a)	Oct. 2009
200829029	13.2(b)	Sep. 2008			

TABLE OF IRS PRIVATE DETERMINATIONS DISCUSSED IN *BRUCE R. HOPKINS' NONPROFIT COUNSEL*

Private Determination	Book Sections	Newsletter Issue	Private Determination	Book Sections	Newsletter Issue
*200930049	4.3(a), 4.3(b), 25.1(b)	Nov. 2009	*200943042	22.3(d)	Dec. 2010
*200931059	4.5(a), 18.3, 27.17	Oct. 2009	*200944053	4.11, 7.6, 8.4, 8.5, 9.2, 20.11	Jan. 2010
*200931064	19.7, 24.4(a)	Oct. 2009	*200944055	20.4	Jan. 2010
*200941038	4.11, 7.7, 11.6, 27.12(b)	Dec. 2010	*200947064	7.2	Jan. 2010
			*200947065	12.4, 24.2	Jan. 2010
			*200950049	18.3, 20	Feb. 2010

Index

IMPORTANT NOTE:

Because of the rapidly changing nature of information in this field, this product will be updated with annual supplements or with future editions. Please call 1-877-762-2974 or email us at subscriber@wiley.com to receive any current updates at no additional charge. We will send on approval any future supplements or new editions when they become available. If you purchased this product directly from John Wiley & Sons, Inc., we have already recorded your subscription for this update service.